In memory of Keith Liddicoat, a man I never met in person but who gave me valuable information, especially on cycling in Russia. Sadly, he died while cycling across the Nullarbor in late 2019.

I would also like to thank anyone who has helped me over the years, especially Warmshower hosts, and those who have given me great advice and support, in particular, in my hometown of Berriwillock.

Finally, I would never have got this far without the help of my parents. Thanks Mum and Dad for letting me be me.

My previous cycling trips

This was not my first cycling tour and I plan to develop more books based on previous and future trips. I am starting with this one because it involves being in countries which many people do not get the chance to travel in, especially by bicycle.

One day I may write about how this all began but essentially it started at La Trobe University, Bendigo, where I did many outdoor activities including hiking, canoeing and cycling. I found cycling to be the best fit for me as it allows me to travel at a relaxing pace without having to carry anything on my back. So, thank you to all during my university time for inspiring me to go cycling in the first place.

After finishing university in 2009, I set off to cycle around my home state of Victoria, mostly following railway lines. Over the next few years, my cycling trips expanded to other Australian states, concentrating on one region at a time.

I went on my first overseas trip in 2013, spending three enjoyable months cycling in France, Britain and Belgium. I haven't been back to Europe until now.

In 2014, I spent five months cycling in the Sierras and Rockies in the United States and Canada, while my four-month trip to North America in 2015, was timed to start by attending some FIFA Women's World Cup matches in Canada.

My last overseas trip was to New Zealand in early 2016. During this tour, I began to notice I was feeling fatigued with cycling, having done a few tours in the previous three years. By not touring for a while, I have recharged my batteries.

Why this trip

The reason for this trip is because the 2018 FIFA Men's World Cup is on in Russia from 14 June. Therefore, the visa requirements for visiting have been relaxed during this period to allow for a longer visit of 52 days from 4 June to 25 July, instead of the normal 30 day tourist visa. These dates span ten days before and after the World Cup.

It's an opportunity to spend more time exploring Russia than normally is allowed, along with experiencing a FIFA Men's World Cup. Having already experienced the 2015 FIFA Women's World Cup in Canada, I'm curious to see if it will be a different experience.

Because of the World Cup, instead of visiting the Russian Embassy with an invitation letter from a travel company, all I have to do to obtain a visa is purchase a World Cup ticket and apply online for a Fan ID. Not only is it my visa for visiting Russia, I need it and individual tickets to attend World Cup matches.

I have managed to buy tickets for Australia's first two matches against France in Kazan on 16 June and Denmark in Samara on 21 June, but I was unsuccessful with finding tickets for the third match against Peru in Sochi on 26 June.

Since this is the first World Cup appearance for Peru since 1982, many dedicated Peruvian fans are coming and I have heard stories of people spending a fortune to come. Even if I could have got a ticket, Sochi is about 2,000 kilometres from Samara which is impossible to cycle in the period between Australian matches, and even a challenge negotiating a route by train.

The only minor issue when applying for my Fan ID, was getting a passport photo to be automatically accepted online. Although once I found an acceptable photo, it was a simple online process. My Fan ID and World Cup tickets were mailed to me within a few weeks, along with an emailed electronic version of my Fan ID.

My Fan ID

My Rough Plan

Having only confirmed this trip a month before, I only had a chance to do a rough plan, which starts with flying into Moscow on 4 June. I will then spend a few days there before using a suburban train to get out of Moscow. This allows me to avoid cycling in suburbia, which also reduces the distance required to cycle to Kazan, in time for Australia's first World Cup match against France on 16 June.

By using trains, this will allow me to slow down and take my time, rather than try to rush everywhere. For me, I want there to be something interesting to see every day, rather than worrying if my ride is all connected. I also enjoy riding trains so will take the opportunity to combine the two when feasible.

From Kazan, I have four days to get to Samara by the 21st for Australia's next match against Denmark. I can travel either side of the Volga River which flows in a southerly direction between the two cities. The eastern side looks more direct but requires a long crossing on the Kama River Bridge, so I'm not sure if it's possible to cycle on this bridge. The longer west side route involves some ferries but less highway cycling, while there are railway lines in case I'm delayed.

From Samara, I have no deadlines except needing to be out of the country by the end of 25 July, which equates to 34 days. My rough plan is to follow the Volga River to Volgograd, formerly known as Stalingrad, a turning point in the Second World War.

From Volgograd, there are a few possibilities depending on time.

I would love to visit St Petersburg, but the sheer distance from Volgograd with the time I have left looks unrealistic without using trains, especially as I could spend days exploring St Petersburg. Perhaps I should save it for another ride from Finland to Estonia on a future trip, as the last thing I want to do is rush around covering vast distances rather than stopping to explore.

A shorter route is to cycle from Volgograd via Smolensk to Estonia. This area has some historical significance, as both Napoleon and Hitler invaded through here when trying to advance towards Moscow.

Another option is to utilise the train system, which would allow me to visit St Petersburg. However, there are issues with taking bicycles on long-distance trains. Apparently they have to be disassembled and I would have to carry all my bike parts and my bags into a small shared compartment, so it's not a simple process.

Since I have to be out of Russia by 25 July but have no reason to return to Australia before October, it makes sense to take the opportunity to explore other countries in the region. Therefore, my aim is to see parts of Eastern Europe especially as their history has been influenced by Soviet Union occupation and subsequent decades under communism.

As an Australian I cannot enter Belarus from Russia, as the border is not open to me. The Belarusians prefer you fly into Minsk for a few days, while the Ukraine and Caucasus are both war zones, so I will concentrate on the countries I can freely visit like the Baltics.

Once out of Russia I haven't done as much detailed planning on my route. I'm looking at Estonia, Latvia, Lithuania, Poland, Slovakia, Hungary and then turning east but don't have an exact plan. I could follow the Danube River or head to the Mediterranean coastline, but it doesn't look like I will have enough time for Greece.

Only Poland has cycling maps incorporated into Google Maps so other countries are a guess, especially Bulgaria. As always, my route is flexible and will no doubt change over time.

For ending the ride, I thought why not finish in Gallipoli in Turkey. Gallipoli is regarded as the first place Australians fought in a war, conveniently ignoring any conflicts between European invaders and Indigenous population of Australia, or the Boer War in South Africa. During my cycling trip in 2013, I experienced the Western Front World War 1 sites so why not see where the Anzacs started.

In April, before deciding on this trip, I read Richard Fidler's book called Ghost

Empire about the Roman history of Constantinople, modern-day Istanbul. It feels like the perfect place to fly home from, as the rest of Turkey isn't regarded as safe by the Australian Government, especially since the crackdown by the Turkish Government in 2016. Two years on many thousands of people continue to be detained, so I don't feel like I should go further until it's safer. I also wish to return to Australia in October for Outdoor Education work and summer sport, so I won't have enough time to go further even if I want to.

From Gallipoli, the most sensible route to the heavily populated Istanbul, is to cross the Dardanelles by ferry and head north to Bandirma where there is a ferry to Istanbul.

My only previous foreign language experience is French so I have no experience with any languages I will encounter on this trip and once I leave Russia, I will be changing countries regularly and so the language and currency will also. This will be a change for me as all my previous tours have mostly involved being in a country for at least a month or more.

Making it even trickier is that Russia, Serbia and Bulgaria use the Cyrillic alphabet rather than Latin. This alphabet includes some different letters and even more confusing is that some similar looking letters make a different sound.

I have downloaded some language apps but as I only decided to go on this trip a month before, I haven't had much time to try to learn Russian or any other language.

My bicycle set-up

I now carry only a handful of items I took on my first trip, as my set-up has evolved over the years. Even the actual bicycle has changed from a mountain bike to a professionally designed touring bicycle called Vivente World Randonneur, which I found at a bicycle shop in Melbourne in 2013.

My current set-up involves three major bags and three smaller ones. The smaller bags include a tool kit on my seat-post and two around the handlebars to store my iPhone and camera separately.

Strapped under my butterfly handlebar is a long horizontal black waterproof bag called Revelate Sweetroll. This enables me to store my tent, air mattress, compressible pillow, inner sheet and rain jacket at the front of my bicycle. This is only a recent change, having previously had most of my gear on the rear rack of my bicycle.

On my bicycle rack over my back wheel, I have two red Ortlieb Back Roller Plus waterproof pannier bags. One carries my sleeping bag, spare clothing, book, journal, electronic chargers and anything else I want to keep clean and dry. The other has my stove, food, spare equipment and basically anything which doesn't matter if food spills on it.

Gear on my bicycle
Cycle computer and two spare batteries
Water bottle cage on the handlebar
Two water bottle cages one on each side of the front fork
Two large water bottle cages on the frame
A smaller cage underneath the frame for the fuel bottle
A 1.5 litre Nalgene bottle, along with two smaller water bottles

Tools
Small shifter
Cycling multi-tool
Spare patches and glue
Spokes
Spare tubes x two
Duct tape
Spare chain connectors
FiberFix spoke kit

Electronics
iPhone 6 Plus and Apple white charging cable
SD card camera adapter for iPhone
My apple USB charger with Euro plug
Cygnet Battery 5200mh
Panasonic Lumix camera with two batteries and two SD cards
Li-ion camera Battery pack charger and cable, that charges by USB
Earphones
OwlEye Solar-powered light with a USB charging cord

Clothing
Showerpass Mountain Elite rain jacket
Blue Jumper with Berriwillock writing on front
Two hi-vis t-shirts, one yellow, one orange
One yellow cycling top
One set of thermal pants and top
My thermal top is Merino Icebreaker GT with hood
Two shorts, one boxer shorts
Three Alpha Coolmax jocks, have found they reduce chafing
Two pairs of socks, one thick, one thin
Shimano MT42 MTB cycling shoes that clip into the pedals
Pocket towel by Sea to Summit
One Helmet

Sleeping gear
Moondance one-person tent
Sleeping bag, Mont Brindabella
Thermarest compressed pillow
Thermarest Neoair mattress
Inner sheet: Thermolite Reactor by Sea to Summit

Sea to Summit kitchen kit that contains
A Spork
A butter knife
A multi-tool with sharp knife
Toothpaste and Kathmandu travelling toothbrush
Soap
Washing detergent
Sponges

Small First Aid Kit with
A few band-aids
Sports tape
Tweezers
Small roll of Fixomull
Blister prevention Kit

Other things in my pannier bags
Brooks saddle cover
Money belt, Sea to Summit waterproof
Two paper copies of passport and Fan ID
Yellow A5 Paper Journal and pens x two
A book will try to swap
Small Sudoku book
A small pack of cards
Trangia stove
Plastic container for spare food
Sunscreen, hand sanitiser and Voltaren
Aerogard, as I have been told mosquitoes are bad
Lip balm
Toilet paper
A Poo shovel
Macpack backpack that stuffs into a small bag
Combination bicycle lock
I will pick up maps as I go

Clarification

Spelling, language or historical information used in this book comes from what I learnt during the ride. Each country spells localities differently, so I've used what I believe the place was called locally, while trying not to confuse people as many well-known names have been anglicised. i.e. Moscow is actually Moskva in Russian. I made an effort to learn the local language, but many people replied in English, while Google Translate was invaluable for communicating.

Most of my tour was behind the former Iron Curtain, which allowed me to compare each country's experiences before, during and after the Second World War. This included the almost 50 years under communism post the Second World War, and changes in the last 30 years since communism fell with many countries having become independent.

Because each country has a different perspective of history, what I describe is relevant to where I was, and how I interpreted it. There is a stark difference between the Russian perspective of the 20th century and that of countries previously under the influence or control of the Soviet Union but now independent.

Therefore, I apologise for any mistakes, especially to anyone who has a personal connection. This isn't a history book with references so if I get a date or event wrong, it's my fault. Whatever I say about a particular place is a generalisation from when I was passing through, so things may have changed since then.

I'm writing this in 2020 using notes from my paper journal and my iPhone. Some days I wrote a lot in detail and other times I didn't. While I didn't always record the names of people I met, since many names were unfamiliar to me, they are harder to remember. Sometimes I took many detailed photos, other times I didn't, while there aren't many photos of me, my bicycle or people I met. Instead of focusing on taking a selfie, I prefer to chat with people.

If I refer to a dollar amount, I'm talking about Australian dollars unless specified. Time in Russia and Europe is known by twenty-four-hour time, but I will try to stick with am/pm to avoid confusion.

Getting to Moscow

A month before my flight to Moscow I went for a week-long preparation ride in New South Wales from Moree to Scone, via Tamworth. After arriving in the evening by train into Moree, I assembled my bicycle from the cardboard box it was in and rode off. I assumed my bicycle light would automatically work as it is powered by the turning of my front wheel using a Dynamo Hub.

However, the light isn't working, nor will it charge a device by USB, so I try fiddling with the connections and googling ideas, but I can't get it to work. When I purchased my bicycle in 2013, it came with the dynamo and has worked okay until now. A few times I have had to adjust the electrical wires for it to work.

After the ride, I dropped my bicycle off at Brunswick Cycles in Melbourne, because they have some expertise with Dynamo Hubs. A few days later I got a phone call telling me it cannot be repaired, so I have to make the choice to replace it or just go with a normal, slightly cheaper wheel.

As most of my tours are in summer, I rarely use my bicycle light and I don't think I will need it very often in Russia because during their summer, sunsets are after 10 pm and sunrises can be as early as 2 am. The light only works when the wheel is spinning so it is no use off the bicycle, so I use my iPhone light around camp instead.

Another consideration is I have found that my average cycling speed isn't fast enough for the dynamo to generate enough power to charge my devices or a battery pack efficiently by USB. Anyway, on most of my tours I can usually find a power source often enough. So I decide to go with a normal wheel which will apparently have slightly less resistance, not that I have ever noticed.

Instead, I find my white OwlEye bicycle light, which charges by USB and also has a small solar panel to help charge it. The battery lasts a while and I usually only have to charge it once a month. It can be taken off the bicycle easily, so I can use it instead of wasting iPhone battery. I haven't used this light for a few years and will see how it goes.

Because my bicycle has been left at the shop in Melbourne, this allows me, a few weeks later, to catch public transport from my home in regional Victoria. Without my bicycle it's much easier for me to just carry all my gear in one light, striped canvas bag.

With Saturday, 2 June 2018 being the first Saturday of the month, there is a public bus from Woomelang to Bendigo via Charlton. With my parents attending netball in Charlton, I organise for them to drop me off there.

After farewelling my parents, with them once again reminding me to be safe and enjoy myself, it is just over an hour bus ride to Bendigo, before a two-hour train ride to Melbourne and a short suburban train ride to Brunswick Station.

Brunswick Cycles is located near the railway station so it's easy collecting my bicycle just after lunchtime. I nearly make the mistake of forgetting to take the magnet off the spokes from the old front wheel of my bicycle. This magnet is critical for my cycle computer to work.

For the rest of the afternoon, I search for a few items, including collecting some mountain bike disc brakes from a bicycle shop for my Warmshower host Daria in Moscow. She asked me via WhatsApp because she apparently can't get them in Russia.

I also find a yellow paper A5 exercise book to record my daily journal, which this book is based on.

Once everything is sorted, I make my way to my sister Brylie's house in Preston for my last night in Australia for a while.

I will be referring to Warmshowers often. This is a website where people offer touring cyclists a place to stay at their home for free. Anyone can be a host and the host decides if they are available.

Warmshowers is a great way to learn about the place from locals, so I have used this on all my tours with many different experiences. I have stayed with people of various ages and family dynamics, from singles to couples to families. The style of accommodation can vary from camping in people's backyards to sleeping on a couch, to having my own room or even a place to myself.

Not all hosts are touring cyclists, some don't cycle at all, while many are aspiring cyclists and by hosting, they get an idea of what cycle touring is like. It's also a way to meet people from around the world without having to leave home, as people I'm staying with are just as fascinated about my own country as I'm about theirs.

In return the only expectation is that you will help cyclists when you're back home. I try to help whenever I can. I hope this book and any other writing I have done can assist and inspire.

There isn't a train to Melbourne Airport, so my best two options to get there are either by bus or bicycle. Buses all require a bicycle to be in a box, as I have done a few times including from Bendigo. However, having cycled from Melbourne Airport a couple of times, I know my way into the airport and I can get a bike box there, so I will cycle as I have plenty of time on this Sunday.

From Preston, it's a simple hour cycle west through the northern suburbs to Melbourne Airport, mostly using cycle paths and bicycle lanes which includes going past old Pentridge Prison to join the Moonee Ponds Trail, before I make my way to Melrose Drive, which is a dead end road but has a bicycle path which connects with airport car parks. From there I'm able to snake my way through the car parks until I'm close to the international terminal.

I try searching for a cardboard bicycle box at the airport arrival area including where I have previously left a box. But I can't find any, so I head to the Qantas service desk and purchase one.

The price appears to have gone up since last purchasing a box, as they now charge me $40, which, if I add the fare of $20 for the train from Bendigo to Melbourne,

Packing my bicycle into a bike box

negates saving money on cycling to the airport. Instead I could have used the airport bus from Bendigo for less than $60, using a bike box I have at home.

People often ask how I fly with my bicycle. It takes about an hour to take it apart by removing both wheels, both pedals, the seat and the butterfly handlebars to fit it inside a cardboard bicycle box. Boxes come in many sizes so sometimes it requires extra disassembling, but thankfully this Qantas one is reasonably sized.

The hardest item to take off are the pedals, as the pressure of pedalling makes them tight and you have to screw them off the opposite way you pedal. With each one unscrewing in the opposite direction to the other it can be confusing as to whether you're turning the pedal the correct way. I try to visit a bicycle shop to get them to loosen the pedal before I fly, otherwise I use a lubricant to loosen them. Since I was at a bicycle shop yesterday, they are loose.

I use bubble wrap, other soft plastics or my clothing to protect certain bicycle parts like the brakes and gears. I have only had one issue with flying with my bicycle, when after returning from Paris, I landed to discover that the box was half-flattened with holes in it but thankfully my bicycle was fine.

I'm carrying some clear packing tape to seal the cardboard box, rather than duct tape which doesn't work as well. Usually airport staff will have some tape.

I ask Emirates staff at the check-in counter if I can put all my baggage gear in the cardboard box together including my tent, stove, helmet and one pannier bag. They say as long as it weighs under 30 kilograms I will not be charged any extra fee as they have the same rule as Qantas, with this being a codeshare flight.

I often hear stories of people being charged extra for taking a bicycle even when they're within the baggage weight limit allowance. I got caught out with this once when I flew back from Paris with AirFrance. They charged me 100 euros to fly home with a bicycle in a cardboard box, despite it being free with Vietnam Airlines on the flight over. This was the flight when the box was half destroyed so I wasn't happy. So before booking any flight, I check the bicycle carrying rules for each airline.

I have to show my World Cup Fan ID at check-in, as this is my visa for entering Russia. They aren't familiar with this yet, so I assume I'm one of the first to do this, as the visa-free entry only starts tomorrow.

Because my bicycle box is an oversized item, I must personally drop it off at oversized luggage. With this being my fifth international flight with a bicycle from Melbourne, I know exactly where the oversize luggage is. It's near McDonald's for anyone else who needs to know.

Since I arrived at the airport with plenty of time before my flight, I manage to sneak into a Qantas lounge. I'm a frequent flyer member but don't have enough points for a lounge so since they charged me $40 for the bicycle box, I will get some of it back by eating their food.

My first flight is to Dubai, but after eight hours I have to get off the plane in Singapore while they refuel and clean the plane. All up it takes about two hours from when we land in Singapore to when we take off, before another six hours of flying to Dubai. I had expected it would be an easier flying experience being able to get off the plane in Singapore for a break, instead of a direct fourteen-hour flight to Dubai. However, the break is annoying as I don't get as long to sleep in between taking off, meal breaks and landing.

Changing planes in Dubai involves some walking and a short train ride between terminals. Otherwise it's an easy four-hour layover without having to worry about my bicycle box as it's checked through to Moscow.

On the five-hour flight to Moscow, I watch The Death of Stalin which brilliantly shows in a satirical, comedic way what happened after Stalin died in 1953, highlighting the bureaucracy which led to confusion once he died. This film is banned in Russia, but we are allowed to watch it on the plane to Moscow. All up, it takes me around 27 hours from Melbourne to Moscow.

After landing in Moscow, I show my passport and Fan ID to customs staff and have a quick five-minute chat with only two questions asked, including which matches I'm attending and then I'm allowed in. I'm not asked about my finances or when I'm leaving the country. I have been asked these questions when entering both the UK and the USA.

I'm expecting I'll have to send all my gear through metal detectors, requiring the opening of the cardboard box and then all my individual bags, followed by answering some tough questions. Instead they wave me straight through without checking anything – a different experience to America or when arriving back in Australia.

Assembling my bicycle is easy having done it a few times. However, finding a place to dispose of the cardboard box is harder. After looking around I eventually end up using sign language with a cleaner who takes it.

Compared to my airport arrival, accessing the airport train involves going through metal detectors, requiring the removal of all bags from my bicycle including my tool bag. This is annoying, as a couple of bags require a few straps to be undone. I have to redo this again at the busy Paveletsky Station in central Moscow. It is frustrating especially when police start asking in Russian what is in each bag, which I don't understand until one officer says "clothes" in English.

I understand they have had suicide bombings at railway stations in the past but find it strange that the airport is less strict. Before leaving Australia, I corresponded with a few people about taking a bicycle on trains and no one mentioned metal detectors.

The actual train ride is easy with a wheelchair area for storing my bicycle on this clean modern train with announcements in English and Russian. There are plenty of advertisements including Lionel Messi advertising Lays chips.

I'm tired from flying so my priority is to figure out a route to get to Daria's home in the western part of Moscow.

A modern train from the airport

As I exit Paveletsky Station suddenly I'm overwhelmed by the numerous tall, square, multistorey buildings and wide multi-lane roads with plenty of traffic. My first issue is figuring out how I'm supposed to cross the road as I can't see any pedestrian crossings. Initially I rush across between breaks in the traffic.

Eventually I figure out there are many stair underpasses, with most having pairs of narrow metal ramps designed for wheelchairs, comfortably allowing me to walk my bicycle up and down the stairs. Often inside these underpasses are shops selling a wide range of products from fresh food to clothing.

Cycling on busy roads doesn't look that appealing or safe but thankfully

An underpasses with ramps on stairs

the footpaths are extra wide with plenty of room. After seeing a small tractor go through the middle of the city, I find a well-built cycle path beside a footpath, which takes me north through the city before crossing a canal to the Moskva River.

Suddenly visible across the river is the famous Kremlin, Red Square and St Basil Cathedral. The Kremlin has creamy-red-coloured walls with red and green towers and plenty of green trees inside the walls. In front of the colourful St Basil Cathedral there are numerous shipping container-sized boxes with glass windows on one side, along with a few other temporary buildings being erected. So Red Square is smaller to explore than usual. I later learn that this is where the media centre was during the World Cup.

In Red Square

Arriving at Red Square is when it sinks in that I'm in Russia. However, being so tired I'm overwhelmed by it all, with so many stylish colourful buildings to see.

I'm planning to spend a couple of days looking around but for now I just want to have a sleep.

Except at the airport, so far I have been unable to connect to any free tourist advertised wi-fi, as they all ask for a mobile number to get a code, even at McDonald's. Since I left my Australian SIM card at home, I can't get a code. I had considered getting a SIM card for emergencies while I'm in Russia, but now it looks like I will need it to access free wi-fi and possibly for private wi-fi as well.

This makes contacting Daria impossible, so I make my way to her apartment block, hoping I saved her address correctly on Maps.me. A cycle path near the western side of the Kremlin, takes me westward, halfway towards Daria's home before some dogleg roads take me to what I assume is the correct address.

I have a look around the old multistorey apartment block, but I'm unsure if I have the right place. After a few minutes, a young man comes outside around a corner and calls my name and introduces himself as Oleg, Daria's boyfriend. He explains he saw me from their window.

After climbing four flights of stairs, I enter a small apartment which has a couple of rooms and a small kitchen, a style of housing I would get used to on this trip. Daria and Oleg speak English well and we share some soup but I'm so tired I'm not really appreciating what they are saying. I soon say goodnight and fall asleep in a spare room, tired from a long day of travelling.

I'm awake by 4 am as the sun is already up and I try to go back to sleep but my body is still on Australian time. After a few hours I hear Daria and Oleg wake up.

We chat for a while over a slowly cooked porridge breakfast about their own travel experiences in both Russia and overseas, including how Daria is into mountain biking. This reminds me to give her the disc brakes from Melbourne. They seem like a nice couple and I assume we will talk more tonight after they get back from work.

The plan for the day is to go exploring on foot using the Moscow Metro, with 1905 Metro Station only a short walk from Daria's home.

The Metro is extremely busy but well organised with metal detectors at every entrance and often, accessing a station involves long escalator rides as some stations are deep underground. Individual tickets cost 55 roubles which allows me to get on and off as many times as I like, as long as I don't leave a station.

I could have bought a card for cheaper rates but since I will only be using the Metro today and tomorrow, it's not worth it.

It feels at times stations are set up like sheep yards with one-way lanes directing people around, which is efficient because you don't have to worry about people walking in the opposite direction. The numerous metro lines are colour-coded, so this helps with directions but still I'm getting lost a few times when walking through stations on the various passages.

Nearly every station has its own unique style of artwork, with several stations having murals with different themes, including military, religious, agricultural or a construction focus. There are also various statues of people including a woman with a chicken and a man with a football. One station has many glass panels just like being in a church. This artwork is found all over the stations, including entrances, on walls, across from platforms and on the ceiling.

At one stage, I jump off at random stops to look at the station artwork; with trains running every three minutes it's a short wait for the next train. On the internet there are self-guided directions to see the most decorated stations.

A range of artwork is all over most metro station including the ceiling

On previous overseas trips I have usually just used free wi-fi but since I'm planning on being in Russia for 52 days it makes sense to get a local SIM card, especially as I still haven't been able to access free wi-fi around Moscow.

I have gone with the mobile company Beeline, which allows unlimited internet for 350 roubles a week and 30 minutes of talking time. Not sure if it is a great deal but it works.

My first place of interest is inside the Kremlin, which requires going through more metal detectors. Once inside there are tourists but it's not packed. Dominating inside the Kremlin Walls is the large yellow and green Grand Kremlin Palace, which takes up about a third of the area However, I'm not allowed near it as it's still the official home of the President of Russia, Vladimir Putin, but it looks quiet today.

Most memorable are a few large gold-domed white churches with Russian Orthodox crosses on top, while around church entrances are amazing detailed religious paintings. Inside is similar religious artwork as this is where tombs of Russian royalty are, which reminds me of Westminster in London but with fewer tourists.

Inside the Kremlin there are also botanical gardens, a large decorative cannon and a large bell with a piece cracked off.

Artwork on the side of a church inside the Kremlin

A decorative cannon is not far from the Kremlin Palace

My method for combating jet lag is to stay awake as long as possible during the day and try to sleep normal hours. By late afternoon, I'm starting to feel tired, so I'm not appreciating the sites anymore.

Instead I will check train times to Vladimir by taking the Metro out to Kazansky Station, as I plan to catch a train to Vladimir in a couple of days. This will reduce the distance to Kazan, making it easier to get there in time for Australia's first

World Cup match. This will also avoid cycling through the spread out suburbs of Moscow and I have been told Vladimir is an interesting city to see.

Just like Paris, Moscow has numerous large railway stations on the edge of the city, with many having names relating to a location where trains depart to, for example, Kazansky Station was presumably built for trains heading to Kazan. However, after searching around multiple parts of this large station complex, I can't find the correct timetable.

Despite ticket machines having English language selection, I'm feeling confused. It doesn't help that my iPhone randomly dies when at 45% battery. After charging my iPhone back at Daria's home, I discover I have been at the wrong railway station all along as there are nine main stations around Moscow.

On the way back to Daria's, I drop into a butcher with some interesting looking meat, so I go safe with some fat sausages. They take a while to cook and aren't nice. Neither Daria nor Oleg are back yet, so I lie down expecting to wake up when they return, except I fall into a deep sleep.

I awake in the middle of the night to a WhatsApp message from Daria asking me to leave in the morning, instead of staying another night because of a small mess in the kitchen. I thought I had cleaned it up, but I must have missed a bit, due to fatigue.

I also left the toilet unflushed after a wee expecting to flush it before they came home. In Australia to save water, I often go with the theory if its yellow let it mellow. I understand Daria's decision for me to leave but my only defence is that I was so tired.

No longer having accommodation in Moscow allows me to make the decision to leave a day earlier, allowing me more time to get to Kazan, which I would find I needed. Thankfully, my Couchsurfing host in Vladimir can host me a day earlier.

Not needing to catch a train until 2 pm, I have plenty of time to spend the morning cycling around Moscow.

After taking as many side roads as I can, I make my way back to the bicycle path I used to get out of the Kremlin on my first day. However, instead of heading towards the Kremlin, I take a cycle path south as it loops around the old part of Moscow. Along the way I pass a few bicycle hire stations, each with a map showing other bike stations and cycling routes around Moscow.

The path eventually ends up beside the Moskva River where there is a large brown-grey coloured pirate ship statue in the river. Turns out it is only a twenty-year-old statue of Peter the Great, celebrating the 300th anniversary of the Russian Navy which he established.

With time getting away from me I make my way back to Red Square to visit St Basil Cathedral. Unfortunately it's closed on Wednesdays but still I admire the colourful building from the outside and have one last look around Red Square

There are plenty of bike hire stations   *A lookout over the Moskva River*

After visiting a lookout over the Moskva River with views of the Kremlin, I make my way to Kursky Railway Station.

For this suburban service, there is are no metal detectors or security at this station. While it's easy obtaining a train ticket to Vladimir as the electronic ticket machine has English language options. I have been told I have to purchase a free bicycle ticket, so I do.

The station's platform is at the right height for rolling my bicycle onto an older style train, electric grey in colour with some red around the doors.

Common style of train in Russia, with old seats inside

After manually opening a couple of sliding doors, I find a tight spot to store my bicycle by taking up an end corner. On this train, seating is made up of rows of basic long brown flat seats. As this is an all stations stopping train, it is a long three and a half hours.

Throughout the journey people are coming through the carriage either busking with a microphone and loudspeaker or trying to sell items like ice creams, clothing or tools. They often leave a mess behind after giving a demonstration, for example, how a knife cuts.

Once out of the considerable suburban sprawl the landscape is green with plenty of forests to see.

Train busker

During the journey, inspectors check my tickets twice, and while there isn't any security to leave Vladimir Railway Station, there are metal detectors to enter it.

Valentina, Roman's girlfriend, meets me outside the station and soon Roman meets us. They both speak English well so for more than an hour we walk around town seeing the sites. This includes many churches and a fire station memorial, with a pump which actually pumps water.

Valentina on the left, with Roman

One of the churches is 1,000 years old, with plenty of decorations on the outside of this white church. It has been surprising so far just how many religious buildings I have seen in Russia – not what I expected.

During the walk at some high points, I can see across the Klyazma River Valley to a road heading through a green forest towards Murom, my likely route tomorrow.

Vladimir was the capital of Russia for a short period in the 12th and 13th centuries, so some buildings still reflect this, including the Golden Gate at the western entrance to the city centre. I

1,000 year old church

have been told this is a rare medieval Russian gate with a long archway and a single gold dome tower on top. Today any surrounding walls are long gone so it is now in the middle of a road, with cars going around it.

So far, I have been falling asleep at 8 pm since I arrived but tonight, I managed to stay up until 10 pm but this is early for Roman and Valentina. Roman teaches English to people by video and since he has a class in the evening, they offer for me to sleep in their bed. I reply I have an air mattress but they insist, while they will sleep on a mattress in the kitchen. This is not the first time this has happened on a bicycle tour.

Finally cycling

I manage to sleep in until 6 am, despite initially waking up at 4 am. Have found sleeping with an eye mask is the only way I can sleep past sunrise, which can be as early as 2 am. I gently wake Roman and Valentina up by 8.30 am, otherwise they probably would have kept sleeping. From my experience, it's common for Russians to start work later in the day than Australians and so they finish later in the day.

Valentina offers to cook me a chicken pasta breakfast, so I take the opportunity to chat more about Australia, my cycling experiences and their lives. I am thankful for all the assistance Valentina and Roman gave me.

Last night while looking at the railway timetables at Vladimir Station, I noticed that there are services further east to Gorohovets, which will allow me to cycle to Nizhny Novgorod, a city which sounds interesting to see and will allow me to be even closer to Kazan. However, I can't find the timetable online, so I make my way to the railway station to check.

Along the way, I visit a log cabin tourist information centre near the largest cathedral. I'm hoping to find a map of the surrounding area, as I didn't find any maps in Moscow but its focus is on selling tourist memorabilia, so no map.

Instead, for navigation I will be relying on apps on my iPhone like Maps.me, Google Maps and the Russian equivalent

Vladimir Tourist Information

called Yandex. Yandex has a useful app which not only shows roads but is also helpful when searching for categories like hotels and groceries. It's more accurate than Google searching but could do with refining between a general store and a supermarket.

The infrequent times I did find tourist information centres in Russia, they generally only had a small amount of information on the city I was in, rather than providing any information on the local region or neighbouring cities.

Back at the very ugly, clearly Soviet era concrete Vladimir Railway Station, I admire the old steam train on display, before locking my bicycle up outside, otherwise it will need to go through metal detectors to get inside the station.

The next train to Gorohovets doesn't leave until 3 pm, so I will stick with my original plan to cycle towards Murom. This will involve taking a more southerly route to Kazan, away from the busier main highway route.

The Klyazma River forms a southern boundary to Vladimir, so a bridge crossing is required to head south. However, the amount of traffic won't allow me to cross to the right side of the bridge, so I take a rough track on the bridge, which eventually involves carrying my bicycle over some small culverts. As soon as an intersection comes up, I cross to the correct side.

By now the weather has changed from sunny to overcast as spitting rain begins. This continues all day with moments of warm sun followed by cold clouds.

The highway is busy, especially at the start as there is a southerly east-west bypass of Vladimir. Once past this point traffic decreases a little but is constant all day, with a mixture of cars and large trucks so not the best cycling conditions. The landscape is mostly large, green pine forests on both sides of the road, which becomes a little open near the end of the day.

One of the first major differences in Russia are the Second World War memorials, which all start with 1941, ignoring the Soviet occupation of the Baltics and eastern Poland from 1939. In Russia this war is called the Great Patriotic War and for the rest of my time in Russia, I will refer to the Second World War as the Great Patriotic War but I will switch the name back once I leave.

Unlike in Australia there aren't references to the First World War. The most obvious conclusion is since their defeat to the Germans led to the Russian Revolution, which ended with the communist takeover of the country, it's not something to be remembered.

Nearly every town in Russia has a Second World War Memorial

I'm also beginning to notice numerous cement bus stops both in towns and in the middle of nowhere, usually with signed pedestrian crossings, even on quiet roads.

Throughout the day plenty of buses are going past, often hourly or even more frequently. However, only once during my whole time in Russia would I see a bus timetable. Locals just seem to know when the bus is coming.

Bus shelters in the middle of nowhere are a perfect spot to make lunch

Have seen many decorated bus shelter in random places

These shelters are a useful spot for a break from the weather and to make lunch, as often there is a seat inside.

Late in the day I begin searching for a place to set up my tent. From looking online my best option is a sports ground in the small town of Malyshevo.

I haven't seen or heard of any official campgrounds in Russia during any of my research, nor have I seen anyone camping yet, so I assume they don't exist. I have no idea what the rules are about wild camping in Russia, but I do know I'm supposed to register my stay at hotels, which I haven't done yet.

On previous trips most of my camping has involved setting my tent up in random places, so I'm experienced with finding places to sleep.

Therefore, I will stop in Malyshevo which, despite being a small town, has two small general stores close to each other. I have found this is common, even if they sell the same pre-packaged food that isn't very fresh. I'm not sure how all these shops, usually run by middle-aged women, survive.

Thankfully most reasonable size towns will have a supermarket or two and they are usually more consistent with fresh food options.

Style of general stores

Often my purchase in general stores was counted using an abacus but then I could pay with my debit card, even for say 30 roubles (60 cents) purchases. For the majority of my purchases in Russia, I was able to use my debit card and there were only a couple of times when it wouldn't work, and I'm not sure why.

Earlier in the day I found some antifreeze which I have been told can be used as a substitute for methylated spirits for my Trangia camping stove. However, when I try it at night, it won't light. Looking closer at the bottle there isn't a flammable sign. Luckily I bought food which won't go off just in case.

As for my camping spot, it is an ice hockey rink with overgrown grass where the ice would be in winter, with a shelter attached which I assume is the player's bench. However, the shelter is covered in rubbish and there appears to be a smear of old human faeces.

Nevertheless, with no other sensible choice and the fact that mosquitoes appear early, I decide to set my tent up in the shelter. Firstly, I have to empty everything out of my Revelate handlebar bag as the tent is tightly packed in the middle of it. I need most of the items in the bag for sleeping anyway.

Having had my Moondance tent since 2014, it's a quick familiar set-up, I then inflate my Thermarest air mattress, unroll my pillow, pull my sleeping bag out and settle in for the night.

During the night I hear people walking past the outside of the rink but have no idea if anyone noticed me or cared I'm here. I'm glad I slept in the shelter as bright street lights come on and the grass in the ice rink becomes dewy.

My first night camping in Russia, is in a hockey rink

As I'm about to leave in the morning, outside a general store a large white van shows up. A man gets out and opens a door to reveal shelves full of bakery items. As he takes a tray of bread inside the store, I follow him inside and find there are now plenty of fresh baked goods available including a jam roll.

Throughout my time in Russia, I would often come across a random

A bread van

bread van. Sometimes I bought directly from them or found some fresh goodies in a general store. Locals know when the van comes because this is the busiest time of the day. Other times there will be fewer bakery options, often only remaining is bread which has been left out in the open, causing it to quickly go stale. Yet when purchasing a bakery item, they will then wrap it in plastic when it has already dried out.

As I approach the city of Murom my rear calliper brake begins to feel sluggish and eventually isn't working, so I stop to investigate. Straight away I can see that the brake cable is really loose, so I tighten the cable a lot. I am not sure what has happened as my bicycle was serviced just before flying to Russia, so I will keep an eye on it.

So far in Russia, I have worked out what supermarkets and pharmacies look like but I'm still trying to find what the likes of hardware stores or sports shops look like. The main item I'm looking for is fuel for my Trangia stove which runs on methylated spirits but which has a different name in nearly every country. I have found a list telling me possible names in Russian but I'm unsure where I can buy it from, so I begin searching.

Type of shop fronts in Russia

However, I don't understand the large Cyrillic Russian alphabet signs out the front of shops and searching on Google Maps isn't helpful because it often takes me to places that don't exist. I'm walking inside random shops hoping it may have what I'm looking for and when I ask no one understands what I'm looking for. So, no luck with fuel for my stove.

The searching takes longer than I expected as the day just seems to get away from me. The weather has deteriorated to light rain as I begin cycling out of Murom.

Sometimes a brand new bridge across a river isn't always beneficial for cyclists as I find out in Murom. Instead of a ferry across the Oka River from the centre of town, I have to cycle out of town on the highway to cross the Oka River on a large cable bridge and then have to loop back to where the ferry used to cross. Driving a car, you probably wouldn't notice these things, but you do when cycling.

A requirement for a foreigner when visiting Russia is to register where you're staying every so often. I have been told every seven days at a minimum or every three days if you're staying in a World Cup host city. Since I haven't done this for my first four days and the rain has become heavier, I will try staying in a hotel.

The first place I find in the town of Navashino says no to me staying, so I make my way to the second one. As I'm about to head inside a man befriends me and then helps me with checking in. The friendly receptionist asks to see my passport, immigration paper and my Fan ID, as she fills in my foreigner registration paperwork.

After paying 1600 roubles, I have a basic room which looks old but has a bed, fridge, kettle and television but all that matters to me is that I'm dry and warm.

I have figured out that a straightforward way to convert roubles to Australian dollars is to treat them as cents and double them, so 1600 roubles equals approximately $32.00.

I'm finding town names are useful for helping me learn the Russian language, for example Murom is spelt Муром. With the different letters I'm having to re-train my brain to remember that y=u sound, p=r, c=s н=n, б=b and в=v. It's easier remembering letters sounds which are not related to Latin letters like ф=f and д=d. The most confusing are letters which either look similar or make similar sounds, Й is different from И so is Ш to Щ and little ь is different from В and Ы is one letter. Some letters are the same including M T A O K.

Newer words are usually easier to understand because they sound closer to English than older words. For example, SIM card is Сим-карта but is pronounced Sim-karta. Translation apps have been invaluable, along with setting Chrome up on my iPhone to automatically translate web pages.

Entrance sign to Murom

In the morning on the way out of Navashino I can clearly see the town square has seen better days, reminding me of the town centre in Back to the Future in 1985. With no one around it feels dead with only a Lenin statue in the otherwise empty cement-based town square. In Russia, most references to communism have been erased from history, however, most towns still have a Lenin statue.

Navashino town square, with a Lenin statue, which is common in most towns

While leaving Kulebaki three teenagers cycle past me. I follow them for five kilometres until they stop at the side of the road, so I assume I will never see them again.

Cycled with these boys for a while

Two hours later suddenly they show up again. We end up cycling together for an hour using Google Translate to ask questions and share Instagram profiles. Thanks to them for being the highlight of the trip so far.

Sadly, the road surface is not a highlight as it is terrible with potholes everywhere, even on busy highways. At Sakony as the highway takes a slightly longer route, I take the shorter route through small rural towns. However, the road becomes dirt with numerous potholes, some full of water, which is okay – just some zigzagging required. Seeing the conditions of roads makes me think twice, when complaining about local roads back home.

Many houses in the towns are wooden and in various conditions, some okay, others falling apart, while often the best-looking building in town is a church, but a handful are derelict. Since I'm in a rural landscape today I'm seeing tractors and cows, but paddocks aren't fenced.

In one section between towns the road has seemingly been abandoned, leaving a rough track. However, with less traffic, it's a more relaxing ride. Out of nowhere a short hailstorm begins, luckily nearby in the middle of nowhere is a bus shelter.

A common site - terrible roads in towns   *Rural life in Russia*

By late afternoon I realise I will make the city of Arzamas by tonight. Using Booking.com I message a few hotels, asking what facilities they have and if they accept foreigners.

ARZ gets back with the best offer, is the first one on the way into town and will cost me 1500 roubles or about $30 for the night. After buzzing my way inside a large gate, I find a quiet, clean hotel with a kitchen. Even with a language barrier, Tatiana the receptionist is lovely; she even does my dishes, despite my weak protest.

I wake to sunshine, so I handwash my clothes and dry them by hanging them on the outside of my bags on my bicycle. However, sunshine doesn't last so my clothes never have a chance to dry.

Near where I'm staying is the old part of town with an outdoor market and a large white church with gold domes. Further north, Arzamas becomes more of an ugly cement city with plenty of people around retail shops. Once again, I search various shops, trying to find either a map or fuel for my stove but no luck with either.

Church in Arzamas

As for cycling out of Arzamas, my route follows the railway line for a while, as the road becomes rough in places especially each side of the town of Vad. The landscape is becoming even more open but on this cold overcast day, I'm focusing on just cycling.

Vad is the first town, where surrounding the war memorial, I notice war vehicles on display including a jet plane and a tank, along with a large human head memorial statue beside a list of names of the dead. It was common for children to use these war vehicles as a playground.

Vad's Great Patriotic War memorial

After asking online for suggestions on what fuel I can get for my Trangia stove, Keith Liddicoat suggests I try asking for spirit at pharmacies.

So in Perevoz I go inside one, finding a small room with a wall of glass from floor to ceiling separating the staff and pharmacy items from me. From seeing other customers, I learn that I have to walk up to an open window and ask for what I want. So, I put a translation on my iPhone and walk up and ask for spirit. I'm given a small 50 millilitre glass bottle and it's cheap at 25 roubles or 50 Australian cents a bottle.

Outside, I try it in my Trangia, and it does light so will see how it cooks. The 50 millilitres should be enough fuel to cook two meals but I will keep looking for another larger option.

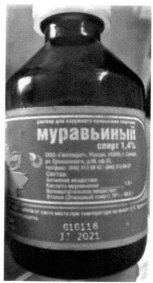

Spirit fuel for my stove

I see online there is a motel in the next town of Burturlino, so I race along as light rain begins. The motel cost 1500 roubles but doesn't have a kitchen so I boil water using the kettle and rehydrate powder potato, rather than use my spirit fuel.

With the sun out for most of the day I fly along despite the landscape feeling noticeably hillier today. However, rather than doing any serious climbing, I'm just going up and down every so often. Using a secondary road on the way to Sergach, it starts as five kilometres of paved downhill before gravel for the next twenty kilometres but with little traffic it's relaxing, despite cold clouds returning.

After some delicious mini pizza buns from a bakery, I leave Sergach with more rolling hills. At one stage, I stop for a pee and discover I'm near a rubbish tip with unchained guard dogs, so I jump straight back on my bicycle and take off as they begin chasing me. Thankfully its downhill.

As I'm making my way east, I have to cross a few rivers, so I need to be aware of where bridges are. However, I'm unsure if the bridge across the Sura River on my route is open, as I have been given conflicting information from online mapping apps and a general search online doesn't help. If the bridge isn't open this will require a 50-kilometre southern detour to the next bridge which, with Russian roads, will take half a day before I have to ride north again.

So, in Pilna, the last town on the railway line, I call into the unstaffed station to see if there is a local train option to get me to Shumerlya on the other side of the Sura River. However, I can only find long-distance trains, which are no use to me. So, I will continue cycling, expecting to camp somewhere randomly twenty kilometres from town, well before the Sura River.

After heading south across the railway line and over a small river before a steep short climb, I turn off my current road and soon I come across a large yellow road sign. After using Google Translate, I think it says that the route to Shumerlya is unsuitable for heavy vehicles, so I should be able to get through.

As I'm about to set off again a cyclist comes towards me, so I put a translation on my iPhone and flag him down. He confirms in Russian that the bridge is open despite not being happy I stopped him.

Not long down the road, I take a loop road through the small town of Tenekayevo to see if there is a suitable camping spot or general store. I can't find either but I'm seeing various farming equipment parked in front of houses. Not something you see in Australia, is a harvester parked out the front.

Every so often on a tour there are times where I feel like I'm flying along not noticing how far I have cycled. For some reason, late in the afternoon returning to the main road was one of these times. The conditions are perfect with a beautiful later afternoon sun, I can hear birds calling, the road is a decent paved surface with no potholes to worry about as I'm slowly descending for a while and every so often cyclists are racing towards me. Some are by themselves, others in groups but none want to stop and chat, so I just keep going until eventually the Sura River comes into view, but I can't yet see the bridge.

I am seeing a few campers beside the river and nearby creeks. However, while searching online I see there is a decently priced hotel in Shumerlya just on the other side of the river, so I decide to continue. Thankfully there is a bridge across the Sura River. I see why there is confusion as it is a pontoon bridge which I assume lies on top of ice during winter but is now floating on top of the water. While stopping to take photos of the bridge, I'm attacked by mosquitoes, so this confirms my plan to continue on to the motel.

The motel looks fancy, but the receptionist rejects me saying they can't accept foreigners because tomorrow is a public holiday. I suspect as a smelly cyclist she doesn't want me to stay. I can't find any other hotels despite searching in fading light, as online suggestions are not making any sense.

Eventually in the dark, I find a spot to camp in the ruins of a sportsground with the vandalised grandstand falling apart. I finally try cooking some food in my Trangia stove using the spirit bottle from the pharmacy and it works fine. However, it uses half the fuel in the small 50 millilitre bottle.

In hindsight, I should have camped by the river, as there weren't many options to do this in Russia. For some reason during my first week, I got in the habit of searching for indoor accommodation when I have a tent. Weather and lack of camping options were a factor, along with cheap indoor accommodation and a better budget than previous tours.

I awake to find a shepherd with three cows on the sportsground, as light rain begins. I can now clearly see how run-down the grandstand is, with graffiti, broken glass and random cement blocks everywhere. Looks like the place has been trashed, which reminds me of my first night camping in the trashed hockey rink. I have seen so much rubbish just dumped in random places.

While checking my cycle computer, it informs me I cycled 149.95 kilometres yesterday. This passed my previous longest day of cycling in terms of distance which was my ride out to Golden Spike in Utah in 2014. Both times, I hadn't planned to cycle that far, it just happened and both were late finishes.

I know people who cycle this distance every day, but many appear to just be cycling, whereas I prefer to stop to look at things along the way. There often isn't enough time in the day for me to cycle that far, rather than being just a physical reason.

Abandoned sportsground, with cement blocks and glass all over the place.

Russia Day Celebrations

Today is Russia Day, a public holiday marking the end of the Soviet Union and the start of modern Russia. Initially, it feels like any other day until I see a sign for a celebration starting at 10 am in a local park.

After undertaking some errands, I enter the park to find various food for sale being cooked on barbecues. A small concert is on, with children performing in traditional dress with an orchestra. Not sure what they are singing but still it's an experience.

For the rest of the day, I didn't see any more Russia Day celebrations.

The toilets in the park are locked so as light rain begins, I make my way to the railway station hoping they have a toilet. I'm not sure if I'm supposed to pay but staff just let me use the squat style toilets. For those unaware, this involves a large white porcelain square on the floor with two spaces for my feet either side of a hole.

As I'm about to leave rain becomes a little heavier, so I stay inside taking the opportunity to charge my iPhone and read my fiction book on the Australian light horseman during the First World War while railway staff are friendly, offering me tea.

The rain eventually eases with overcast clouds continuing all afternoon. My route is hilly with some traffic, nothing serious but still busier than I hoped on this cold day.

Near Azim-Sirma, I leave the highway to head south, as it looks like a quieter route, which it is. The trade-off is that this route involves a small section of gravel with potholes to be dodged, especially through Azim-Sirma. Once out of town the pavement returns all the way to Kalinino.

In Kalinino, there are a few small grocery stores, but they are all selling similar pre-packaged food with a small selection of okay semi-fresh bread. While snacking away I meet a cycle touring couple about the same age as me, but they appear not to speak English and are not interested in talking to me at all. So I'm not sure where they are going except in the opposite direction to me.

Leaving town, the weather deteriorates so a few bus shelters through the afternoon are useful.

By the end of the day, I find myself in the town of Yamashevo with a small war memorial, surrounded by a few buildings including what I assume is a school or the town hall. Importantly, with light rain around, there is a large enough spot to set my tent up in an entrance way to one of the buildings.

Nearby the small general store is open until 10 pm, which was a common closing time in Russia. After a brief explore around Yamashevo, it looks like a run-down town, with many buildings abandoned.

While cooking dinner, a mob of cows are chased past me, reinforcing the rural lifestyle they live by here. So far I have seen plenty of cows, either chained up outside houses or in unfenced paddocks with shepherds watching their herd.

Staying dry in Yamashevo

It appears in the rural communities that men dress in trousers and older women dress modestly, while farming practices are more hands-on with animals, many have their own veggie gardens and it's common to see homemade farming equipment. All this reminds me of how my grandparents used to live.

In the morning a man drives past me on his presumably homemade vehicle. It is a small trailer being towed by a rotary hoe motor on two wheels, with him steering while on a seat above the toolbox at the front of the trailer. This is definitely something my grandfathers would have built.

I assume a homemade vehicle, while many woman are dressed conservatively

It takes a while to motivate myself to leave my sheltered camping spot in the morning as it's another cold rainy day.

The building nearby which I thought was either a public hall or school, turns out to have a hardware store inside, along with photos showing the local community in Yamashevo. Seeing the photos reminds me not to judge a town by just looking at the outside of buildings. A downside of not understanding the language, is not being able to easily chat with locals or read in detail about a town's history.

On my ride to Shikhazany the rain eases slightly but still it's all about getting there, as I'm feeling like I'm cycling with blinkers on, focusing on staying dry, rather than the landscape.

After enjoying a type of kebab-style food at a roadside stall, I begin making my way to the city of Kanash. With ten kilometres of busy highway cycling to get there, I have found a back road into town. Unfortunately, it is a dirt road and with the rain, it is now mud so I'm slipping a few times as my calliper brake on my rear wheel is becoming jammed with mud.

Since I'm feeling frustrated and exhausted with the weather and Russia in general, I will see if there are any hotels nearby to have a rest afternoon to refresh myself. Firstly, I make my way to the railway station to charge my phone.

With metal detectors to get inside, it's easier to leave my bicycle outside locked up to a rubbish bin. However, all the power outlets are being used by waiting passengers. I still have some battery, so I head back outside to my bicycle and start searching online for accommodation.

While I'm searching, a young police officer comes over. As soon as he realises I'm a foreigner, he pulls out a piece of paper with Russian to English translation phrases. I assume this is a World Cup initiative. He asks me what I'm doing and where I'm going.

Once I explain I'm an Australian cycling to Kazan and show a copy of my passport and Fan ID, he is friendlier, with other people coming over to chat as well. I have had no issues with police, it has been more the requirement of them needing to check paperwork.

I have found an apartment on Booking.com in the nearby town of Yantikovo so message them and begin making my way through Kanash. I am finding it a busy city but I'm so focused on getting out I'm not appreciating it. While in a supermarket, I receive a message from the apartment host with the location not making any sense, so I message again. I receive another reply which informs me that the apartment is located near Georgia, 2,000 odd kilometres away rather than twenty, which adds to my frustration, as nothing is going well.

After another brief online look, I see a hotel in Yantikovo, but I can't find any contact details. Since it's on my route anyway I will check it out in person.

Once I get to Yantikovo, I can't find the hotel despite a road sign saying it exists. I do, however, find a free power point in the bus station which allows me to charge my iPhone and begin searching more thoroughly online for options. This helps to calm me down and allows me to work out a plan to get to Kazan by tomorrow night.

In the meantime, the sun has come out so I decide to continue cycling with no plan of where I will finish the day, just with the idea if I get far enough tonight, this will allow me to make Kazan tomorrow. Despite some headwinds initially, I'm still making reasonable time. During a snack break in Khozesanovo, two young boys around ten years of age appear. After a hand gesture chat, unprompted they show me to a water tap to fill my water bottles. I have been told to be careful of water in Russia as most locals buy bottled water but have had no issues with drinking this water, so I'm not sure what I should be doing.

Once I meet a road heading east, it's enjoyable cycling, as it is now more a tailwind and I only stop when I make the town of Bolshiye. On each corner around the main crossroad, are four similar looking general stores. After looking inside all four I find some delicious fresh cake snacks. While snacking away I can see down a hill a park, so I head down to investigate. Compared to previous parks this one has a contemporary playground and a large, modern, enclosed blue ice rink building.

Modern playground

I soon spot a cement path beside a small river which goes under the road, so I follow it. This path takes me to a separate larger sportsground, with numerous small buildings scattered around a central area, it reminds me of showgrounds back in regional towns in Australia. This looks like a decent place to stealth camp but I will have to wait for people to leave as its busy with locals exercising.

In particular a group of teenage boys are playing futsal in a purpose-built basketball-size court. So I make my way there to watch, while writing in my paper journal. However, the boys stop playing and come over to me. Using Google Translate I explain I'm from Australia and I'm heading to Kazan to watch the World Cup. They then invite me to join the game, where I score a few goals.

Afterwards, they all ask me if I'm on Instagram, so we connect online. On this trip, Instagram was the preferred social media people wanted to connect with me on and some still respond to me now. In a way, they are more excited to say they have met an Australian, as I assume few foreigners visit Bolshiye.

Their coach Valiullin, who shows up later, then invites me to stay at his house. One of the boys Almaz coming along.

However, for some reason, we go via the ice hockey change rooms as Valiullin coaches ice hockey as well. They then find me a towel and shampoo among all the hockey gear, and I have a shower before we go to Coach's house.

Meeting "Coach" after playing futsal in Bolshiye

At his house, I'm given soup and some liquid to try which burns my throat; turns out this is what vodka tastes like. On local television, the World Cup is being promoted on the news. The expectation of people I have met is that Russia will not do well.

Almaz wants me to go for an evening walk as he takes me to the public park to show me off to his slightly older friends, with one of them speaking some English. I'm offered some black sunflower seeds, which aren't particularly tasty and look like birdseed, but is apparently a common snack in Russia.

Initially, I was feeling a little apprehensive being out late at night with strangers but everything works out fine, with one of them giving me a lift in a car back to Coach's house, for my first car ride in Russia. I'm sleeping in a modern spare room, so not sure why I couldn't shower here. What started as a terrible morning, turned into a memorable day.

I will be in Kazan tomorrow, a World Cup host city, the first big city since Moscow and I presume I will see numerous Australians compared to the past week where I haven't seen any tourists.

Having to be in Kazan by a set date has been a good motivator especially when it was cold or raining. I am not sure how I would have gone if this had been my first bicycle tour.

Hockey sticks in the garden

After a lovely breakfast with Valiullin and his wife, I walk my bicycle past his vegetable garden with old hockey sticks helping prop up his vegetables, while Valiullin points out a milk cow in a small shed in his backyard. The neighbours are out the front of their house, as I wave goodbye to all who helped me out.

Kazan is only 75 kilometres away with only the Volga River in the way. The direct route involves a ferry which only runs a few times a day, while there is a more regular service but to a location ten kilometres from central Kazan. Therefore, I'm aiming for the 1 pm direct ferry.

Vladimir to Buturlino (Google Maps)

With this in mind, I race along not really soaking in the landscape as the road is initially quiet with just a few gentle 100-metre climbs. What changes is when I meet a highway, where the traffic and noise increases considerably. Helpfully the road shoulder is not too bad. So I plug in some podcasts to help get me through.

In the previous two years since my last overseas cycling trip, the number of podcasts I listen to has increased considerably. I now use podcasts to keep up with news and sport, more than reading newspapers online. I'm trying to not allow them to distract me from the trip, but they are a useful distraction when noisy roads are terrible.

There is one small break from the highway with a short loop road section through small towns. However, when I return to the highway, I begin a 200-metre climb but with two lanes it is okay and a gradual climb, with traffic respectful.

After 25 kilometres, I leave the highway as it travels over the Volga River on a bridge further west of the ferry. Instead, my quieter route is through the town of Verhnij Uslon on the inside corner elbow of the Volga River. However, since it's close to 1 pm I keep going with a short steep descent as the wide Volga River comes into view – my first view of this river I will get to see a lot more of.

The Volga is the longest river in Europe as it takes a horseshoe route through European Russia. Starting north-west of Moscow, it flows in a rough easterly direction through Nizhny Novgorod to Kazan, then south to Samara and continues in a south-westerly direction through Saratov and Volgograd before emptying into the Caspian Sea.

With many cities on this river and its tributaries, the Volga was the main navigational route in this region for millenniums, and even today many cargo ships still travel along the river. It's the equivalent of the Murray River in Australia or the Mississippi in the USA.

At the ferry terminal, there are a couple of ferries waiting so I'm unsure which one to take. After putting a translation on my iPhone asking for a ticket for the direct ferry to Kazan, I show my Russian translation to the first ticket office and he says da (yes in Russian) and sells me a ticket straight away so I board the nearest ferry.

Soon after starting to cross the Volga, the ferry starts heading in the wrong direction. I have either been sold the wrong ticket or I got on the wrong ferry.

Buturlino to Verhnij Uslon (Google Maps)

Kazan

Once across the Volga, I realise I will now have to cycle ten kilometres through suburban Kazan. However, I can see a spectacular looking church nearby which reminds me of St Basil Cathedral, so I go for a look.

From the outside it appears to be a collection of randomly added colourful buildings with towers of various shapes, sizes and colours. These include round towers, pointy towers, a red egg-shaped tower and one with blue balls on top of each other. There are also various shaped glass windows, that could be found on Play School, and what appears to be an open door for me to go inside.

The Scenic Temple of All Religions, the front cover of this book

Example of artwork still being added

Inside, I discover it's not a church, but the Temple of All Religions, an art space designed using various religious art features, including Islamic, Russian Orthodox, Egyptian and Jewish. Different art techniques are being utilised, including drawings, paintings, mosaic tiles, photos and dolls dressed up in various cultural outfits. Artwork is still being added, which I assume is regularly updated. It's well worth a look outside and inside.

Information inside Temple of All Religions

"The symbol of togetherness through Art and Culture! This is the idea of this Temple. The main point is that people unite regardless of their religion, ethnicity to create instead of taking part in wars, discord and hatred. We are all one, all the religions were given to us from the one divine source, but at different times, to different nations and though different teachers (Muhammad, Jesus, Buddha, Moses) The source is one!

The idea to create the Ecumenical Temple came to Ildar Khanov, as he said, in a dream. He said that the image of t blessed him to build the Temple.

Construction works have been carried out on donations, and it can be called "public construction". Construction works are ongoing on now, led by Ilgiz Khanov together with like-minded people.

The building complex includes the following rooms: Genghis Khan Hall (Pagan Hall), Orthodox Hall, Egypt hall, Islamic hall, Concert hall (Gothic), exhibition halls, Japanise tower, mosaic and woodcraft workshop. There are plans to create workshops for different art crafts and different directions, and new space is being developed.

It is open to visitors: both individual and tourist groups, guided tours are provided."

A railway station is near the Temple, but instead I begin cycling to Kazan initially on the road. I soon come across a levee bank beside a railway line with enough space to cycle on, so I join it to see where it will take me. As the levee bank goes around a corner, I see it is a dead end with a railway bridge blocking me. However, rather than backtracking, I carry my bicycle up some stairs and across the railway tracks to the busy road. From here I cross the Kazanka River into busy, central Kazan.

It feels strange to be back in a busy city compared to the relative quietness over the past week. From first impressions, Kazan is like a mini Moscow with a high-walled Kremlin and the first references to the World Cup since leaving Moscow.

Once past the large, busy railway station I search for where my hotel is supposed to be, but I can't find the entrance. After walking around the block, I discover it is right near where I first thought it should be. Turns out it is smaller than I thought, more like a hostel with small single rooms and just enough space to store my bicycle in my room, but no kitchen facilities at all.

From looking at maps I can see how the Kazanka River splits the city in two with the northern part being the more modern side with a large shopping mall, the FIFA Fan Fest and the World Cup stadium, while the southern part is the city centre and looks older with a large Kremlin area beside the river. A long pedestrian mall begins south of the Kremlin and connects with a large lake and gardens in the south of the city centre near my accommodation. The western boundary of Kazan is the outside elbow of the larger Volga River, with the main railway station beside it.

With the cable on my bicycle's rear brake still randomly loosening itself, I leave my gear behind and begin searching for a bicycle shop. Initially, I struggle with finding one, as a suggestion by Google Maps, is in fact a supermarket.

With the help of Nail, the son of my future Warmshower host, he suggests a shop across town on the north side of the city. My route across the Kazanka River goes past the FIFA Fan Fest which is starting to become busy with only a few hours before the opening match of the World Cup between Russia and Saudi Arabia.

I'm also beginning to notice many people dressed in green and gold and speaking English in an Australian accent, along with a few Australian journalists I know from back home. Feels strange after spending ten days barely hearing English, let alone seeing Australians since I arrived in Russia.

Once at the bicycle shop, they easily fix the rear brake and refuse payment for it. With it now nearly 6 pm I make my way back towards the Fan Fest, arriving just after the first World Cup match has started. Surprisingly, there are dedicated bicycle racks outside.

Each World Cup host city has a Fan Fest, which is an enclosed outside area, with sponsor tents and a big screen showing every game. To get inside requires going through security including metal detectors, and no outside food or liquids are allowed inside. This is a way for FIFA's sponsors to make even more money.

It's packed inside with plenty of people enjoying the game, including Australians I know from Daily Football Show, an Australian podcast I was listening to but which sadly doesn't exist anymore.

FIFA Fan Fest in the north of Kazan

Credit to Toby Zerna

During the first half, I randomly check Twitter, seeing a message from Huw, an Australian journalist hoping to meet me. I have only sent one message on Twitter about my trip and he found me. After replying, Huw asks to meet at half-time outside the Fan Fest.

Once back at my bicycle I'm surprised to see Toby the cameraman shows up as well. After a brief chat, Toby suggests it will look better with all my gear, so I cycle back to my hotel becoming briefly lost trying to find it. We re-meet at the bridge near the Fan Fest.

For the next half an hour, I cycle numerous short rides of twenty or so metres while Toby gets his perfect shot, the actual interview with Huw take less time. What an interesting experience as the interview takes place while being able to hear Russian fans from the nearby Fan Fest, cheering each of the five goals they score against Saudi Arabia.

After the match finishes many happy fans are going past me, with one Australian assuming I'm a Russian tradie because I have on one of my hi-visibility t-shirts. Since I only confirmed coming to Russia in May, I hadn't the chance to organise any Australian attire.

The next morning, before my hotel checkout time, I go for an explore around Kazan on foot via some fresh food markets, to the large brown railway station. With plenty of Aussie's getting off the train, I provide information about Kazan to a few, as they tell me about how they got here. Many have just flown into Moscow in the past few days and then caught an overnight train.

If I hadn't taken my bicycle, I would have also been using trains to get around Russia, especially as some free train tickets were offered to travelling fans. However, few train services make sense, as many require backtracking to Moscow rather than a more direct route between Kazan and Samara.

The main pedestrian mall is quiet before 10 am, with a few French fans in blue but it feels like there are more Australians in Kazan.

For the World Cup, they have set up temporary tourist information centres in half-spheres in the middle of the mall and near the railway station. However, at this time of the morning the only person inside is a security officer on a fold out stretcher, who presumably slept here overnight to stop tourists sleeping inside.

Later in the day I went inside a tourist sphere, finding a few volunteers who are helping with World Cup enquiries, or giving out information or a map of Kazan. This information has World Cup logos on it, so it has been specifically developed for the World Cup visitors and I hope this may lead to more permanent information for future visitors.

The main permanent tourist information is in an actual building in the mall. With more detailed information on Kazan but nothing about further south I still don't have a decent map.

With nothing of interest opening before 10 am, I return to the hotel to cycle to my Warmshowers host's home in the south of Kazan. Along the way I pass a few man-made lakes, before finding myself near a large two storey house beside another scenic lake.

In front of Kazan's Railway Station is one of a few temporary tourist information spheres

My host, Ildus, is away on an eighteen-month cycling trip around the world; currently he is in Vladivostok in the Far East on the Pacific Coast. Ildus is aiming to be home in late September, the same time as I fly home from Istanbul. Istanbul is closer to Kazan than Vladivostok, despite me having to cross numerous countries to get to Turkey, while Ildus will be just cycling through Russia. This highlights just how big Russia is and how I will only get to see a small part. I followed his ride on Facebook and he got home in October. Left behind in Kazan are his wife Gulnara who is a doctor, his around twenty-year-old son Nail and his ten-year-old daughter Jan.

Nail meets me outside their modern two storey house and takes me behind his house to a granny flat built by Ildus specifically for cyclists. Inside the main room is a fold out couch to sleep on, a sink, a yellow and green Australian boxing kangaroo flag and many more features I discover during my stay. Out the back is a room containing about a dozen bicycles, with plenty of tools to allow me to clean my bicycle and relax here.

Nail is volunteering at the World Cup, so he is invested in it.

Over the next two days, my Warmshower family makes me feel welcome in their home, letting me do laundry, offering to cook me meals and in the evenings, we watch a couple of World Cup games on television together. This included the enthralling 3-3 match between Spain and Portugal with Cristiano Ronaldo having an amazing individual performance scoring a hat-trick.

A granny flat built for cyclists

In the afternoon I return by bus into Kazan, finding it is now much busier as I meet up with Matt and Chu, two Australians I randomly saw on a television report on SBS World News before I left. They have also brought their bicycles but just for two weeks of cycling and the rest of the time are travelling by train with their bicycles. I'm interested in learning about their experience with having to disassemble their bicycles when travelling on long-distance trains.

Matt is dressed in a 1999 Men's Cricket World Cup shirt as they tell me they had to take both wheels off and find a spot inside their small shared sleeping compartment to store their bicycles. Sounds like it takes a lot of organising to get on the train and having two people would be easier. Maybe next time bringing a folding bicycle would make it easier to use long-distance trains.

We meet at Chak-Chak Museum where we enjoy learning about Tatarstan culture, as Kazan was the Islamic religion's western most point of influence in this part of Russia. Therefore, Kazan has both Russian Orthodox and Islamic faiths which, in the past, led to conflicts. During the Soviet era, Tatarstan culture was suppressed so now they are trying to re-educate people on their culture.

Our female guides are dressed in traditional long dresses, as they guide us through the museum in their okay English. We then sit down and have some local food and tea, including Chak-Chak which is a delicious baked yellow sweet.

This is what I enjoy about touring, learning about a previously unknown culture while hearing about the historical changes in Kazan.

Tea and Chak-Chak with Matt and Chu

Another museum has various items from the Soviet era on display including luggage, toys, board games and arcade games, similar to what my parents' generation grew up with, along with showing posters from that era in a nostalgic way. As someone born in 1987, the Soviet Union is history for me, so it's fascinating seeing some familiar things found in Australia and some quite different items.

In the evening on my way back to my hosts home, a conductor tries to tell me I'm on the wrong bus. Using Google Translate I stupidly argue I'm not. However, it turns out she is right as just before my stop, the bus turns right instead of left.

The conductor is great helping me find the correct bus and she contacts other conductors so when I change buses, the conductor knows to be on the lookout for me.

An example of toys from the Soviet era on display

On the actual day of Australia's first World Cup match against France, I spend the morning experiencing the Kremlin area which, for the most part, is free to visit.

The Kremlin is on a hill, so I walk around parts of the walls viewing many surrounding interesting sites on this beautiful sunny day. Inside the Kremlin are many buildings, some with a religious focus, including both a church and a mosque, with white and blue being the dominating colours.

While visiting my first ever mosque, I'm required to wear a skirt to cover my knees, while women have to cover their heads as well. In this part of Russia, many older women will be wearing a headscarf.

The mosque has a lot less artwork compared to churches with no humans present in the artwork. Instead there are plenty of Islamic Arabic symbols around this prominent white building, while hanging from the middle of the ceiling is a large, blue glass, flower-themed chandelier. In contrast, the church has many colourful paintings of religious people and crosses everywhere.

Visually I prefer the mosque because it's not in your face religion, just scenic artwork. From what I understand, one of the Islamic rules is that you cannot show religious figures like Mohammed.

The Kazan Kremlin with both churches and a mosque inside

Chandelier inside the mosque   *A Christian next to a Muslim*

Nearby are two statues together, one a Christian, one a Muslim, symbolising the meeting of two cultures in this region. Kazan still shares religions, something other parts of the world could learn from.

Nearby is the large semicircle curved agricultural ministry building with a large tree sculpture out the front. With many more interesting

Agricultural ministry

buildings to see, I make my way north to a busy riverside area beside the Kazanka River. It looks more like a lake with a pedestrian mall, restaurants and people collecting World Cup tickets here, with the Fan Fest visible across the water.

Kazan has a small one line metro underground train service which goes under the Kremlin, and like the Moscow Metro, each station is decorated with individual artwork.

Artwork inside the Metro

The metro connects with the larger tram network which takes you towards the World Cup Stadium. However, for some reason, the tram to the stadium stops over a kilometre away, despite the tracks continuing right past it.

Since I have spare time before the match starts, I search for a screw for my cleats in my shoe due to one having fallen out. It takes some time to find a hardware store before everything is sorted out.

Heavy security to get inside

There are long lines to get into the stadium with two security gates to get through, each person's Fan ID and ticket both scanned individually and then we go through metal detectors. Liquids or any kind of food is not allowed to be brought in, even apples, despite my attempt to sneak it in my pocket. I'm forced to eat it quickly as they won't let me in until my mouth is empty.

Security staff apologise for this saying in English it is Russian rules.

Once inside there are long lines for the limited fast food which is available. However, stadium staff don't care if you have shoes on.

Next to me high up in the stadium is a man from Kazakhstan, along with many other nationalities. In many parts of the stadium it's a sea of golden Australian shirts, who are making themselves known vocally.

As for the match, I'm enjoying the atmosphere with Lucas Hernandez the French left-back, being booed every time he touches the ball, after diving early in the game. After half-time, France is awarded a penalty due to a video assistant referee decision. This leads to Australian fans shouting out "bullshit", "bullshit" to the decision which then leads to other fans repeating "bullshit"; nice to know Australians have taught locals a new word.

Soon after the French penalty, we are awarded a penalty too. Mile Jedinak with his Ned Kelly beard scores for Australia. For the next twenty minutes, it feels like Australia is staying in the match until a deflection off an Australian defender, loops over our goalkeeper and just goes over the line directly in my line of sight, with the goal confirmed by video.

I thought Australia played well against a strong French team so am hopeful for an even better game against Denmark on Thursday. In the other match in our group, Denmark beat Peru 1-nil.

After the match, stadium stewards are lined up to shepherd us to certain exits and this continues once out of the stadium, with stewards lined in rows.

Wish they did this in Australia.

Staff line up to guide us out of the stadium

The volunteer stewards are smiling and are happy for us to give them a high five, but the police lined up in between them are stone cold, not smiling or offering a high five.

Some Australian fans are more carefree than the more reserved locals as many are singing loudly as we leave the stadium, with a few climbing up onto rubbish bins.

While walking back to the city centre, in a bookshop I finally find a decent paper map which will be helpful as I make my way south to Samara tomorrow. I also see that the article by Huw on my trip has been published online.

"Aussie pedalling 8000 kilometre to see World Cup"

The 31-year-old from Berriwillock — 330 kilometre Northwest of Melbourne — has joined thousands of Australians in Kazan for today's Cup opener against France, but none have experienced a journey like his.

Emonson is riding all over Russia on his bicycle for 52 days during the tournament, going to the Socceroos games in Kazan and Samara. And he won't stop there, saddling up for a further 10 weeks through Eastern Europe.

It's him, his bike, a tent strapped to the handlebars and two bags fastened at the back, holding his clothes, food supplies and a portable stove.

Try reading these figures without just cramping up in the calves: 120 days, 8000 kilometre, 12 countries, 100 kilometre a day and in the saddle for eight hours a day.

Emonson — proudly decked out in the fluoro tradie shirt he wears on the road — admits that most people are shocked when he tells them what he's doing, but to him it's the best way to travel.

"Most people can't understand the principle or actually doing it. I don't think about Istanbul. I'm just thinking about tomorrow, where I'm heading the next day," he says.

"You get to see a country. Not just big cities. Cycle touring is such a rewarding way of travelling."

His journey which started on June 7 in the town of Vladimir — three hours out of Moscow — will take him all over Russia before heading south through Estonia, Lithuania, Poland, Slovakia, Hungary, Serbia, Romania, Bulgaria and Greece before flying home from the Turkish capital of Istanbul on October 2.

The diciest moment so far?

"There was a truck coming towards me, overtaking while I was on a narrow shoulder. So two trucks heading towards me at speed. That wasn't fun," Emonson says.

Still it's not as scary as the time he came across a mountain lion in Canada, apparently. This is not the first time he has undertaken such an arduous trip.

In 2015 he followed the Matildas around Canada during the Women's World Cup and next year he's planning on doing the same in France before heading to the Ashes, Wimbledon and the French Open.

It's been a week so far and no crashes or major issues with his bike, not even a punctured tyre.

The Socceroos can only hope their ride through Russia will be just as smooth.

Towards Samara

Since crossing the Volga into Kazan, the weather has been beautifully sunny with not a cloud in the sky days, very different weather to last week.

It's another sunny morning but I will wait until 9 am for breakfast as my host family don't want to wake up until then. Since they have been so accommodating to me, I'm more than happy to wait and will always be grateful for their wonderful bicycle granny flat and all the help both Nail and Gulnara gave me.

With their home in the southern suburbs of Kazan, it is easy getting out of the city by taking some dogleg roads, before finding myself at the highway on the way to the airport. This busy, smooth surface, dual lane highway has a wide roadside shoulder to cycle on but once past the airport, the highway becomes single lane with some traffic.

I'm still experiencing vehicles not considering me when overtaking another vehicle especially when coming towards me. At times it feels like they are playing chicken with me. Thankfully, a wide shoulder makes me feel safer but still its unnerving when it happens. This would continue in Russia, possibly because they are not used to cyclists. Other times when there wasn't a road shoulder this was more dangerous, forcing me off the road.

Just past Imenkovo beside the Kama River is a large group of people in a grass paddock with cars all along the road, so I stop and walk to see what is going on. Finding a cultural gathering around a circle, with teenage boys wrestling, along with horses on display and food stalls, I'm not sure exactly what is going on, so I will continue cycling.

Cultural gathering near Imenkovo

Soon the Kama River Bridge comes into view. When planning this route between Kazan and Samara I had been concerned about whether I could cycle across this bridge, as there is no alternative once leaving Kazan. Thankfully, the bridge is a dual lane highway with a wide roadside shoulder. With little traffic it is a relaxing crossing with a gradual descent, as the wide Kama River is bright blue on this clear day.

Once over the bridge, there is a small roadside café with some tasty food including a baked chicken with tomato and cheese on top and a cold hot dog with jam in a bun. Cafés/restaurants in Russia often sold similar food to those back home, just with slight menu variations but still usually fresh, delicious food. So I'm trying as much new food as I can.

The direct route south involves continuing on the highway, but I have found a quieter route via Alexeyevskoye, which is a quiet town on the southern shoreline of Kama River with many shops. I can't find a place showing the World Cup but have found noodles to try to cook with my spirit fuel.

Leaving town, I pass a large, gold coloured church with reflective golden domes. In this region, churches are so colourful.

The road south is quieter and once I turn off towards Sukhiye Kurnali it becomes silent. The couple of shops in this small town are closed on this Sunday evening, while up a hill, a tall single tower building dominates the town, so I head up to investigate.

Golden coloured church in Alexeyevskoye

It's a mosque and in the courtyard, there are power points, water in a bucket and an outback dunny. With no one around it is a perfect spot to camp. Being surrounded by farm paddocks there aren't many other camping options and either no one has seen me or cares that I'm camped here.

After successfully cooking dinner, on my evening walk through a town with dirt roads, some with deep dry puddles, I see people chasing sheep through town, reminding me of back home on the farm. So far, I have seen more cows than sheep, while often animals are chained up outside houses. If animals are in a paddock, there is a shepherd with them as there aren't fences.

Mosque in Sukhiye Kurnali, has a dunny, water and power, this is all I need

Dry biscuit

In the morning, after trying some dry biscuits with a sour flavour at the small general store, I leave Sukhiye Kurnali using a farm track to connect with the small town of Levashevo, crossing the highway from Kazan straight away onto a secondary road route.

Shelter in the middle of nowhere

While stopped at a random roadside shelter for a snack, I discover that a bolt is missing from the frame of my left pannier bag. It is one of only three bolts which hold the frame onto the bag so it's an important bolt. The frame then hooks onto my rear bicycle rack.

I have been cycling with Ortlieb pannier bags for five years and this is the first time a bolt has disappeared on me. However, this is a relatively new set after my first set became wrinkled inside and was replaced. Previously I snapped a frame on an Ortlieb bag when I hit a gate while cycling on a rail trail on Prince Edward Island in Canada. In that case, I used some string to tie it until ordering a new part.

Fixing bag with cable tie

This time it should be a simpler fix as I just need a bolt. I carry a few spare cable ties and small bolts just in case but none of my bolts are suitable. So I cable tie the bag to the frame and continue on hoping to find a hardware store in Dimitrovgrad tomorrow.

Today I'm only going through small towns with general stores which, if I'm lucky, may have some fresh bread options and packaged food but not much else.

My original plan for today is to cycle south directly towards Dimitrovgrad as there is nothing I'm aware of that I wish to see. My finishing point is wherever I end up. If all goes to plan, I will be in Dimitrovgrad by lunchtime tomorrow.

However, around midday I pass another sign for the Bolgar Museum, this time only 30 kilometres away. Since I have a spare afternoon in my schedule, I decide to visit. This will mean a detour and a longer day tomorrow but Bolgar turns out to be worth it.

Bolgar State Historical and Architectural Museum-Reserve is a large, spread out complex with many religious buildings, both Islamic and Christian. I can cycle between them all and leave my bicycle at bicycle racks outside some of the attractions.

A large all-white mosque with dome roofs and large skinny twin towers, dominates the landscape, with a large reflective pool out the front, similar to what I have seen of photos of the Taj Mahal.

This time I'm required to take my shoes off to enter the mosque which is quieter and less decorative compared to the one in Kazan, as it's all white inside.

The bread museum next door isn't as interesting with old wooden buildings set up like a pioneer settlement, so I don't recommend paying to visit. As I'm about to leave,

Bolgar's White Mosque

there are two buses with signs saying they are Australian football fans on tour, obviously travelling between Kazan and Samara.

Nearby I cycle through a large wooden gate made with horizontal logs with a wooden pyramid roof, and find myself now in a wide open grass plain with paved paths to cycle around. I'm seeing numerous remains of stone medieval religious buildings, mostly with Islamic heritage but some Christian. I know this because there are information panels around, written in Russian and English.

There are a few single cream brick towers with a cone-tiled roof with just a single window at the top and a small balcony. Does Rapunzel live there? These are called minarets and at this

Wooden Gate

stage in the trip they are just another medieval building. It isn't until I get to Turkey that they would have a larger significance on my trip.

The first minaret I come across is by itself next to Khan's Shrine in a small complex among the open grass plain area with no one else around, including museum staff. It appears anyone can just climb up the minaret to an open ledge with no safety barriers, so I do just that while eating an orange.

Khan's Shrine, free to climb up

Near the wide and deep Volga River valley, close together are numerous medieval religious buildings. There are more minaret towers and a few large tombs of former leaders in buildings of various shapes and sizes. Some buildings are well kept, others in need of repair. Under a large square shelter is an open archaeological site showing layers of history. The whole complex reminds me of visiting Roman sites and clearly is important for the settlers of Tatarstan.

A collection of various old buildings in the Bolgar State Historical Museum

The current town of Bolgar is on the edge of this heritage site having been re-established in the 1950s when the Kuybyshev Reservoir caused low lying towns beside the Volga to be flooded. In town I have found more spirit fuel at a pharmacy but I can't find a hardware for a bolt for my pannier bag.

Since it is only 5 pm on what has been a warm day with the weather now cooling off, I decide to continue because cycling 30 odd kilometres tonight, will make a shorter cycle to Dimitrovgrad tomorrow, allowing me to arrive earlier as its predicted to get warmer. The evening cycling is relaxing with an enjoyable temperature and quieter traffic but worse road surface than the morning. However, it is better than most roads I used in the first week of cycling.

As for where I will sleep, late in the day I begin randomly searching in a few towns without finding anything decent until looking on Maps.me, where I see there is a possibility of camping at a church four kilometres away at Kokryat.

I find a dilapidated tall white church surrounded by a metal fence with two teenagers watering the gardens. Once the teenagers leave, I settle in for the night as mosquitoes make me seek the tent early. There is a dunny out the back but unlike last night no water or power.

Before leaving in the morning a bread van shows up randomly on the

Less facilities than last night

street outside the church with ladies waiting for him, so I purchase a snack. Also throughout the day I have to purchase extra water, as it is the warmest day so far.

While cycling along beside the road I pass a woman in her forties dressed like she is going to the shops. Not long afterwards, a blue tractor goes past me and I see the woman in the back of the tractor. Further down the road, I see her again waiting by the road and for a while, we leapfrog each other as she is hitchhiking using a few different vehicles. Hitchhiking appears to be common in Russia, with people of various ages doing it.

The track slowly disappears into a paddock

My cycling route towards Dimitrovgrad involves some quieter back roads and a short cut which turns into a dirt farm track, which soon vanishes as it has been ploughed over. To find my way, I end up using GPS on my iPhone, where a blue dot tells me where I am on Maps.me. I can see that I'm in the correct location as I'm still following a dotted line through paddocks.

On the edge of a paddock I soon spot a sandy track, which is my suggested route. However, the track is the hardest section to get through as my bicycle is getting stuck in the sand, so my only choice is to get off and push. I have no idea when the sand will end, I'm just hoping Maps.me is correct that a town is five kilometres away.

Eventually the sand eases off and the track becomes a more stable harder dirt surface before becoming a paved road just before the next small town on the edge of the city of Dimitrovgrad.

This short cut saved me twenty kilometres and cycling on a busy highway but having to walk my bicycle through sand is slow and frustrating, so the short cut wasn't worth it.

Having camped out the past two nights, indoor accommodation is preferred in Dimitrovgrad. However, I have an issue with a fake apartment listing on Booking. com which leads me to a random apartment block which makes no sense.

During my time in Russia, I had a few similar experiences with online accommodation not existing or people just randomly listing their apartment online but with no way to communicate.

I did manage to find a bolt for my pannier bag at a local hardware store, so I'm hoping it will hold. If it doesn't the cable tie option has worked fine so far.

After receiving a message from Matt and Chu, saying they have also just arrived, they tell me about their hotel called Tepemok. So, I make my way over there hoping the hotel has a spare room. They do, along with a bicycle rack in the backyard and free breakfast in the morning. While I'm informed that the Samara region including Dimitrovgrad is an hour ahead of Kazan so this is my first time zone change in Russia and I will cross back an hour in a couple of days.

Farewell Chu and Matt

My evening is spent with Chu and Matt in a sports bar, sharing an evening meal while watching a couple of World Cup matches along with a few locals. We compare our cycling routes from Kazan, as they took a different, longer route. From their description they took the correct ferry from Kazan in the reverse direction to me, then followed the western side of the Volga south before a long dam crossing across the Volga at Ulyanovsk.

Cycling back in the dark with Matt and Chu feels different as I'm not used to riding as a group.

Having finished my paper book, I leave it here, so now I have nothing to read in English – wish I had thought of purchasing an eBook reader before this trip.

Chu and Matt are aiming to cycle to Samara today, further than I plan so they leave slightly earlier than I do. It was delightful to meet fellow cyclists even if it was only a couple of times. We never meet again.

After a delicious crepes breakfast at Tepemok Hotel, I leave as soon as I can as a midafternoon storm is predicted. I don't spend any time exploring Dimitrovgrad, as, from what I saw yesterday and today, it looks like an ugly industrial city.

It's already warm when leaving town but soon clouds appear as wind is picking up. Once over the Bolshoy Cheremshan River which provides a border to the south of Dimitrovgrad, I leave the main road as I turn right into a headwind blowing into my face and onto a more cracked road. For the next 30 kilometres, the headwind is annoying until I can turn away from the wind.

It appears that farming is still collective here, as I understand it was during communist times. During the day I pass large scale farming operations with plenty of modern tractors and ploughs, just like at home. Or maybe they just have large family owned farms with a few workers, which is becoming more common in Australia. I asked Warmshower hosts a couple of times but never got a clear answer whether farms are still collective or not.

My arrival into Divnyy is well timed as another bread van shows up outside the general store. While eating a delicious fresh Apricot Danish I spend time chatting to locals of various ages using sign language to help communicate my trip and their questions.

After leaving town, I notice the replacement bolt in my pannier bag has fallen out. I try another spare bolt, but it won't tighten so I cable tie it again.

Not long afterwards I hear a squeaking noise and realise I have my first flat tyre of the trip. After taking all my bags off and turning my bicycle upside down,

I replace the front tube, pump the tube up and set off, as clouds are becoming darker and wind stronger with another 30 kilometres until Tolyatti.

I'm hoping to get as close as I can before the storm arrives but another flat slowly develops, this time in the rear wheel. There is nowhere safe to change the tyre off the road because there are trees and ditches on both sides and the road has suddenly become very busy despite no noticeable big towns on my route, so I begin walking my bicycle.

After a few minutes, I spy a gap between trees leading to a paddock with enough space to change my tyre, so once again I take all my bags off, turn my bicycle upside down and begin changing the tube. This is the back cover of the book.

A storm is clearly imminent, so I rug up and wish I had found a bus shelter as the storm begins, while I'm pumping up my tyre. Thankfully, there isn't any lightning, simply hard rain for fifteen minutes. Once the tyre is fixed, five minutes down the road I find shelter under a veranda of a small general store.

When the rain clears, the road is slightly flooded as I set off focusing on just getting to Tolyatti. It isn't much fun dealing with a busy, noisy road, while a couple of times, cars are still using my road shoulder lane to overtake in both directions and I'm also trying to avoid potholes full of water for the last 25 kilometres.

When I finally arrive in the suburbs of Tolyatti, I make my way to my Warmshowers host home in the suburbs. Finding a large double storey, gated home, an elderly woman speaking in English welcomes me in.

Evgeniya and Aleksei are a lovely elderly couple who are looking after their four-year-old grandson Leva for a couple of weeks. I'm staying downstairs in my own apartment which is larger than what many people in Russia live in.

Evgeniya serves up a delicious pasta meal as we still use Google Translate for certain words. Aleksei tries to get me to drink vodka but I explain how it burns my throat and I prefer to just drink water which is always served from a bottle.

I had a few delicious meals with Aleksei, Leva and Evgeniya

Instead of cycling to Samara, I have decided to get public transport from Tolyatti and back in a day. This will save me from cycling a busy highway in suburbia to Samara and by staying in Tolyatti, this will hopefully allow me to cycle quieter roads towards Syzran by crossing the Volga by ferry. It does mean missing a national park on the inner side of the large bend the Volga takes between Tolyatti and Samara, but I don't have enough time. I would have missed a longer memorable Warmshower with Evgeniya, Aleksei and Leva.

However, there are issues with public transport to Samara. The train from Tolyatti to Samara isn't running according to the time found on Google Maps, which isn't always as accurate here in Russia. Thankfully Aleksei offers to drive me halfway there, dropping me off at Samara Airport with the idea to hopefully catch a shuttle bus to Samara from the airport.

At the airport are numerous maps showing bus routes to Samara just for the World Cup. However, despite being told buses are leaving every half-hour, they aren't showing up and staff at the airport are no help. I'm not the only person hoping to get to Samara. Geisel from Perth has just flown in, so we decide to Uber to Samara together.

We end up spending the morning together exploring Samara, seeing the okay space museum with a full-size rocket outside. Inside is plenty of space equipment, including space suits, parts of rockets, many models and information about Samara's role in the space race. Samara used to be a closed city during the Soviet era due to being where space vehicles were built. They also have World Cup references including a model of the World Cup stadium.

Space museum, with Geisel in yellow, looking at model of Samara's World Cup Stadium

While walking along the scenic Volga River esplanade with a green bicycle path on this sunny day, we are seeing plenty of people using the river like a beach, with sunbakers, beach volleyballers and a few swimmers. I could be walking on any European Mediterranean beach.

As part of the World Cup, they have human-size Babushka dolls decorated in symbols from each nation playing in Samara, placed in a park near the river. The Australian one is cream and has the Sydney Harbour Bridge above the Great Barrier Reef on the front with Uluru and a beware of kangaroo's road sign

Samara's Volga beach

on the back. Nearby is the predominately red Danish one.

Babushka dolls decorated in symbols from countries playing in Samara

My highlight of Samara is a popular guided tour of the fascinating Stalin Bunker, which today is busy with Australians and Danes. Stalin Bunker was the fall-back location for the government if Moscow fell during the Great Patriotic War, but it was never used. The bunker was only declassified in 1990.

The bunker's stairs go down many levels with information on Samara's role during the war and afterwards. It also has information about Samara when it was a closed city, with one reference to an Australian building.

On the bottom level is the unused cabinet room set out as it was in the 1940s, with long green tables, wooden chairs, a large map showing the eastern front during a period of the Great Patriotic War and photos of important communist people.

Stalin's Bunker in Samara

I wish I could have spent longer in Samara but with Samara Arena a fair way out of town we need to leave at 1 pm. Thankfully there is an excellent light rail line which takes me close to the stadium but just like in Kazan I still have a kilometre walk to the stadium as I farewelled Geisel after an enjoyable morning.

As for the game against Denmark, Australia plays okay but can't score in open play. This time the video assistant referee helps Australia by awarding us a penalty, with Mile Jedinak once again scoring. However, it is a frustrating game as it finishes a 1 all draw, meaning to go through to the next round, we must beat Peru in the next game and hope Denmark loses to France.

After the game, Aleksei has organised a ride for me back to Tolyatti with his friend Serge and his family, who have been at the game and are dressed in 2018 World Cup shirts. It's an interesting car ride with the teenagers knowing English words better than their parents.

Aleksei talking to Serge and his family

When we get back to Tolyatti, I show them my bicycle set-up and they give me a couple of snacks and stickers.

Aleksei offers for me to stay an extra day and to take my pannier bag to get a new bolt at his engineering job, which he fixes well, with a strong Allen key bolt.

During my rest day I realise I needed it, having been

Aleksei fixed my bag

focusing on doing something every day since arriving in Russia. When you're away for months, sometimes you need to relax and not do much, otherwise you will burn out.

Most of my day is spent lying in a swing chair in their backyard, working out a route from now. With no more World Cup matches for me to attend unless a miracle happens with Australia qualifying for the second round, I can go wherever I want until the 25th of July.

With today being the 22nd of June, I have 33 days to see as much as I can. My plan at this stage is to continue following the Volga to Volgograd and then figure out a way north from there. It has been okay cycling between Kazan and Tolyatti, with some quiet back road options, so I'm assuming a similar experience to Volgograd.

For a brief period during the day, Evgeniya drives Leva and me to a few sites including the war machinery museum with various former Soviet era war vehicles on display including many tanks, planes, helicopters and a large submarine. Many children find it normal to play on these former war vehicles.

Evgeniya taking a photo of Leva playing on war vehicles

In the evening, we enjoy another lovely meal of meat and potatoes. I ask Aleksei about how the fall of communism affected him and he replies that it was hard for him to adjust for a few years. From all the people I stayed with in Russia, they appear to be the most well off with a large home.

While investigating my route before leaving home, I found a possible ferry across the Volga from Tolyatti but wasn't sure if it existed. This ferry will save me cycling 40 kilometres, including avoiding cycling twenty kilometres through the spread out greater Tolyatti and across a dam wall before taking the only road to Syzran. As this is the main road west from Tolyatti I am presuming it will be busy.

Being unsure about the ferry was my initial reason for contacting Aleksei and up until the night before leaving his home, we still aren't sure of the correct ferry time or location it departs from. Eventually, we figure out the only morning ferry service leaves nearby at 8 am, so I organise with Aleksei to leave his home around 7 am.

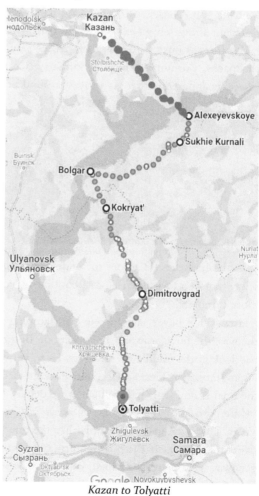

Kazan to Tolyatti

Leaving Tolyatti

Evgeniya cooks me a crepes breakfast despite me saying I'm happy with my own cereal and she gives me a Tupperware container to carry the crepes in. This container becomes useful to carry leftover food or to protect fruit or other spare food and it made it home to Australia.

I have found my hosts in Russia have been extra accommodating for my needs, even when I say I can manage by myself. This continues with Aleksei driving the ten kilometres to the ferry terminal as I cycle behind. We find that the site where the ferry departs from suggested by Google Maps is not correct.

Thankfully, the correct location is nearby as suggested by the Tolyatti tourist map along with the Yandex navigation app. I could have figured this out myself but I'm glad Aleksei is here to help me out.

Thank you Aleksei and Evgeniya, I will be eternally grateful for all your help; you went above what I expect of a Warmshowers host.

The ferry is busy with heaps of people wanting to get on. Many have hiking backpacks, presumably heading off to go camping and a few are mountain bikers, as apparently there is a forest around here you can ride in.

Many mountain bikers and hikers are on this popular ferry

As the ferry travels across the wide Volga on a bank among pine trees I spot a few tents, so I assume that as I continue following the Volga I may encounter more campers.

However, I never saw anyone else camping after this point in Russia. Along the way, the ferry stops at the locality of Berezovka, which appears to be just a paddock in the middle of nowhere. However, with a dozen cars waiting, clearly it's an important local service, as numerous people are leaving the ferry here, so the boat is now only half-full when we depart again.

After two-and-a-half hours, we arrive at Usolye on the southern bank of the Volga. However, instead of a pier like the one we left from, there is just a sandy riverbank To get off the boat requires negotiating down steep steps on a narrow gangway with guardrails which, with all my gear on my bicycle, is a challenge.

Thankfully with the help of fellow passengers, we manage to get my bags and my bicycle down the steps.

I follow the mountain bikers for a brief period before they take a different route. Usolye is an actual town with a small outdoor Saturday market on, so once again I go through the process of explaining to sellers that I don't need a plastic bag for my fruit when I have pockets.

The narrow gangway to disembark the ferry

By now it is 11:30 am so I set off on a warm day with an okay road surface. Close to Shigony, I suddenly hear a loud squeak and feel my rear tyre go flat straight away. This is my third flat in two days of cycling, so I hope it's not a sign of tyre wear as they still look like they have plenty of tread left. A bus shelter is nearby so there is some shade to change the tube.

Other than a short 80-metre climb, the rest of the ride to Syzran is uneventful through an open landscape, as over time traffic builds up the closer I get to Syzran. My arrival into Syzran is through the ugly industrial part of town with plenty of railway infrastructure around. Thankfully, the city centre has nicer and cleaner looking buildings, along with the remains of a former small Kremlin area beside an inlet which is now a park.

My only climb of the day   *Where the Kremlin was in Syzran*

I have organised a Couchsurf host in Syzran but once I'm told the address I realise it is eight kilometres in the wrong direction and the host messages me that he isn't going to be home, just his brother. It doesn't feel like a sensible place to stay especially as his profile is bare and he contacted me after I posted a generalised message. Couchsurfing is a bit hit and miss so I tend to use it if there are no Warmshower hosts. I'm more vigilant about hosts after a terrible experience in Dallas in 2015. In saying that most hosts are friendly, helpful people.

If I finish the day west of Syzran, this will allow me to get further tomorrow rather than getting distracted in the morning, which will hopefully allow me to be into Saratov earlier in a few days' time. As suburbia doesn't end until the road meets the main highway, I assume there won't be any stealth camping options and if I stay in a hotel tonight the foreigner registration requirements will be reset for another seven days, with it being four days since my last registration.

However, the first motel I try messages me to say they are having issues with electricity, another option is out of town beside the main road and has terrible reviews, so I find one closer to town. It is basic, more a dorm room style and my room is warm because the sun is shining on my side. I should camp the next two nights and I have a Warmshower organised in Saratov the evening Australia plays Peru.

I awoke to a flat rear tyre, so I replaced the tube. However, both my spare tubes, have holes that I haven't been able to seal successfully with patches. So I make my way to the only shop I can find that may have bicycle tubes.

The general sports store has bicycle tubes but none that are in my size, so I google to see if any bicycle stores are on my route. There is a store in Balakovo a day and a half away, with their website saying they have the correct size. I have also had no luck with finding a map for my ride to Volgograd, despite a few bookshops having maps, but none in the area I need.

My route out of Syzran involves taking a short cut by crossing a large pipeline on a small bridge, through a poor looking area of town. Once again, I'm seeing numerous blocks of brick storage sheds with large metal doors and small metal chimneys. I was never sure if they were just for storage or if people lived in them, as I never saw anyone near them.

Blocks of small rundown sheds, while many apartments looked like this

Leaving town is okay through an industrial area and once out of town, the scenery improves with a deep river valley on my left and the railway line to my right. I'm hoping it will stay like this today, with decent scenery and roads.

However, once I meet the highway it all changes, with the traffic increasing considerably, the main concern being the numerous semitrailer trucks going past me with barely a road shoulder to cycle on. I'm not surprised about the traffic, but I had been expecting a road shoulder similar to the ride south of Kazan. On a warm day having been delayed because of visiting the sports store, this section is not much fun nor am I feeling safe despite the scenery being okay.

As soon as I find a dirt track leading away from the highway and the river, I take it. Despite the dirt surface, it is a relaxing descending ride through farm paddocks without needing to worry about traffic. This takes me to the small town of Severnyy.

Consistent road through farmland   *A different way to stack hay bales*

From here its enjoyable cycling through a few small towns, while crossing a railway line three times and seeing rural farming practices. Eventually I have no choice but to return to the highway as the road becomes a grass track, which I'm still able to cycle, despite it being slow.

Once back on the highway I search for the first opportunity to leave it. The first track which Maps.me suggests down to Khvalynsk doesn't exist, so I continue on the highway until finding a second option. This involves a steep descent to the Volga on an abandoned road with potholes and motorcycle mud tracks crossing it often. For a descent it is okay, but I would suggest taking the main road if going in reverse.

Once in town, a convenience store is selling strawberry milk in a carton, the first time I have found flavoured milk on this trip. Often in Russian shops they only keep water and full cream milk refrigerated, so as an alternative to water, I have started drinking cold full cream milk. This isn't something I normally drink back home, and I have continued drinking plain milk since returning home.

An excellent cement levee bank beside the Volga goes around the edge of Khvalynsk, with many people swimming in the Volga or sunbaking on small beaches. Once the levee bank finishes, I have to decide whether to stop here or continue on. Once past the next town of Alexseyevka, the road re-joins the highway and there doesn't appear to be any places to stealth camp or food options available for a while.

With plenty of daylight left in the day I decide to cycle to Alexseyevka but I'm not sure what grocery options are there so with this in mind, I backtrack into town to find a supermarket.

The next twenty kilometres to Alexseyevka is scenic with green views of the Volga as it's at a similar height as the river with low traffic. Despite feeling exhausted from the day's heat, I'm appreciating the scenery and I wish the whole ride beside the Volga could be like this.

Scenic section beside the Volga River

Alexseyevka is a spread out town without a supermarket but with a few general stores so I can get an extra packet of pasta but not a lot of fresh food is available.

I'm not sure where I'm sleeping. I thought about camping at a large church but its gated, while a park on my map turns out to be private property, a small swimming spot beside the Volga has plenty of rubbish and people around it, while it was fairly open landscape on the ride in. Eventually I go with the idea to camp up a hill behind the ice hockey rink in the centre of town as it looks out of the way. It isn't perfect, especially with many locals still out enjoying the evening so I assume I will have to wait until dark to set up my tent.

While cooking pasta in the hockey rink, a woman and her two primary school age sons come to play football in the dry cement rink and then they leave. As I start to pack up my gear a man shows up and introduces himself in okay English as Aleksei and tells me that his wife saw me when their sons were playing. He then asks me if I wish to camp in their backyard. His offer will mean a safer and quieter night's sleep, so I say yes and follow him in his car.

Compared to my Warmshower experiences in Kazan and Tolyatti, this place is more basic with a wooden house, a wooden shed with a smelly drop toilet and a separate wooden shower block. It feels very much like going back in time, especially as they have many vegetable garden beds out the back. Aleksei offers for me to sleep inside but since it has been a hot day it will be cooler outside and as most Russians go to bed later than me, I may get a longer night sleep in my tent.

I do take the opportunity to have a wash, which requires water to be heated by a wood-fired stove and then using a bucket to wash myself.

Before going to bed Aleksei asks what time for breakfast and I say 7 am as my iPhone has changed back an hour to Moscow time. Instead his boys wake me up just as sunrise begins, as apparently I'm still on Samara time. I hope I haven't made them wake up earlier just for me, but I suspect I probably did.

I'm wanting breakfast at 7 am is that it is predicted to be even hotter today, so the earlier I can start the better. Breakfast is in their modest wooden home, where I'm served various delicious home-cooked food options, many of which would be served for lunch or dinner in Australia rather than for breakfast.

After breakfast, I'm told to wait while the whole family dresses up in local cultural attire and then performs local songs with a triangle-shaped guitar. This is what I love about touring – meeting people who show you a small glimpse into their lives.

The family dressed up and performed for me in a backyard full of veggie gardens

It's warm even before I leave and once out of Alexseyevka there is no choice but to return to the same busy highway as yesterday. The highway is high above the Volga, so I'm gently going up and down long climbs on a decent surface with some traffic.

As soon as I leave the highway to go via the small town of Shirokiy the road surface deteriorates to a sandy potholed road. Town roads and highways must be under different government authorities, as often once I hit town limits the roads conditions change straight away, usually for the worse.

Rougher road through Shirokiy

I'm hoping that once I'm across to the southern side of the Volga the traffic will decrease. To do this involves crossing the Volga to the town of Balakovo with a long section of single lane road, with traffic just as busy as the highway. The crossing of the Volga is on an ugly dam wall, where I go under an overhanging for half a kilometre with a tempting path next to the road. However, many support posts are blocking the path so it's easier to return to the narrow road.

Once across the Volga, I can't find a safe way to exit the highway so I keep going until I see an exit to a supermarket. I want to get out of the heat as it now feels like 40 degrees and it is only midday.

In the centre of town is a modern shopping mall which has the sports shop I found online a few days ago. They have bicycle tubes which aren't a perfect size but should work. Having taken my bicycle through the shopping mall, the shop assistant lets me use their foot pump to pump my tyres up.

While making my way out of town, suddenly there is a loud bang and my bicycle stops. Straight away I can see that my front tyre has blown. I assume a combination of too much air from the pump despite having a gauge and the hot temperature has caused it to blow. I replace the tube and return to the bicycle shop to get another spare tube, along the way stopping for ice cream.

My hot afternoon ride is now on the southern side of the Volga on a terrible potholed surface, where tar used to repair potholes is melting so I have to be careful I don't slip. There is slightly less traffic but still too much to relax, especially as many drivers are not used to cyclists.

Initially, there are plenty of cool drink options using roadside truck stops even if it requires drinking liquids I don't particularly like the flavour of, on this now stinking hot day. However, for the last 30 kilometres, I can't find any shops on the highway or even on the couple of times I leave the highway to search in towns. I do still have water, but it is so hot it makes me feel sick.

Making it even harder is that all towns are off the highway and none appear to have connecting secondary roads, so accessing towns is often by one road or a horseshoe loop road which ends up back on the highway only a kilometre down the road. Going into a town just takes more time with no guarantee of finding supplies so I'm not bothering.

Despite the heat, numerous people are selling handpicked berries beside the road and this would continue for the rest of my ride in Russia. Often the sellers are women between 40 and 70 with an umbrella for shade, but other times it is children. My Tupperware containers become useful for storing the berries.

Being exhausted from the heat, finding somewhere cool is desired. Fortunately I have found a hotel next to the church in the small town of Zorkino which also has a small general store closing soon.

Roadside fruit sellers out in the hot weather

Thankfully, the hotel has air-conditioning, a restaurant and a bath but no fridge or kitchen. I'm feeling dehydrated so I just have ice cream and cool milk for dinner. After a cool bath, I head to bed exhausted after one of the warmest days I have spent cycling. Reminds me of cycling in California in May or Australian summers.

In the morning, I try to leave as early as I can to beat the heat but it's still warm by 7 am. Initially I try to use a sandy road between towns, but it is just too sandy, so I return to the highway. The surface hasn't improved, in places it is okay but other times it is full of potholes and what should be the road shoulder is the worst section of the road. I also have to be aware the whole time of fast traffic which isn't used to cyclists on the road, so this feels like hell.

At one stage, I leave the highway and head into the small town of Podlesnoye but the road is a worse surface and anyway, it just loops back onto the highway once I'm through town, so I haven't saved any time but this does allow a break from the traffic.

The only decent surface for the day is a road into and out of Marx, a town actually near the Volga, with a small park beside the river. I take some time to try to cool off in Marx and on another day, I may have spent longer here before continuing. However, I'm aiming to get to my Warmshower hosts home in Saratov by midafternoon to watch Australia's last World Cup match against Peru at 5 pm on TV, so I need to continue before it gets too hot. On the way out of town a stranger comes out and gives me some much-appreciated cool water as I return to the highway.

After crossing another creek, I finally leave the highway permanently to travel through Leninskopye.

The road surface is even more bumpy but with less traffic, and it would be a relaxing ride if it weren't so hot. Thankfully, I'm now passing through a few towns, which allows me to often stop to get a cool drink and/or ice cream, while trying to stay cool in each store for ten minutes at a time.

Bumpy potholed roads

To get into Engels involves some industrial suburban cycling before I'm finally beside the Volga, where I can utilise a levee bank to get me into the city centre. From the levee bank I'm seeing numerous people enjoying the various beaches.

Serge, my Warmshower host, has asked me to contact him when I arrive but I have been having an issue with sending SMS messages with my Beeline SIM card. When I see a Beeline store, I go inside to see if they can help me, but despite using Google Translate to explain my problem, I'm not sure they understand me so I still can't send SMS messages. However, I can make phone calls and Serge just understands me and suggests we meet on the bridge over the Volga.

This long bridge is busy with pedestrians. In the middle of the river is a sand island full of beachgoers which is only accessible from the middle of the bridge.

Serge meets me on the Saratov side of the river with his bicycle and then I follow him through this large open city area to his home. For a few hours I'm able to relax in a modern apartment with air-conditioning as Serge offers me mash potato, my favourite food and I'm feeling rejuvenated.

The football doesn't go as well with Australia having its worse match at the World Cup losing 2-nil to Peru. This means Australia is now out of the World Cup, while Denmark and France played out a dull nil-all draw, so even if Australia had won, we wouldn't have qualified.

However, I'm told I must go stay at Serge's friend's house, as his unseen wife doesn't like people to stay. After squeezing my bicycle into the tiny elevator to get up to Serge's friend's apartment, I find this apartment is much smaller, older and there isn't any air-conditioning. I do enjoy chatting to Serge's friends despite some language barriers, but I have a terrible humid night sleep.

My original plan was to follow the Volga to Volgograd but after three days of cycling in 40-degree heat on terrible highways with narrow shoulders and plenty of fast traffic, I have decided not to go to Volgograd.

I'm disappointed that I won't see where the Battle of Stalingrad happened but the weather has dictated my plans, especially as Volgograd is predicted to be 40 degrees Celsius for the next seven days. With at least four to five days of cycling to Volgograd, it doesn't feel like it's worth it, especially as I have felt dehydrated each day, constantly stopping at grocery stores for cool liquids.

Even if the weather was cooler, looking closely at online maps, neither highway on either side of the Volga is near the river at all. Also, going by the last few days, I assume any non-highway options which do exist will involve unpredictable surfaces, and I have no idea if I can cycle them.

I can't find any train options to Volgograd outside of long-distance trains which require me to disassemble my bicycle. With the heat it's not worth it to even try; besides, going to Volgograd will make me further away from my planned exit of Russia into Estonia.

Now my rough plan is to travel north towards Nizhny Novgorod using suburban trains where possible to rest and save time, but I will be mostly still cycling. Being further north I'm hoping for cooler weather and more interesting places to see as I follow the Volga upstream in a westerly direction. This will take me on a route a couple of hundred kilometres north of Moscow and hopefully, eventually to St Petersburg.

In the morning, my first point of call is the railway station to confirm train times. After walking inside an ugly cement building, I find a suitable train for tomorrow. In the meantime, having found an apartment online with air conditioning for $35 Australian, I will have a rest day in Saratov.

While waiting for the apartment to become available, I have my beard shaved and obtain more bicycle tubes. The shop owner is excited to meet a foreigner and he takes my photo as I assume they don't get many touring cyclists here. I also try finding the Gagarin Museum but can't find it. The Gagarin connection is because the Vostok 1 capsule landed back on earth near here after the first human space flight. Instead I visit an okay art gallery.

The woman who meets me outside the apartment wants me to pay in cash, but all my roubles are too large an amount for her to take so we head to a supermarket to exchange money. While in the supermarket, I find ingredients to make Bolognese, having previously not found the right ingredients in Russia.

After resting inside my apartment for a while, I go for a midafternoon walk to the Volga for a swim – it's not the cleanest river but with numerous locals swimming I assume it's safe. Otherwise, I just rest in the apartment, watching a couple of World Cup games, while recharging my exhausted body.

There is a shock in the World Cup with South Korea beating Germany which knocks them out. The second goal becomes memorable as the German goalkeeper, Manuel Neuer, is caught stuck up the pitch, losing the ball while searching for an equaliser, allowing the Koreans to score an easy empty net goal.

This rest day allows me to plan my ride north in more detail, including finding suitable trains to plug gaps to enable enough time to see as much as I can without rushing. I don't want the same situation as the last few days where I felt like all I was doing was cycling as far as I could, instead of stopping to smell the roses.

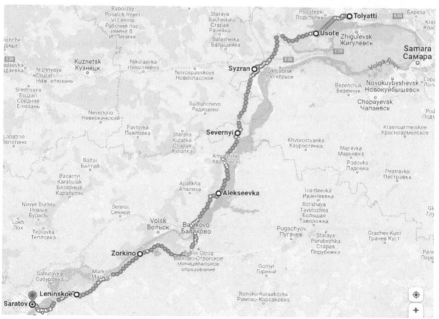

Tolyatti to Saratov (Google Maps)

Heading north

I'm feeling better after yesterday's rest, but I still feel like another day of not cycling will do me good. Fully assembled bicycles cannot go on long-distance trains in Russia so instead I will take a slower suburban service to leave the still warm Saratov. I will be heading in a northerly direction to Penza which hopefully will allow me to get away from the heat and find quieter roads.

I have to lift bicycle onto this train

Going through security at the ugly block railway station once again requires the removal of all my bags from my bicycle and then each bag is individually put through metal detectors. I make my way through an underpass to a bare railway platform, where an old-looking blue train is waiting. With steps to negotiate to board, it's easier to take all my bags off again, then lift my bicycle up onto this empty train.

It is a similar leisurely ride as the train from Moscow to Vladimir except it's quieter without buskers. With a change of trains required in Rtishchevo, I have a few hours to explore between trains. While inside the waiting room confirming the train times to Penza, I have another quick chat with railway security, using the timetable board to explain which train I'm taking in the afternoon and they wished me well.

Waiting room in Rtishchevo

There isn't much to see in Rtishchevo but most memorable is how they have covered their above-ground steel pipes with decorations and advertising. In Russia, steel pipes are often visible above ground, especially in towns. When these pipes cross a road, they go high over the road, allowing cars to pass under. I presume these pipes are for water and they are above ground due to cold winters.

Above-ground metal pipes are common in most towns

There is a museum in town, but it isn't open, so I just cycle around visiting some parks and a memorial to railway workers during the Great Patriotic War, as this is a railway junction town.

Outside a grocery store is a plastic bottle recycling bin, one of the few times I saw recycling in Russia. Due to me having to buy water often, this meant I created more plastic waste than normal with no way to recycle most of it.

Railway war memorial

Back at the railway station, a long-distance train is here for a short refreshment stop, with many people selling food on the low floor platform including ice creams.

For my second similar style old train ride today, the train stops a couple of times at railway stations in the middle of nowhere, whose names are just kilometre distances. At 192-kilometre station, there is only just a low floor platform, with no buildings or towns in sight.

Rtishchevo Railway Station

Penza is a larger city than I expected, with a busy railway station complex as I set off in the evening to find a place to sleep inside. Once again I discover that I can't find the apartment found on Booking.com, despite looking around for a while.

After another look online I make my way to Lastochka Hotel which is up a steep hill. The receptionist uses Google Conversation on her mobile, where her voice is translated into English to communicate with me. This was something I didn't realise Google Translate did until now. She also lets me put my bicycle in a storage room, while I sleep in a clean, modern room.

The next morning, I spend time exploring Penza including the informative local history museum which is up a 20% gradient hill. People are driving past me laughing at my failed attempt to cycle up this hill.

The museum is informative as they actually have references to ill-fated events in Russia, like World War One, the Soviet invasion of Afghanistan and the end of the Russian Royal Family. There are also references to wars they won including the Napoleonic and Great Patriotic War as well as many animals remains and local history about Penza.

Once again while visiting an art gallery in the governor mansion, staff follow me around the whole time. It is common throughout Russia for staff, who are usually older women, to follow me around a gallery until the next person takes over, so I'm never really alone. It is a little spooky even if they are friendly and helpful, despite the language barrier. This means there is often more staff than visitors, in this case six staff when I'm the only visitor.

Penza has a long, quiet pedestrian mall which starts from the main church and heads north with rows of trees on both sides to explore on this warm day, with a temperature gauge telling me it is now 30 degrees already. This clock style temperature gauge also allows for 40 degrees below.

Leaving Penza requires travelling through an industrial area, crossing a few railway lines on busy roads until sixteen kilometres north of Penza, where a loop road begins. This allows eighteen kilometres of a decent, quiet, paved surface road through small towns, the type of relaxing cycling I enjoy. Even once I'm back on the highway, it is okay for ten kilometres to Lunino.

During the afternoon, I have two interesting interactions purchasing food. Firstly, at a roadside fruit stall, the man is surprised when I say I want to put apricots in my back pocket instead of a plastic bag, so he washes the apricots and gives me extra fruit. He then becomes excited when I say in a combination of broken Russian and hand gestures that I'm from Australia and I explain where I have cycled. This is a similar experience to anywhere else in the world where people are amazed by how far I have cycled and where I'm from.

The second interaction is when buying an ice cream in a cone, I notice I'm being charged by the weight of the ice cream, down to the grams. This isn't the first time I have noticed this when buying assorted items not normally charged by weight in Australia, including various bakery items. When I take a photo of my ice cream being weighed, this causes local people to laugh at me. I'm happy once again as I have made people laugh.

Roadside fruit stall   *An ice cream sold by weight*

The next 45 kilometres is one of the most enjoyable periods of cycling in Russia so far, as the road is quiet on a paved surface where I can't recall having to dodge any potholes. With gentle climbs followed by gentle rolling descents, this allows me to relax and admire the views without having to worry about dodging potholes or traffic. I had been hoping most of the cycling in Russia would be like this but sadly it has not been.

Quiet roads to cycle along, while I'm often passing animals chained up outside houses

Along the way I pass animals chained up around towns, acting as lawnmowers, while also seeing more modern harvesters. It's a nice temperature as I arrive at the small town of Bulychevo with only one of three general stores still open.

My best option in the general store is a large frozen chicken breast which I soon learn is too much for me to cook all at once, as my spirit fuel runs out. Hopefully, what I can't cook tonight will stay frozen enough until arriving in Saransk by lunchtime tomorrow.

While cooking dinner at the basic railway station, with the help of Google Translate I have an interesting chat with a trio of young men who are smoking and dressed like bogans. I'm initially a little apprehensive around them but we all relax as I explain my trip. They are all surprised I'm from Australia and cannot relate to someone cycling around Russia. So far, everyone I have met has heard of Australia even if many have never met an Australian before.

Once they leave me alone after dusk, I find a quiet spot on the edge of town near a church to stealth camp.

I leave as early as I can to beat the heat and travel via a quiet road to Issa. A busy Saturday market is on, with a wide range of items from clothing to food available, including some delicious fresh pizza buns. By bringing my own bread bags left over from previous purchases, this helps reduce my plastic waste and makes it easier to explain that I don't need them to wrap bakery items in plastic.

Saturday market in Issa, with pizza buns

A few people are arriving at the market on very old-style bicycles with different methods for carrying items. Some just have plastic bags hanging off their bicycle, while others have baskets attached. In my time in Russia, I saw a wide range of people riding old clunker bicycles as a form of transport to get around, often carrying groceries home or dressed in work gear. However, rarely did I see locals riding bicycles for fun or exercise. I never saw Lycra-clad people with skinny road bicycles outside cafés having a coffee.

The ride into Ruzayevka involves a small section riding through a natural arch of trees reminding me of similar rows of trees back home on the Sunraysia Highway north of Avoca.

Ruzayevka is a large town with an even larger red and white railway station complex with a steam train on permanent display along with many closed pop-up souvenir shops. There are still a few World Cup volunteers around, despite the last World Cup match in nearby Saransk having finished two days ago.

After using the large footbridge over rail tracks and into the station, I'm surprised to encounter Colombian fans singing while waiting for a train. This causes a rare sight where railway staff are smiling, laughing and taking photos, as often they seemed to be jaded with their work.

The railway station is at the bottom of a hill with the older part of town up a steep climb to the main church area. Once up, I'm glad to get a cool drink on a warm day in a Pyaterochka, the most common supermarket in Russia, whose symbol is distinguished by the number 5 with a leaf at the top.

Ruzayevka Railway Station   *A common supermarket is Pyaterochka*

Jaiwei is from China

From here the flat road is busy but with a decent shoulder to Saransk, as they really are two cities slowly joining up. Close to Saransk, a small dot appears coming towards me. I soon realise it's another touring cyclist. Before I can slow down, he crosses the road towards me.

Jaiwei is from China and is all covered up dressed in baggy long sleeves and pants and his bicycle setup is the classic four pannier bags and gear over the rear rack. His English is okay, so we chat for a bit. He flew into Moscow and cycled to Saransk to watch a World Cup match and is now on his way south to Georgia. Then he plans on cycling west through Turkey and on to Spain.

I suggest the quiet route I took yesterday and wish him well especially as it looks a warm route to take in July. It's delightful to meet a touring cyclist in Russia as they are rare and I have only met a handful so far.

The first apartment I booked on Booking.com wants me to pay 50% more for my bicycle to be stored inside so then I thought of searching on Airbnb. Finding a cheaper place in a better location, I am not sure why I haven't used Airbnb before. I can also pay in Australian dollars straight away online with no need to have the correct roubles.

I have found staying in apartments costs a similar amount to hotels and I get more facilities – in particular, a kitchen and laundry, while my bicycle is normally allowed inside. There have been a couple of issues with staying in apartments; they are less dependable with contacting in the first place, and they don't appear to register me with authorities like hotels are supposed to do.

The ride to Saransk was quick this morning having left just after 6:30 am to beat the heat, so I'm in my Airbnb apartment by 11:40 am. It's now above 35 degrees, so I stay cool in the apartment for a bit while cooking the rest of my frozen chicken breast.

By midafternoon, I go for a barefoot walk in this World Cup host city. Because it was a host city it actually has an informative tourist information centre with helpful volunteers. The city is small so it's easy to walk around this scenic, colourful city which doesn't have a Kremlin but does have many interesting single buildings, dotted around. In a way Saransk feels more European in style with fewer dull buildings from the communist era.

The most striking is the new, large, round orange World Cup stadium on the edge of the city centre. While the red and white railway station is similar in style to Ruzayevka. There are many more buildings to admire in the main square, including the red and white opera house with reflective windows, while I put my feet in a large fountain on this warm day.

There is a small local history museum but without English information I'm relying on photos to try to understand.

Colourful buildings in Saransk including the Orange World Cup stadium and an opera house

Homemade swing

The history museum is near a scenic green park beside the small Saranka River, with the FIFA Fan Fest up a rise, so I head up there to end my day as I watch France comfortably beat Argentina, despite a late Argentinian comeback.

By taking a dogleg route it's a quiet relaxing morning cycle out of Saransk to get to the highway. Soon I'm able to leave the highway to pass through small towns. However, once again, the road becomes terrible especially just before re-joining the highway as the road crumbles and I only get through because I can walk my bicycle. A car would have no hope.

Compared to the secondary road, the relatively quiet highway has a decent surface all day but involves more roller coaster cycling with some long gentle climbs and descents due to constantly crossing creeks throughout the day. It becomes a little steeper in the afternoon. It's cooler today becoming overcast with light rain a couple of times especially around lunchtime.

When I have been beside the Volga, the highways have mostly been bypassing towns. However, today the highway passes through a few towns, which allows me to stop for refreshments and interact with locals. This is the style of touring I prefer rather than just highway cycling.

While stopping for a snack in Pervomaysk, I chat using the limited Russian I know to a family who is driving to Nizhny Novgorod to watch the Croatia-Denmark World Cup match tonight. If Australia had been more successful, they would have been playing instead of Denmark and I probably would have found a way to be there.

I make the mistake of not obtaining more water in Uzhovka as I assume there will be a general store or service station on the way out of town but the only service station I see has no store attached. Many service stations in Russia only sell fuel, nothing else.

The lack of water becomes a bigger issue because the afternoon ride involves 40 kilometres of not seeing any towns from the road. It feels even more remote as the road is surrounded by forests, with long climbs which mostly involve descending to a creek crossing and then climbing straight back out again. At one stage, there is the option of diverting away to Tolskiy Maydan, but it is three kilometres off the road, so I decide to continue, as I'm unsure if any shops exist anyway.

By the time I make Lukoyanov I need water and thankfully there is a decent red Magnit supermarket, one of the two regular main supermarkets I utilised in Russia. Often inside were free lockers, with keys, not sure why.

Because Russia is playing Spain in a round of sixteen knockout match, I search for a café or bar showing the World Cup on television. This takes a while until eventually I find a Kafe restaurant, where I have to ask if they can show the match, while I enjoy some normal restaurant meals served with French Fries.

A common supermarket is Magnit

It isn't until the match goes to penalties, that the locals appear to be interested. When Russia successfully scores all four of its penalties and Spain misses a couple, the waitress claps and the previously unseen chef comes out celebrating loudly doing a mini dance shaking his hands. Generally Russian people are more reserved than Australians, so it's nice to see them excited.

I could stay at the hotel next to the café, but I feel like camping. I'm not sure exactly where until I find a church three kilometres from the café, which is still in town as suburbia stretches along the road towards Arzamas. Along the way I stop at a bakery, where I find some delicious mini pizzas for a second dinner.

Camping behind a church

Thankfully, there is an open gate into the backyard of the church for me to sneak in and stealth camp.

It's straightforward flat cycling towards Arzamas with the railway line beside the highway for most of the morning on this humid day. There has been spotty rain a couple of times so once again bus shelters are useful as a mini break. The highway passes through a few towns but also visible in the distance are a few, large blue churches in towns off the highway. When I see one which looks particularly interesting, I decide to go for a look.

Once again, the road off the highway is in terrible condition with a few potholes and dirt sections but the church looks fine. I find it strange, the priority churches seemingly get over basic things in towns like decent roads.

The large church in the town of Krasny Bor looks like it has recently been repaired, so I open a metal gate and have a look inside a window. Before I even have the chance to have a proper look, an elderly woman comes out yelling at me in Russian and chasing me out the gate. I have no idea if I did something wrong so I will just move on. On the way out of town, once again, I pass more houses with vegetable gardens, as I return directly to the highway.

The rest of my ride gradually becomes busier as the highway takes me back into Arzamas, as I see the same large white church and outdoor markets from my first visit a few weeks ago.

Since I have plenty of spare time before catching my train to Nizhny Novgorod, I decide to explore more this time, firstly seeing if the road beside the river is scenic. It isn't as I can rarely see the river through trees, and it becomes industrial before I cross a railway line to visit Arzamas 1 Railway Station.

Arzamas has two main railway stations with trains using certain stations depending on where they are going. This is common in Russia with many cities and towns having a few railway stations often with names only differing by adding a number. While there, policemen ask me questions, but it is just another seemingly friendly inquisitive chat.

With my train not leaving until 4 pm, I continue exploring by visiting the local park and obtaining some supplies but I'm still at Arzamas 2 Railway Station by 1 pm to double-check train times. While waiting for the train to leave I spend some time recharging my iPhone, cooking a rice-based dinner and redefining my route after Nizhny Novgorod.

Decorative Arzamas 1 waiting room, while I wait outside Arzamas 2 railway station

Getting my bike onto a train

No security is required to get on this predominately red train but because of a low platform I have to take all my pannier bags off and lift my bicycle up onto the train just like at Saratov. However, this time the train is a little more modern as it has a space for a wheelchair which is perfect size for my bicycle. Just as I get my bicycle up a woman starts chatting to me in okay English, beside her quieter adult son.

It's not until you don't use your native language for a while, that you realise how much you miss it.

However, when only the son joins me on the train, the chat dies off, as he doesn't speak English. We try using Google Conversation Translate but it doesn't work once we lose mobile service, as we are passing through more pine forests.

The reason for getting the train is to avoid a busy highway which my Warmshower hosts in Nizhny Novgorod have told me to avoid. This also saves time, allowing more time to explore other parts of Russia. Crossing the wide Oka River by rail is a highlight as the bridge is high above providing a wide view before entering suburban Nizhny Novgorod. Seeing how stretched out the suburbs are, I'm glad I'm on the train rather than spending time cycling through suburbia.

It's simple departing the train onto a same level platform but then I have to deal with security, where I have to take all my bags off my bicycle for them to go through metal detectors. I then become confused about how to get out of the station, eventually figuring out a way using a few lifts and stairs to get out.

My Warmshower host Vasilii, has organised to meet me outside the station, so while waiting I chat to some Argentinian fans, also seeing World Cup signs everywhere. When Vasilii shows up with his bicycle, he then guides me to his house which I assume, going by his Warmshower profile, is close by.

However, we head off in another direction re-crossing the Oka River on a long bridge which then leads to a curvy 5% gradient climb for a kilometre, before heading south while dodging puddles on a smooth busy main road. I never have a chance to ask Vasilii how far to go but eventually after eight kilometres (I worked out later), we make his small apartment, where I meet Vasilii's wife Anastasia and their two noisy large dogs. I knew about the dogs beforehand, but they are still confronting.

Anastasia and Vasilii are both quiet, in their mid-twenties and scientists, who are easy to talk to. It's fascinating learning about how Anastasia does research in the Arctic. Vasilii tells me he was part of a 1,000 kilometre race a few weeks ago, after I mention I saw a group of cyclists near Pilna, and he confirms they were part of this race. This makes sense as to why cyclists didn't stop to chat.

Once I figure out where I am, initially I'm a little annoyed at having gone so far from where I thought I was staying. However, it turns out I'm on the correct side of the Oka River for visiting the old city centre, for tomorrow's rest day. With buses running from here to the city regularly, it works out well in the end.

In the evening in my room away from the dogs, I stream the end of the Belgium-Japan World Cup knockout match on my iPhone. With the scores at 2-2, Japan has a last-minute corner to win the game. However, the Belgium keeper catches the ball and the Belgians quickly counter-attack running the whole field before a brilliant dummy by Lukaku, leads to Chali scoring the winning goal for Belgium.

Nizhny Novgorod is where the Oka River meets the Volga River, upstream of where I first saw the Volga at Kazan. I first crossed the Oka near Murom on the second day of cycling and I have followed the Volga in a downstream direction from Kazan to Saratov. Now because of my route north I have met it again and I plan to follow the Volga from here upstream for a while.

The Oka is the largest tributary of the Volga and the Moskva River flows into the Oka, making the water connection between the city of Moscow and the Volga. I have been in the Volga River Basin since arriving in Moscow and will only leave once I'm close to St Petersburg.

At 10 am the brick-paved mall is quiet as I walk along seeing what I can find. In a bookshop, I finally find a decent collection of maps. After a decent look I select two maps which should help me navigate out of Russia and while I could have bought more, two is enough.

The Kremlin is at the end of the pedestrian mall, with the Fan Fest area beside the outside of the Kremlin Wall so I may revisit in the evening to watch some World Cup matches.

The red-bricked Kremlin is free to enter but some sections require payment, while half the area is fenced off to visitors as it is still being used for governmental purposes. Parked under the red-bricked archways of the Kremlin Wall are many vehicles from the Great Patriotic War era, alongside artwork and historical information about the Kremlin's past.

I'm allowed to walk on parts of the top of the Kremlin with spectacular views of the city, the harbour and visible across the Oka River is the large World Cup stadium and a yellow church.

On the outside of the Kremlin are many steps to walk down to the Volga riverside area with plenty of people out enjoying the wide pedestrian esplanade on this beautiful sunny day with plenty of ice cream sellers around.

Quiet morning in the mall   *War vehicles on display in the Kremlin*

Under a red-bricked archway from a distance this artwork is just a tank but when I get closer, I realise it is made up of a collage of smaller photos of Great Patriotic War victims.

Oka River flowing into Volga as Kremlin Walls go halfway down to the rivers

Hero Boat is on display below Chkalov Stairs

Along the esplanade is a tugboat-sized boat on display, which is known as the Hero Boat, as a memorial for the Great Patriotic War.

Next to Hero Boat is Chkalov Stairs which is a salmon coloured figure of eight pair of stairs leading back up to the pedestrian mall. But this is blocked off because the back of the Fan Fest is temporarily in the way.

The Kremlin is on a hill

Tramlines go around many parts of the city with one taking me around the old part of town, including the bottom outside of the Kremlin to the port area. This helps show that once again, a Kremlin is on a hill.

By now it is late in the day so I make my way back to the now busier pedestrian mall area for a snack, before entering the Fan Fest area to watch Sweden beat Switzerland on one of a couple of big screens. In the evening England finally wins a penalty shootout in a World Cup prevailing over Colombia.

After the first match, I walk back through the busy mall area with many people out enjoying this evening with a few buskers performing English pop songs, including trumpeters.

Inside the FIFA Fan Fest, while the mall is busy in the evening with performers

I have been surprised by how much I have enjoyed exploring Russian cities, especially learning about their varied history. Because there isn't traditionally a lot of international tourism, locals appear to appreciate me visiting rather than seeing me as someone to make money off, as I have found elsewhere.

On most other cycling trips, I have preferred cycling away from cities but here in Russia with the terrible roads and mostly plain landscape, I'm looking forward to visiting cities.

(

Penza to Arzamas (Google Maps)

The Volga again

I'm back following the Volga again, this time upstream towards its source. From looking at both my new paper maps and on my iPhone it does look like a better route this time, with quiet roads through interesting towns and hopefully nice scenery to admire.

After leaving Vasilii and Anastasia's home, randomly outside an apartment building is a large blue water bottle filling station, allowing me to fill all my bottles for twenty roubles. I have no idea if this exists anywhere else as I never saw another one.

Instead of following the main road back towards the city centre, I make my way down to the Oka River using a steep, narrow, zigzag path through trees. It is undeveloped beside the river, with a rough track which follows the river under a couple of bridges back towards the city. In theory, you could stealth camp here, but it looks like a dodgy area.

Once close to the city centre, I leave the river track to climb up to a bridge to enable a crossing of the Oka River to the newer part of the city, where I first arrived by train.

Dominating the landscape on a corner where the Oka River flows into the Volga is the brand-new World Cup stadium and a large yellow church. Nearby is an old market area which looks closed today so instead I stop at a supermarket next door. This newer part of Nizhny Novgorod feels less interesting, so I leave.

Initially I'm able to avoid a busy highway on my way out of Nizhny Novgorod, until just before crossing the Volga. For the next five kilometres I'm on a long viaduct with a decent road shoulder to cycle on, while below it's a swampy area until the next town of Neklyudovo.

From Neklyudovo I leave the highway behind to join a quiet road which travels through a few towns, follows a lake and crosses over levee banks. From looking at Maps.me, I can see that soon there will be two route options; either I continue on this current road which will shortly meet a highway or I take back roads which will allow me to avoid the highway for a while longer, but I'm unsure of their condition.

However, I'm unsure exactly which road is the short cut as a few small tracks are going off the road. Therefore, I turn GPS on my iPhone to work out exactly where I am. Even then some roads aren't as accurately mapped on Maps.me so it is a lottery to find the correct road, while my paper map is too large a scale to help me.

This sign could be for nearly every road

Roads are a mixed bag in this region

The first time I thought I found an actual road to take, it turns to sand, so I backtrack and continue for a little bit more. I soon try another quiet road, which starts paved but ends up being a farm track which passes by some large plants in flower until suddenly in the middle of nowhere the bitumen returns and this being Russia there is also a bus shelter. Once I re-join a highway, it is busy for ten kilometres to Gorodets and I realise how relaxing the previous section has been.

Gorodets isn't as interesting as I hoped. Maybe Russians would find it interesting but due to language differences, I can't figure out what makes it interesting, despite there being signs directing me to a few well-kept older style wooden buildings. After further looking around, I think it is religious-based tourism.

Australian shirt

There are plenty of tourists around, including a man in a yellow Australian cricket shirt with Warnie on his back. For a minute, I'm excited to think I will be chatting to an Australian, but he is in fact Russian. He has no idea who Shane Warne is, as someone just gave him this shirt. For anyone not from a cricketing nation, Shane Warne was one of the most famous cricketers in the world.

North of Gorodets the Volga is dammed, forming Gorky Reservoir. I'm on the eastern side which doesn't have any decent road options further north, so I cross on the dam wall to the western side to the town of Zavolzhe. Zavolzhe feels like an industrial town which probably had something to do with the Gorky Reservoir being built. Gorky is another name for Nizhny Novgorod, as many Russian cities changed names especially during and after the communist era.

I thought about camping here but the main sports ground is busy with plenty of people out exercising or teenagers being teenagers. It is the same with the park next door so I make my way to the next town only five kilometres away called Pervomaysliy. Finding a small town with a small community centre to stealth camp behind, with rain looking likely overnight, I place my bicycle under the veranda in front of the community centre while I sleep behind it.

In the morning with no rain around, I leave my tent to dry, while I walk to the nearby general store for some breakfast supplies.

After returning to pack up my gear, as I'm about to leave a man shows up. Using Google Translate, Ukhanov talks to me and while we chat, he organises a few local community members to come over, including a woman who speaks some English. He shows me inside the community centre where I'm shown local toys and crafts, I'm dressed up in a heritage white shirt and given a chocolate bar snack. Finally, a photo is taken of me in front of the war memorial with a few locals.

This is what I enjoy about bicycle touring – for me Pervomaysliy was just a random town until meeting the locals who make me feel like a celebrity.

Pervomaysliy War Memorial

Ukhanov inside the community centre, as I'm dressed up and shown toys.

It is still a cold overcast day as I start cycling, my route involving highways, with rain off and on for a few hours so it's not much fun.

The town of Chkalovsk is okay to visit, with a decent lookout of the wide Volga as the sun briefly comes out. However, soon the heaviest rain of the day begins so I find shelter in a supermarket for a while. While sheltering I find a hotel online not far away in the next town of Puchezh, so I continue as thankfully the rain soon clears along with the traffic as I leave a highway behind. However, the hotel appears to be permanently closed and since the sun is now out, I take it as a sign to continue cycling.

Before leaving town, I visit the most scenically located war memorial I saw in Russia. It is on the banks of the wide Gorky Reservoir, with a tall white monolith memorial in a larger open public park, with a few park benches.

War memorial beside the Volga

For my evening ride, the traffic is light except for an old small green harvester with its comb still attached to its front, which is keeping pace with me.

Today's ride finishes in the town of Segot, where my best camping option is a small single storey church. It looks more like a house, with the addition of a small green round pointy tower to make it look like a church. Of more interest to me is that there is a small veranda to settle under for the night as rain is looking likely to return.

While relaxing in my tent under the veranda, a man shows up and insists that I should stay at his house nearby. I carry my tent over but he insists I sleep inside.

Igor's English is okay as he explains that he looks after the church, so he is

religious. He asks me about my own lack of religion, while he gives me another meal.

His home is a wooden shack similar to the family I stayed with in Alekseyevka, with a stinky drop toilet in a separately attached shed. However, his actual home is a comfortable place to stay, as I sleep well in the spare bed he offers me. Once again, people have been so friendly and helpful, especially today.

Igor wants to leave at 7 am for an appointment but he still insists on making me a fish and pasta-based breakfast. He gives me so much I end up carrying leftovers in my

Igor fixing his car, while his church is in the background

Tupperware container.

I set off on a sunny day making my way to Yuryevets through a mixture of trees and open views of the Volga on my right. I arrive at a high point of Yuryevets with a war memorial and a lookout providing views of a scenic town on an elbow of the Volga. With a steep one-way road into town, it is easier to just leave my bicycle locked up near the war memorial and walk down some stairs to find a large white church tower and a local market on. However, once again it looks like the river is separate from Yuryevets as there is a barrier between town and the wide river and there isn't any infrastructure beside the river, which was common in Russia.

Yuryevets war memorial is on a rise, with stairs lead down to town

The rest of the day is similar to other times I have been following the Volga, where I'm only occasionally seeing the river, but instead I'm going through forests and small towns. I have been surprised how roads don't seem to follow rivers compared to previous experiences in other countries. At one stage, there appears to be a secondary road possibility. However, when I try it, I find a muddy track with numerous puddles causing my bicycle to become clogged with mud, so I turn back.

In the afternoon clouds return with occasional showers of rain and then the sun will come out for a fleeting time but by the time I make the city of Kineshma rain appears to have settled in. So instead of admiring the waterfront and markets, my priority is finding inside accommodation, especially as the first two World Cup quarter-finals are on tonight.

I have had no luck with Airbnb but have managed to find an apartment on Booking.com. This time the listing exists, and the owner lives next door, so I end up sharing a meal and watching the first two quarter-finals with Gena, his wife and two young children. During the break between matches, Gena takes me around the block to introduce me to his friends.

Gena and his family   *Fixing my bicycle in my simple apartment*

In the morning, I spend time doing some bicycle maintenance in my one main room apartment, including fixing a front flat tyre and a rubbing rear brake, so I don't leave until 9:30 am.

Further west from here there aren't any decent roads on the southern side of the Volga. Luckily, there is a bridge to the northern side, the first one since Gorky Dam.

Once on the northern side I'm cursing my map at the start as the rough, slippery, sandy dirt road is full of large, bumpy potholes so it's hard going especially on my body and my map suggests this goes on for 40 kilometres. Thankfully over time the road slightly improves, becoming less bumpy, and eventually after the only town on the route, it becomes enjoyable as there is little traffic, the sun is out and I can occasionally see the Volga

This rough road is improving now   *Log houses being built*

Along the way, I pass a couple of log houses being built with actual round logs forming the walls in a square overlapping process. I imagine this is how they used to build log cabins listed as heritage in Australia.

Now that I'm close to being directly north of Moscow, people come here for holidays, which is why I can see a tourist resort for the rich and famous called Plyos across the river.

Once the pavement returns, the afternoon cycling is relaxing on this sunny day as I make my way to a Russian holiday park, where I have found a cabin for $25 Australian, with dinner and breakfast buffet included. This holiday park is busy with families and has a pool to relax by, while my cabin is basic with just a bed.

In the evening Russia is playing Croatia in a World Cup quarter-final so in the bar along with about 30 adults I watch the emotions of the local's ebb and flow, while the children are in the dining room watching the game on a slight delay internet stream so as the game goes on, we hear a delayed reaction next door.

Russia scores first, before Croatia equalises as the game goes to extra time. Croatia scores in extra time before Russia equalises, forcing the game to penalties.

At midnight, the atmosphere in the bar is intense especially as Russia misses the first penalty but then Croatia misses their second. However, Russia then misses their third penalty and unfortunately Croatia successfully score three in a row including their fifth and final penalty which knocks Russia out of the World Cup, 3 penalties to 4. Suddenly it goes quiet in the bar as devastated people drift away.

Since I have to wait until 9 am for the delicious pancakes and hot dogs breakfast buffet to open, I FaceTime home, learning that Sue Digby has died. I knew her from back home and she had been following me on Facebook; life goes on while I'm away.

The route to Kostroma involves some of the best roads so far with a decently paved shoulder on a busy highway. As I reach the city centre I arrive into an open square which is busy with pedestrians and tourist vendors. Dominating the skyline is a large yellow fire tower, which looks like a lighthouse on top of a building with white columns out the front. Inside the fire tower are a couple of museums including a firefighting one.

Across the road is a grass square, on each side are two large white buildings with green roofs, and numerous white archways forming a veranda, which goes around the whole building forming a rectangle. Under the veranda are various shops, while in an open area in the middle are numerous fruit stalls.

Using a paved path beside the Kostroma River, I'm able to admire the predominantly white Ipatiev Monastery, which has a mixture of gold domed and green coned towers. It's okay to visit but for me it's just another religious building which is more interesting from the outside.

Kostroma's fire tower

Before leaving Kostroma, I have plenty of choices of fruit from the numerous stalls in the markets. Some of the friendly older ladies speak some English as I explain I'm from Australia, while I fill my Tupperware containers and my pockets. The sky is looking dark with thunder around but thankfully no rain so far.

Ipatiev Monastery

Fruit stalls inside the markets in Kostroma

My afternoon ride is back on the southern side of the Volga on a busy highway with a decent road shoulder and fewer potholes than normal. However, a heavy thunderstorm begins but I can't find a bus shelter so instead my best option is a large tree off the road which sort of reduces how wet I get for nearly an hour. Once this storm drifts away, I continue on a now shiny reflective road.

Looking at maps on my iPhone, I thought there might be the possibility of camping in the town of Tunoshna.

The first open space I look at isn't an appropriate place to camp, because it's a memorial to Lokomotiv Yaroslavl, a local professional ice hockey team, whose plane crashed here in 2011, after taking off from the nearby airport. This impressive memorial is a round open area next to a small river with numerous Lokomotiv Yaroslavl scarves tied on the outside railings, along with a small chapel with photos of the people who died.

Lokomotiv Yaroslavl memorial

Another option is a nearby church, but it has locked gates and looks uninviting, so I'm still not sure where I'm sleeping tonight. In the meantime I start cooking dinner in the centre of town and begin searching online for options. Finding a hotel near the airport for $11 Australian, I go for it because it will allow me to get dry.

The receptionist isn't that nice as she insists I leave my bicycle locked up outside, so I find a space under some stairs near the entrance to try to keep my bicycle dry. My room is fine but I soon learn why my room is so cheap – it's on the highway side and the noise and light from the traffic comes straight into my room all night, so I don't get much sleep.

On my morning ride towards Yaroslavl I come across roadworks, where there are diagrams showing how to get around them. However, unlike in Australia, workers don't usually have hi-visibility clothing on.

My cycle into Yaroslavl is busy with a three-lane highway taking me to a railway station with Moskva in its name. Yaroslavl is relatively not far from Moscow so many people will do a day trip from Moscow especially as there is a fast train service connection.

Yaroslavl has a reputation as the capital of the Golden Ring tourist area. The Golden Ring name comes from a list of old Russian cities including Vladimir, which are located around Moscow with the majority north of Moscow. The list was only made in 1967 with the original idea to preserve historic buildings but it has become a tourist route.

It does feel more touristy than other places with religious pilgrims travelling here. However, I have only found one small visitor information centre which doesn't have much information useful for me, except for one English map of Yaroslavl.

One of many churches

I struggle with the power and influence religion has on people and how freely religion can discriminate. In Russia many churches I visited would require my sisters to dress differently to me.

My reason for visiting religious buildings is to see the varied scenic architecture and usually I only visit if they are free, as I prefer not to give my money to religion. I do make an exception if they have a specific historical feature or a scenic view.

From the top of a 360 degree belfry lookout I can clearly see why pilgrims come here as it has lots of churches. I count thirteen and each is slightly different – some are red, others are white with gold or green domes and all have various towers. On top of each church tower, are a variety of objects – some with crosses, others with a golden ball with numerous golden spikes sticking out from it. From the belfry, I can see a storm is imminent.

View from top of the belfry of various churches

The highlight of Yaroslavl is the Millennium Park built on what is presumably a man-made peninsula where the smaller Kostrol River flows into the Volga. This park has a few fountains and gardens in a long row stretching out towards a church visible across the Kostrol River. In a grass square is the symbol of Yaroslavl, which is a bear holding a sceptre, along with the number 1008, as Yaroslavl traces its history back to 1008.

Above the Millennium Park in Yaroslavl is a promenade with food vendors

From the millennium park there is a nice promenade to walk alongside the Volga with food vendors and a few tourists now that I'm in the old part of town. By visiting the nearby history museum, I learn more, including how a moat used to go around the old part of town.

After exiting the museum, I continue exploring when suddenly a heavy thunderstorm begins so I seek shelter under a walkway as flash flooding begins in places. While sheltering an elderly gentleman starts trying to explain something to me in Russian which I don't understand but I assume he is trying to be helpful. He eventually takes me into a café for a cup of tea and a snack.

Since rain looks like continuing all afternoon and I'm not enjoying cycling Russian roads even when it's clear weather, I decide, rather than dodging potholed puddles in the rain, I will use a local train to head west to Rybinsk.

Where I have found an apartment on Airbnb as I need to do laundry and I'm tired from last night's terrible sleep. I'm enjoying that in many apartments there are dedicated heated pipes to dry my clothes, which is useful after doing laundry.

With this apartment high up in a tower block it's quiet, so I have a decent night's sleep.

Heated pipes in my apartment

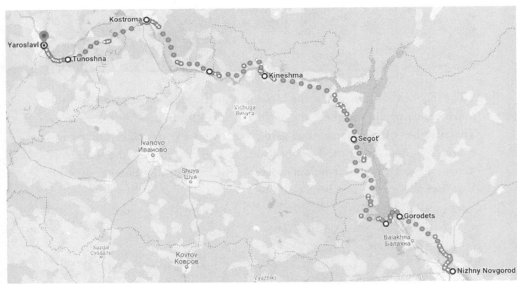

Nizhny Novgorod to Yaroslavl (Google Maps)

Leaving the Volga Basin

Compared to Yaroslavl, Rybinsk looks a younger city with less religion or tourism and feels like a town in need of a makeover as I pass some derelict buildings on this overcast morning.

Once I'm at the river it improves as there is a wide path beside the Volga with people out rollerblading or walking. Alongside the path is a mural of planes and tanks attacking during the Great Patriotic War. There are also plenty of parks and gardens, including a large monolith war memorial holding a plane propeller.

War mural beside the Volga in Rybinsk,

Upstream, west of Rybinsk, the Volga is dammed causing a large lake to the north-west, but the Volga flows in from the south. I can take a short cut to re-meet the river at a ferry upstream of the big bend. On the way, I go through an industrial part of town, including passing the local smelly sewage farm on a rough road.

I believe this is a farm

The ferry ride is uneventful, except that whenever the ferry docks, two men, both smoking but with hi-vis vests on, get off first, and with shovels physically build a dirt mound to enable vehicles to depart. It may keep more people in employment but with this regular ferry service, they will be doing this all day.

Building a mound to depart this ferry

Randomly, after a railway crossing, one of my water bottle cages falls off. Straight away I can see that one of the two holes on this cage where a bolt goes through, has broken off. Luckily, only one hole is required to attach it to my bicycle along with a cable tie, so I re-attach it using the second hole. As I search for a cable tie, I also discover that a bolt on one of my pannier bags has disappeared, just like what happened earlier in the trip to my other pannier, so I cable tie again.

As I'm about to leave, a train carrying brand new farming equipment passes by. This causes two sections of the road to lift up by hydraulics to form a physical barrier blocking the whole road, preventing vehicles from entering the crossing. Not sure why we can't have this in Australia, as there

Barrier rises to block the whole road   is no way to drive around this.

As I make my way south it's a delightful ride as the sun comes out and the road surface is great. As I enter the town of Myshkin at a bicycle/chainsaw store with modern tools and brands I recognise, I find a screw to fix the pannier bag and hopefully it will hold.

As I re-meet the Volga I see along with a large cruise ship docked here and a small souvenir market nearby, there is a delightful brick-paved path on top of a high grass embankment beside the Volga for me to cycle on. Myshkin is an example of what I expected when visiting the Volga. I It feels like people actually live by and use the river, along with encouraging visitors, rather than just happening to be near the river as I have found in other places.

With the first World Cup semi-final on tonight, I have found a hotel in Uglich, the next town upriver. As it's on the other side of the river, I have to make a choice when to cross. I can either stay on what looks like the quieter, longer, western side where I will have to cross on a dam wall before heading through the city to get to my hotel, or cross on a ferry here at Myshkin and cycle what could be a busier but shorter route. With my hotel in the northern part of Uglich, this seals the deal to use the ferry here.

Scenic Myshkin

With a ferry leaving soon I race to the dock but as I arrive, I have another flat. While accessing my bicycle pump I discover the bolt on the head of my pump is missing, so it is slightly harder to pump up my tyre. Thankfully, I manage to fix the flat just before the ferry is ready to leave. This short ferry ride is scenic as I look back at Myshkin with a large white building in front of the church and a cruise ship on the river.

Once across I fly along on a quiet highway to Uglich. Along the way, I leave the highway for a short loop road, which soon becomes a dirt road, with certain sections full of puddles and for some reason, toys have been left beside a puddle.

My hotel exists and is in a nice quiet location with one small communal kitchen. After obtaining some food nearby, my

Toys left in a puddle

evening is spent relaxing watching, in the hotel lobby on a television with terrible reception, the first World Cup semi-final as France beat Belgium by a single goal.

In the morning, I find a hardware store to search for a replacement bolt to put in my bicycle pump head. It's easy finding the correct size as every available bolt is laid out on display with size labels.

My route into the centre of town involves a relaxing ride on a path beside the Volga, with views of colourful attractive buildings stretching alongside the river with a dam in the distance. Looking around I find a rare sight, a permanent tourist office. This one actually has local information in English, with friendly staff who speak English, clearly a place many tourists visit as Moscow is only a three-hour drive directly south of here.

While exploring Uglich I visit a couple of museums including a bicycle-based one which has a wide variety of bicycles from different ages, sizes and uses. I have to walk my bicycle to enter the main church area. The church is small, but of more interest to me is the archaeological dig outside. I'm not sure what they are looking for but it's still fascinating.

Tourist office in Uglich, with some nice churches around the city

A range of bicycles are in the museum, including firefighting ones

My way out of town involves crossing the dam wall and a lock before visiting a supermarket on this warm day as I'm unsure how far until the next shop.

My route now will be away from the Volga as it becomes more meandering from here, so I will be taking a short cut.

On the way out of town, I notice a man using a Whipper Snipper trimmer to cut a whole paddock of grass, when a lawnmower would be more efficient. This makes me wonder if I have seen lawnmowers at all in Russia and I don't recall if I have, yet I would see more Whipper Snippers.

After leaving the Volga behind, it is a quiet paved road to Ploski, with three delicious chocolate buns in the general store.

Sometimes I can tell by maps if the next section will be a challenging surface, other times what is on the ground does not relate to maps. For this next section, my paper map predicts it will be challenging but I'm hoping instead it will be okay like Maps.me suggests.

Unfortunately, the paper map is correct as for five kilometres it is the worst bumpy, muddy, potholed surface of the trip so far. In a few places I have to walk my bicycle through puddles but thankfully in a few places, red house bricks have been laid across them, presumably to help cars cross. Randomly there are also plenty of light green butterflies foraging on this muddy track.

When I'm across the worse section suddenly light rain begins so I race as

quickly as I can. Eventually an old paved section returns but it's still a terrible, rough surface but thankfully without mud. At the same time, rain becomes heavier and with no cover, I have no choice but to cycle in the pouring rain.

Eventually, the rain eases and the sun comes out as I meet what I assume is the main road. However, the surface is worse than the section just cycled. It's still paved but in need of repair with plenty of potholes and this continues until the town of Kashin where, for once, roads are better in town.

Dodging puddles

The best bit of road on the way to Kashin

Before I came to Russia, I expected the people, police or Russian culture to be the main challenge, instead they have all been fine compared to roads.

In saying this some terrible roads were okay to cycle and part of the experience. The worse times are when dealing with traffic at the same time so despite the terrible roads, today is okay cycling because there isn't traffic to worry about and it is sort of fun.

The weather reports for the past few days have suggested showers all day but usually this has involved one heavy shower for half an hour then the sun comes out in the afternoon, so I have managed. I'm never really getting soaked, just the unexpected nature of not knowing when or for how long it will rain for is distracting from the experience, especially when needing to consider the road conditions.

Kashin is a nice-looking town with a Lenin statue and an old-looking market square which is now a car park surrounded by the same style two storey brown brick buildings looking mostly unused. Just visible behind the square is a scenic blue and white church.

The Kashinka River snakes its way through town and has some paths beside a green riverbank to explore. Because the sun is now out this provides a scenic upside down reflection of the white church with the blue roof in the river.

Old market square in Kashinka   *Kashinka River in Kashin*

I could stay here but I have found indoor accommodation down the road to watch the England-Croatia World Cup semi-final.

Thankfully after Kashin, the next 30 kilometres involves a decent, flat paved surface through forests to the quiet town of Verkhnyaya Troitsa. I thought the hotel is in town but with no mobile reception, I can't find it. Thankfully, a man gives me directions to a location two kilometres out of town on a dirt road as I dodge shallow puddles.

They haven't received my online booking but then a local politician who speaks some English assists me with check-in. It isn't really a hotel, rather a set of cabins with individual dorm-type rooms located beside the Medveditsa River, with the main clientele being fisherman. Dinner is included which is okay but I'm just not sure what meat I ate.

It's quiet with only a few people staying here as I relax by the river. It's also refreshing not having mobile reception. Always having access to the internet has been distracting, normally on bicycle trips I just use wi-fi because this reduces how often I have access to it. There is a modern television in my cabin which allows me to comfortably watch the second World Cup semi-final between Croatia and England. Croatia wins after extra time, so now the only match I wish to watch left of the World Cup is the final in a few days' time.

Some days can feel like a moving day where it's all about getting to somewhere else rather than there being anything in particular of interest to see that day. While cycling towards Tver it feels like I'm cycling through forests all day with some lakes nearby but mostly out of sight with the landscape feeling the same after a while. Thankfully, road surfaces are okay and with light traffic, it is easy relaxed cycling.

I even pass a rare site – a fence, as most livestock in Russia are kept more like pets at home or chained up outside rather than being allowed to roam in a paddock freely without a shepherd. This fence is made out of tree limbs lined up horizontally as rails, so it looks old school.

Again I'm seeing wooden houses, some which require major repair as they are on a lean and the roof is about to collapse. I'm also encountering older farming equipment which back home in Australia would have been found 30 years ago.

A rare site a fence in Russia, while it was common to see house falling down

Throughout the day, I come across many roadside fruit sellers, sheltering under an umbrella, with most being either older ladies or bored teenagers. All have many two litre plastic bottles full of blueberries, while other fruit including watermelon is also available.

Near the end of the day, I come across a classic Russian roadside experience – a bus shelter, a random cow and people selling fruit. The availability of fresh fruit from the roadside sellers helps as I haven't seen any supermarkets today.

In one small town of Goritsy there were four small general stores all selling the same pre-packaged food so I didn't starve but some variety would be nice. I have no idea how all four are economical.

Just before the last town of the day I come across a well, which I assume is drinkable water, so I fill my bottles up.

A classic Russian roadside, while I have found water in a well

I end this day camping in a playground in the town of Slavnoge, waiting until nightfall to set up. Some towns will have a decent playground, often surrounded by houses or apartment tower blocks, while others will have no green spaces at all.

It's my first night camping in a while after paying to sleep inside six days in a row through a combination of

Camping in a park in Slavnoge

wanting to watch World Cup matches and terrible weather. On previous, similar length cycling tours, I have often only paid to sleep inside six times for the whole tour. However, it has been a lot harder to find stealth camping options and I'm yet to see a paid campground. With most indoor accommodation around $30 Australian a night, this fits within my budget and I would rather be comfortable then miserable. Once out of Russia I assume I will camp more.

Having deliberately stopped early last night before the city of Tver, it's a short ride into Tver during the busy morning peak hour.

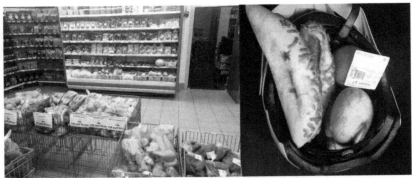

Every piece of fruit is wrapped in plastic, sometimes I use my helmet to collect food

When I finally find a supermarket, it is a type I haven't seen before and I'm shocked to find that every piece of fruit is wrapped in plastic, including some individually wrapped and then wrapped again. I can't even buy a single piece of fruit if I wanted to. This was the worse situation I saw in Russia but overall, I struggled with how much plastic is used for covering food and I know I shouldn't be expecting Australian standards, but I still tried. People find me strange when I try to avoid plastic by reusing bread bags, or using my helmet or storing fruit in the pockets in the back of my cycling jersey.

The Volga is back as it flows through the middle of the Tver with a long riverside park with plenty of statues, decorative gardens and a large war memorial obelisk. Maps and English information signs inform me about the various modern-looking buildings rebuilt after the Great Patriotic War as this city was occupied for a couple of months in 1941.

Tver is on the main railway route between Moscow and St Petersburg so the railway station is busy. Inside is a long mosaic showing the history of Tver, including its rail history.

I'm not finding Tver that appealing, and with nothing opening until around 11 am, I leave town by lunchtime. Once out of the city the afternoon ride involves a busy scenic flat highway with the Volga on my right but always out of view.

My day ends at Saritsa, where once again, the Volga splits the town in half, with the water low here in a deep valley, the town is high above away from the river. So, there is plenty of space beside the river for people to go swimming, as many are doing.

Near the bridge is a large monastery with white walls around it. It is okay to look inside during opening times with a wide range of religious buildings built at various times, with distinctive styles, colours and sizes but the best find is a flushing toilet.

Back in town, a park surrounded by high modern apartment buildings is a suitable place to cook dinner. However, unlike last night, it's too busy to camp here as there are many families enjoying the evening, with toddlers inquisitive about my bicycle.

Since the river area is undeveloped there is plenty of quiet space to camp as I find a grass area outside the monastery wall to set up my tent.

During the morning ride to Rzhev, I notice some strange shapes coming towards me. For the first and only time in Russia, I encounter professional cyclists, who give me a brief wave but continue on. Otherwise it's uneventful, straightforward cycling to Rzhev, my final city on the Volga. Once again, the river splits the city in two and just like last night, the river is down below in a valley.

Rzhev is the first city I'm visiting that was occupied by the Germans for more than a year during the Great Patriotic War. So, there are many war references, including a display in the main park of a steam locomotive war memorial, highlighting the role trains played during the war. Another memorial has war vehicles and bombs on display, set up like a park, while there are many more war references near the river, including another war memorial on a high point above the Volga.

Railway war memorial in Rzhev   *One of a few war memorials in Rzhev*

On the southern bank of the Volga is a museum focusing on the occupation, with plenty of English information helping explain the impact the occupation had. There are numerous artefacts on display, along with photos and maps explaining the impact of the occupation, which caused much of the city to be destroyed, as the front line was around here for a while.

The main display is of an amazing 3D panorama with a combination of physical objects and a background painting showing a battle in detail. It looks like trench warfare with barbed wire, dead bodies and numerous destroyed buildings.

Rzhev during German occupation

Included in my war museum ticket is entrance to the local history museum across the road, so I go for a look. However, unlike the war museum, this one is all in Russian, so I have a quick look around, rather than learning anything in detail.

I have been travelling in a westerly direction for the past few days but from Rzhev I will begin travelling in a northerly direction as once again, the Volga is nearby but out of sight due to being a windy now as I'm close to its source. Once again, I feel like I'm cycling through forests.

During the afternoon, I pass a few small war memorials beside the road and a couple of artillery bunkers. However, there is not as much visible evidence compared to Normandy as fighting was nomadic with the front line moving often, so Germany never had the chance to build the equivalent of the Atlantic Wall.

A bunker from Great Patriotic War

After arriving just in time to visit the Yelsty general store, I find a white church with a black roof beside a small man-made lake to camp at. Outside the church is a park bench to cook dinner, there is room under the church stairs to hide my bicycle and once again churches are the best place to find a toilet. This one is in a blue wooden shed with a toilet seat over a hole in the ground.

I have been asked if locals cared if I camp near churches and for the most part since people are not used to encountering people travelling on a bicycle, they are more curious than worried about me camping there. Young children often laugh at my small blue tent. I was only chased away from a church once in Russia and in that instance it was in the middle of the day when I wasn't looking to camp.

As for alternative options, there weren't many, certainly I never saw a paid campground. Outside towns, mosquitoes appear in the evening and I have been told to be aware of bears but unlike in North America, I never saw a bear.

The drop toilet behind a church where I'm sheltering my bicycle under the stairs

I estimate, I crossed the Volga seventeen times on this trip with the final time being a symbolic return crossing of a bridge in the town of Selizharova, knowing this would be the last time I will see the now smaller river, with its source not far from here.

Today is World Cup final day, so I have timed my ride to arrive in the resort town of Ostashkov on the shoreline of Lake Seliger to enable me to watch the Final as a thunderstorm is imminent.

I have found a pink guesthouse, where the host family allows me to watch the football with them upstairs in their lounge room. It's a tight first half with France 2-1 up at half-time before France becomes comfortable in the second half winning 4-2. With the World Cup now over, I have ten days to leave Russia

North of Ostashkov is a small uninhabited peninsula on Lake Seliger, so in the morning I go exploring. Water is visible on both sides of this quiet, forested peninsula, with a few trails connecting to beaches, for me to enjoy cycling around. I could spend longer here but my time in Russia is now running out.

On the way out of town, I stop at the Tele2 mobile phone shop, as last night my battery pack wouldn't charge. Since it replaced one with the same problem back in Australia, I decide to purchase a new one. I'm often away from a power source for a few days so a battery pack is useful for charging my iPhone, especially as it has become my main form of navigation due to the challenge of finding decent paper maps. I also buy another SD card as my digital camera is almost full.

For 60 kilometres, I'm following Lake Seliger on quiet, paved, potholed roads, through a forested area with occasional views of the lake. Along the way, rather than fruit being sold beside the road today, I pass a smelly but busy fish market in a few permanent wooden stalls. Otherwise it is an uneventful ride.

At Svapushche, I'm enjoying lunch beside Lake Seliger when a man who is clearly drunk shows up. He isn't dangerous; it is just my first encounter with a drunk person in an otherwise sober population.

Nearby on a car's roof rack, there is a brand-new looking mountain bike on one side and a brand-new looking Whipper Snipper on the other, showing just how important a Whipper Snipper is in Russia.

Dodging potholed road beside Lake Seliger   *A place for a Whipper Snipper*

I know the next section of road will be dirt having found a journal online by Bart and Jan who cycled this route a few years ago. I suspect this is due to crossing between two Oblasts regions, which is where I will leave the Volga Basin for the first time.

Quiet sandy section, no potholes and only a few houses on this quiet route

Despite having to dodge some sandy sections and a short shower of rain, it's an enjoyable ride with little traffic. After seeing a blue sign saying I'm changing Oblast, I assume I have crossed out of the Volga Basin. So now water flows away from the Volga.

However, once a form of pavement returns so do the potholes. At one stage, I overtake a log truck as the potholes force it to go so slow. The worst part is back on a highway which has even more potholes and so a slow cycle means I don't make it to the quiet town of Demyansk until just before 7 pm.

After cooking dinner in the town square, in fading light I begin searching for a place to camp. My best option appears to be an open area beside a river. To get there requires walking my bicycle on a narrow dirt track through an open high grass area.

When I reach the river, I see a narrow pedestrian bridge and I'm suddenly not alone anymore, as there are plenty of people out swimming on this warm evening. I'm tired, so I turn around, leave the track and begin dragging my bicycle through the grass until I feel I'm hidden enough to set up my tent.

In the morning I need to find supplies as I'm unsure if there are any food options until Staraya Russa, 95 kilometres away but most shops aren't open yet. Whereas in previous regions supermarkets were open by 7 or 8 o'clock, now its 9 am or later. After searching around, I manage to find open a fruit market and a small grocery store, which allows me to leave by 8:30 am.

Due to many sections having recently been paved, today is a quick ride on the best surface of the trip so far, which is even more relaxing because there isn't much traffic to worry about. With no shops for the whole ride, I'm glad I took time to get food before I left.

Best road surface I saw in Russia

Along the way are a few Great Patriotic War memorials, with the most impressive one being just off the road among trees. Around this memorial are many large red triangles pointing to the sky, each with numerous names of the dead recorded on the side, along with a memorial to paratroopers. Placed around the memorial are photos of

Great Patriotic War Memorial

soldiers, along with flowers, while trees have been freely allowed to grow among it.

On a warm day, after crossing a few rivers, I'm into Staraya Russa by 2 pm, which allows me plenty of time to explore. Staraya Russa is a pleasant surprise especially the large open brick-paved market square, which has a tall red-bricked clock tower. Taking up more than half the square are half a dozen rows of

Scenic square in Staraya Russa

straight trees which have recently had their limbs cut off.

In between the trees are paved bricks, with the widest path leading me to a tourist office. The visitor information centre gives me an excellent English map and a guidebook which recommends visiting a war museum and some natural spring on the edge of town for a swim.

The Museum of the North-Western Front is one of the better set up informative war museums, where I learn about the impact of the German occupation during the Great Patriotic War, as this area was occupied for two-and-a-half years.

On display are numerous physical weapons, cartoons negatively depicting Germans as well as photos showing before, during and after the war.

Being watched in the Museum of the North-Western Front

The photos show just how devastating it was to this community and that some things never fully recovered, including the large market square which had many more buildings pre-war before the Germans destroyed them.

Once again, there are more staff at the museum than needed, with me being watched as I go around. It feels like staff would be happy if I left as soon as possible, as I'm the only visitor.

The natural springs are on the edge of town and once I find a track between houses, I'm able to follow groups of people dressed for swimming using eroded tracks through an open grass field. The tracks lead me to a large vertical pipe in the middle of a pond. On this warm day, the water is refreshing.

In the evening while cooking Bolognese dinner in the busy market square, a dishevelled man comes up to me and speaks in Russian, which initially I don't understand, until he mimes he is hungry, so I share my dinner. It's karma for all the help Russians have given me. I assume he is homeless, and this makes me ponder that I have rarely seen homeless people in Russia. I have no idea if this means there are less of them or they are not allowed to be as prominent as I see elsewhere in the world.

I do however have to repeatedly tell him in Russian to go away from me while he smokes. Not sure why but I haven't discussed smoking in Russia yet. It is terrible as there isn't much respect from smokers who will light up right next to me. Thankfully, most indoor places are non-smoking but if it's raining or on a train, people will start smoking inside.

Having seen plenty of open space around the natural springs, I return in the evening. With only a couple of people here, I sneak away to set up my tent among the grass with houses far away in the distance. Just before bed, I try the new battery pack, but it won't charge my iPhone for longer than a minute before turning itself off.

Sharing a meal   *An open grassland with a natural spring*

I'm awake early so make my way to the railway station to charge my iPhone as it is now dead. I can't find any power points so I head next door to the bus station, which thankfully does have some. I need my iPhone to be able to contact tonight's Warmshower host Peter in Veliky Novgorod. Besides, I'm waiting for a nearby supermarket to open in about an hour and a half.

While it charges, I spend some time online organising my last week in Russia. This will have to involve a train ride as it is too far to cycle to St Petersburg and Estonia in the time I have left.

Thankfully, I have found a direct suburban train from Veliky Novgorod, which will allow me to spend a few days exploring around St Petersburg, before cycling to Estonia by 25 July, the date my Fan ID visa expires.

The morning cycle is easy with little traffic as Lake Ilmen comes into view. The lake is so large that it looks like a sea with nothing visible on the horizon except water, while the wind is starting to pick up blowing in from the lake. However, with a tailwind to lunch it is fine.

After lunch in Shimsk, I change direction knowing the next 50 kilometres is in a direct line with no bends to Veliky Novgorod. Of course, I get a headwind, I shouldn't complain too much, as I have barely had any wind to worry about on this trip. Also the traffic has increased considerably and I still have to be aware of drivers who feel it is okay to overtake while coming towards me, so it is a struggle getting there.

While taking a break in a bus shelter, I notice an actual paper bus timetable on display, the first time I have noticed one. I still have no idea elsewhere how locals know when buses are coming.

Thankfully after 25 frustrating kilometres, I'm able to divert away onto a quieter but longer loop road closer to Lake Ilmen. With a little more cover, there are times when I'm out of a direct headwind so it's easier cycling while passing through small towns. Closer to Veliky Novgorod the wind picks up, so I'm relieved when I finally make it to this scenic town for a rest day tomorrow.

I'm surprised once I make the city centre to find a large World Heritage Kremlin, with red-bricked medieval walls, and a few cone towers as well, all with tin roofs and slots in the wall.

Peter, my Warmshower host, meets me at the Kremlin entrance and we walk our bicycles across the dry moat, through the medieval archway gate, past some well-kept gardens and out the riverside gate to where the large Volkhov River appears. This river clearly divides the city in two, with only a scenic pedestrian bridge to take us across to a more open park area referred to as the trade side.

Riverside of the Kremlin   *Away from the riverside of the Kremlin*

From here I follow Peter to his apartment using a signed bicycle path alongside the river. Peter and his girlfriend Elena make me feel welcome as we share a delicious meal and they tell me some history of Veliky Novgorod. As this city is regarded as the birthplace of modern Russia in 862, it has a long history

The quieter eastern side is the trade side with remains of a market wall with a large row of white arches which remind me of an aqueduct. Surrounding this white wall are botanical gardens cared for by half a dozen men, who are all using Whipper Snippers to cut a large grass area.

The western side of the river used to be the religious side, but today it is a large World Heritage Kremlin surrounded by a dry moat. By using an English audio guide on my iPhone, my experience is enhanced. On certain parts of the medieval wall, I'm allowed to walk at a height which provides views of the river, with plenty of people sunbaking today on the sand below.

The walls of Kremlin on the west side, while the trade side is on eastern side

Millennium Monument

At the end of the walls are a few towers with small museums, each showing a part of the history of this area, with weapons and armoury from different centuries a particular focus.

The dominating feature in the middle of the Kremlin is the 1862 Millennium Monument. It is a large metal bell-shaped monument which has many life-size historical Russian figures represented around the bell on a few levels, telling the story of Russia.

It was destroyed by the Germans during the Great Patriotic War, as the front line was here for three years. Along with other buildings in Veliky Novgorod, it was rebuilt after the war.

Near the Monument in the largest building inside the Kremlin is the main museum, which covers a wide range of history from the establishment of the city to the present day.

There are plenty of paintings and numerous objects from the past 1,000 plus years on display, helping to explain how the city developed and has changed.

Veliky Novgorod is a splendid example of why I enjoy visiting Russian cities with plenty of history to experience.

The monument after WW2

Before catching the train, I visit a Tele2 mobile phone shop with a receipt for the battery pack which isn't working with the expectation of replacing it. However, they tell me through Google Translate they won't replace it since I purchased it in Ostashkov. I try arguing that it was in the same brand of shop, but they won't replace it. So, I end up purchasing a new battery pack, this time checking if it charges my iPhone first. Neither is that expensive, its more I just have no use for one that doesn't work.

In the evening, I catch a modern fast train with the platform at the same height as the train and a dedicated wheelchair space to store my bicycle. This train reminds me of my first train ride from the airport to Moscow with both Russian and English announcements and rolling electronic messages in both languages.

This train is travelling to St Petersburg, but I get off at a suburban Kolpino on the edge of St Petersburg because it is closer to Pushkin where Catherine Palace and Gardens are, which I'm looking forward to visiting tomorrow.

Rybinsk to Veliky Novgorod (Google Maps)

St Petersburg

From Kolpino to Pushkin I try to use a mixture of cycle paths and side roads where possible but still at times I have to use the busy road. This includes crossing over highways and a busy road on a long overpass to make Pushkin.

Firstly, I visit the Pushkin Railway Station to check train times to St Petersburg. Seeing there are regular services I have plenty of time to visit Catherine Gardens, without having to worry. From the railway station a few roads fan out, with one leading to the southern part of the large, fenced off, former royal gardens.

I'm unsure where the entrance is so I begin cycling alongside the gardens on my left, until a large row of fancy looking, multistorey white and blue buildings with gold detail features appears in front of me. There are plenty of people around including those dressed up in heritage clothing, a few horse and carts and a cream building which crosses the road as it narrows through an archway. This all confirms I'm near the entrance.

I'm told I can't bring my bicycle inside the gardens, so I leave it locked up outside to a steel fence. I discovered later there are proper bicycle racks around the back of the palace, but no one thought to tell me. My bicycle was fine, while I'm inside for hours.

In Russia I never felt like I had to worry about my bicycle being stolen, I just used my cable bicycle lock when away from it. I always left my bags on my bicycle, just taking my wallet, camera and iPhone.

Catherine Palace is quiet before noon

The Catherine Palace was one of many former royal residences around St Petersburg and now is a tourist hotspot which doesn't open until noon for individual visitors with people lining up outside at 10 am. Organised groups are now going into the palace, so instead I will go for an explore around the gardens and will come back later.

Attached to the palace is a small museum with royal clothing on display. Anyone can enter at any time and there are only a handful of people inside.

Walking around the large well-kept green gardens is enjoyable as there are less people, allowing me space to admire how large these gardens are for one family. Around the gardens are numerous statues, decorative water fountains, man-made lakes and hedge rows, with many references to how the royal families used certain parts of the gardens.

There are several smaller buildings around the gardens which were built for the royal family over the centuries and many of these buildings are now excellent museums. My favourite is the white Martial Chamber with the striking green roof, found right at the back of the gardens, with only a few people around.

Martial Chamber

Inside is the only dedicated World War One museum I saw in Russia. It's fascinating seeing the Russian perspective of a war seemingly forgotten in Russia, which started as a hopeful war led by the Tsar but ended with humiliation, the end of the royal family, a civil war and eventually communism.

Using an audio guide, I learn a lot and see many artefacts especially guns, vehicles and colourful military uniforms including those from the Royal family.

Throughout the walls of the museum is barbed wire, which makes me feel like I'm on the front line. There is also an advertisement for the name change from St Petersburg to Petrograd during World War One, due to the German sounding name. After Lenin's death, it was changed to Leningrad in 1924 before returning to St Petersburg once communism ended.

Airplanes and a horse-drawn green kitchen dual carriage are both from WW1

Barb wire is around the museum along with uniforms and weapons

Also, in the gardens is the Arsenal, a building containing a fascinating collection of weaponry collected by various Tsars, from Arabic, Asian and European foes, with distinctive styles depending on the region it was collected from. On the walls of this octagon building are layers of different centuries of war equipment, including a range of swords from different regions and various knight's steel armour which changed over the years.

Arsenal building with a range of weapons on display

The gate at the back of Catherine Palace

The backside of the palace is visible through a large decorative gold, white and blue gate, where I can see a large open space. In the distance the back of the palace looks very similar to the front with the same gold, white and blue colours.

When I return to the front of Catherine Palace the line is even longer, so I will leave and head to St Petersburg by train instead.

The railway from Pushkin to St Petersburg-Vitebsky opened in 1837 and was the first railway built in Russia. This enabled the royal family to travel to their residence at Catherine Palace.

Ramps on stairs are helpful to get down

Leaving the old-looking St Petersburg-Vitebsky Station requires me negotiating getting down some stairs. However, with two wide metal ramps specifically designed for wheelchairs, it is easy for me and an elderly lady with a wheeled basket to get down the stairs.

This is something we should have in Australia.

Despite many Warmshower hosts listed in St Petersburg, I can't find anyone available so instead I have found an Airbnb apartment just south of the old part of the city, which is fine.

St Petersburg is a shock, as it looks so different from the rest of Russia. Many buildings are architecturally different and feel more European compared to the rest of Russia – I could be back in Paris. The biggest difference is how touristy it feels with more international visitors here, along with numerous spruikers trying to sell me various tourist things like boat rides and supposedly cheaper tickets to attractions and museums.

There are a couple of canals which go around the southern part of the old city with numerous tourist boats going through them and out onto the main wide Neva River. The Neva River splits the city in half, with numerous bridges crossing this river and many scenic buildings are visible from the river. I did try once to get on an English guided boat cruise, but it departed at a different wharf than I thought so I missed out.

Before leaving for Russia I read a book about how, during the Great Patriotic War, Leningrad as St Petersburg was then called, was under siege for 900 days by the Germans which was devastating for the people and buildings here.

There was also a lot of teamwork and thinking outside of the box to resupply the city. In particular how the city was resupplied by travelling over frozen ice in winter.

After seeing a few photos showing the damage, I'm amazed how well St Petersburg has been rebuilt but disappointingly the museum focusing on the Great Patriotic War is closed for renovations.

Compared to the rest of Russia, many tourist sites have long lines and it feels like there are more international visitors,

Photos of Leningrad under siege

yet other sites have barely anyone there. The island Peter and Paul Fortress is busy by 10 am so I visit the nearby informative State Museum of Political History of Russia spending a couple of hours there, with only a handful of people inside.

This museum is in the building where Lenin organised the Communist Party during the Russian Revolution and it was originally set up post the Russian Revolution as a propaganda museum highlighting the party. Most of the information details propaganda from the Soviet era, along with general life under communism; food, lifestyles, culture and a display on the space race. However, with a few recent additions added to displays there is a more critical view of the Soviet Union and there is even a little on the post-communist era but once it catches up with the present day, it becomes less informative.

State Museum of Political History of Russia, with many communist era displays, including a man on the top left, erased from a history because he had fallen out of favour with Stalin.

A former railway station

Just like Moscow, St Petersburg has a few railway stations around the edge of the city, including Finland, Baltijsky and Moscow stations, names which refer to where trains originally departed to.

Finland Station was where Lenin arrived when he returned from exile, with the help of the Germans in 1917 during World War One via Scandinavia. Vladimir Lenin became the leader of the Communist Party which won the Russian Civil War which was a consequence of the Russian Revolution. Before this trip, I read an informative book called Lenin on the Train about his return from exile in Switzerland.

St Petersburg Metro is not as old or decorative as Moscow but still has some interesting historical mosaics with many focused on shipping. To access the metro requires using metal token tickets, while some routes travel under the main river which is useful when it starts raining.

Artwork in St Petersburg's metro stations

The highlight of my time in St Petersburg is two railway museums. One is in a house which has been open as a museum since the late 1800s with large models of bridges and trains built at the same time as railways in the late 1800s.

140-year-old model train

There is a Russian guided tour but for me they just have an English brochure informing me about the numerous objects on display which is adequate for me to look around at my own pace

As well, there is plenty of history on Russian railways up to the modern day including a few locomotive cabs, railway equipment, information displays on various events and a large map showing that most railway lines were built in western Russia, with only a couple of lines heading east.

In contrast, the other railway museum is in a former railway station complex near the Baltijsky Railway Station. It only opened here in former rail sheds in 2017. Therefore, it is much more modern, with videos, audio and electronic displays along with a collection of locomotives and carriages throughout history in a larger complex with a few large former rail buildings to explore. Some of the rail vehicles on display include military vehicles, including a 1980s missile train reminding me of the train in the James Bond film Goldeneye.

War railway vehicles on display

I have missed investigating railway history on this trip. Usually this is a major focus on my cycling trips and was the reason for starting my first trip in 2009, where I followed railway lines in Victoria.

In the central part of St Petersburg is the open Palace Square which isn't actually a square because on one side is a large yellow horseshoe-shaped multistorey building with an archway in the middle of the horseshoe. This leads to a narrow, busy pedestrian mall, which during the day becomes busy with tourists.

On the other side of the Palace Square is the former Hermitage building which was the royal residence in St Petersburg and has a similar style and colours as Catherine Palace, except it's green with white and gold rather than blue. Today it is a busy museum with long lines stretching out of the indoor courtyard all day, so I never went inside as I prefer to visit quieter places.

Nearby is a shipping container that had been set up as a visitor information centre for the World Cup and is still open a week after the World Cup finished and long may it stay open.

Runners outside the Hermitage, which is opposite a horseshoe shaped building

As I leave St Petersburg on this Sunday morning, I pass the Hermitage again, noticing an organised running event is on around the city, with thousands of people involved. With a few roads closed, it's easy cycling while looking around at more architecturally interesting gardens, buildings and a couple of museums.

To enable enough time to visit the Peter the Great Palace and Gardens at Peterhof, I catch an older style suburban train out of St Petersburg as its all suburbs between the two. Not far from the scenic Peterhof Railway Station is Peterhof Gardens with some small, former royal gardens free to visit but the main gardens require a payment. It is a short line to get in, with bicycle racks outside to lock my bicycle up.

Once inside the gardens, there is another line to get inside the yellow and white Peter the Great Palace which is smaller than Catherine Palace and this line is shorter too. However, I begin with exploring the gardens and from first glance I can see that the whole complex is clearly much smaller than Catherine Palace but there are still plenty of people.

The main feature of the gardens is the staircase outside the front of the palace. These black-and-white-chequered coloured stairs descend to a large round pool, which then stretches through the gardens in a 600 metres long canal out to the Baltic Sea in the distance. Around the staircase are numerous golden human statues and water fountains as I walk down the stairs to see the larger golden fountain in the pool. Further around the gardens are more fountains, black-and-white-chequered staircases, pools, statues, plenty of hedgerows, trees and other features throughout.

View from the palace patio with so many fountains and golden statues

In the gardens, there are also photos showing the extensive damage caused during the Great Patriotic War because the front line during the Leningrad Siege was in this area. It's amazing to see just how damaged it was and yet now I can't tell that it was damaged at all.

Around the gardens are a couple of small, former royal buildings, which

Great Patriotic War damage

are now museums showing how certain buildings operated when the royal family used this area. Most have something to do with maintaining the palace and gardens. Some museums require me to wear special covers over my shoes, so I end up keeping a pair as a souvenir rather than getting a new pair each time. Somehow I end up with an odd-coloured set.

Shoe coverings required to visit many of the museums around the gardens

The scale of these gardens and the Catherine Gardens not far away shows just how affluently the royal family lived and were out of step compared to the rest of the population. This is reinforced when I go inside the Palace, after lining up for 45 minutes.

Seeing the former royal palace is an experience with fancy furniture, fancy wallpaper and numerous paintings. However, with narrow passageways it feels very much like being herded like sheep through the palace with barely any space to breathe due to the number of people inside, and staff constantly pushing everyone along. Still interesting but not something I wish to do every day.

There are many fancy rooms to see while being herded through the palace like sheep

After the past few days of busy tourist attractions, I'm looking forward to getting back on the road as all this has become overwhelming. Not sure how people do this every day, just going from tourist spot to tourist spot on things like Contiki tours where you're being led around by umbrellas, being told where to look and for how long – not my style of exploring.

The final two days of cycling in Russia from Peterhof to Ivangorod involves some decent roads after a suggestion from Arkady, my Warmshowers host in Peterhof.

Koporye Castle

His route takes me past some old buildings including Koporye Castle, a 16th century stone castle with round twin tower entrances and a stone archway bridge over a dry moat. It is a different style of castle compared to the kremlins I have already seen in Russia, and feels more English in style. I'm passing many memorials to the Great Patriotic War, as once the Leningrad Siege was lifted, the Red Army advanced through here. Throughout history, many other battles have also happened here causing the Russian border to change a few times, so the style of buildings are different.

Randomly in a town, I see an older touring cycling couple having not seen any other touring cyclist since Jaiwei near Saransk, more than 3 weeks ago, so I head over to chat. However, after starting to chat, they abruptly just ride off. All I know is that they are riding from Riga to St Petersburg, the opposite direction to me, so I assumed we would share information but apparently not.

My bicycle is now making a clicking noise when I pedal. I suspect a bearing in the crank but it won't make the noise when my bicycle is on a bicycle stand so the first bicycle shop I visit can't help, despite staff being so helpful even when using Google Translate.

The next bicycle shop a day later suggests changing the chain and cassette which appears to have fixed it. Considering the chain has done between 8 and 10, 000 kilometres since it was last replaced, it is time for a change anyway. I will keep an ear out to see if the clicking noise returns.

Near the end of the day, I pass a large lake, but it is too close to a road to camp, so I continue as a rainbow comes out.

After having to jump over a highway barrier and cycle the wrong way on a one-way road, I make the town of Kotelskiy. Due to not being able to find spirit fuel for my Trangia, for the last time I go into a Russian general store in the town square to get some bread for dinner. I end my evening camping among trees in a paddock close to town.

My last night in Russia

Five kilometres before the border I have to show my passport to get to the border town of Ivangorod. After a brief look at my passport I'm waved through.

As I approach Ivangorod there is a lengthy line of trucks waiting to cross into Estonia as this is the only road crossing. Otherwise, Ivangorod is quiet.

After using up my last roubles at my final supermarket, I'm feeling a little emotional as I have become used to visiting two major supermarket franchises. They have been a consistent place to visit in an otherwise inconsistent Russia.

Just before the border is Ivangorod Fortress which is open for the public but looks abandoned as there is limited information around the castle and some steps to negotiate in the dark. However, it does provide decent views of a taller white castle across the Narva River into Estonia.

Ivangorod Fortress, looks into Estonia

Estonia

Finding the customs office for cyclists and pedestrians is simple. Along the way I pass a pharmacy, so I duck in to purchase more spirit for my stove, as I have no idea if I can get fuel in Estonia. With it being Russia, the road leading to the customs office has potholes.

To leave Russia I show my passport, Fan ID and immigration card I kept from arrival in Moscow. After what feels like ten minutes but was probably five, they let me out and I walk on the pedestrian part of a high fenced bridge across the Narva River, where there are plenty of cars lined up to get into Russia. I'm still not at the halfway mark of this trip. From Estonia I will start cycling south passing through numerous countries rather than concentrating on just one.

After being briefly questioned about how long I will be in Europe including enquiring about which countries I'm visiting, they let me into Estonia. Before I even have a chance to assess Narva, an elderly couple comes over and asks me in English about what I have been doing in Russia. I explain my trip and leave them amazed.

After the chat, straight away I notice tourist direction signs and a large map directing me to the visitor information centre nearby. Inside are helpful staff with brochures in English and maps of Estonia, including towns in the region. Such a contrast to Russia where finding a paper map has been a challenge.

While wi-fi is easy to access, no SMS code is required and from now on, I will be relying on it. As a visitor it already feels different to Russia especially as Estonia has gone out of its way to welcome me.

The Narva Castle is in the centre of town and is better set up for tourists compared to Ivangorod Fortress. The first noticeable difference to Russia is there aren't any security guards or old women hanging around rooms Information is provided in English alongside Estonian and Russian.

Standing out is a tall, white, square tower with red triangle sloped roof and surrounding balcony compared to the presumably older surrounding cream buildings which are similar to Ivangorod Fortress.

Narva Castle on the Estonian side of the Narva River

Trinkets on sale inside the courtyard of Narva Castle

As I walk around appreciating history, staff in the outside courtyard are dressed in medieval attire undertaking tasks from that period, including making small items. When paying my entry fee, I was given a small token to exchange, so I use it to purchase a small yellow bag.

I don't normally buy tourist souvenirs but since I will soon be posting home items I don't need any more from my time in Russia, it can be included.

On a few levels inside the castle are various artefacts, photos, historical information and large-scale 3D maps of the area, showing how Narva and Ivangorod have evolved over the years. Throughout history this has been a strategically important river crossing because the Narva River and Lake Peipsi south of here form a natural barrier, which has often led to conflicts to control this crossing. Today this makes up most of the Estonian border with Russia.

From the rooftop, I can see across the Narva River back into Russia, including the bridge where I crossed along with Ivangorod Fortress. This is when it sinks in that I have left Russia and I may never get to return. For all its challenges it is still an amazing opportunity to visit.

While leaving Narva I come across my first blue cycling sign, with both local Estonian and EuroVelo route numbers. Velo is French for bicycle, with routes in various stages of development depending on where you are in Europe. I'm hoping to follow EuroVelo routes if they are going roughly my way.

Having seen numerous cycling signs while in France and Belgium in 2013, these signs are making me feel even more like I'm back in Europe.

I followed these cycling signs throughout Estonia and sometimes they go on tracks through paddocks, which is still better than most roads in Russia. I'm now feeling confident enough to take side roads knowing they will be okay to cycle and go where they say they will.

A EuroVelo sign in Narva

While following the Narva River north to the Baltic Sea, I'm passing a few war cemeteries and memorials, including some which are about the 1918 to 1920 War of Liberation, when Estonia successfully fought for independence against Russia.

The main memorial I see is a tall, skinny, stone square-based pyramid with a cross on top, which was blown up by the Soviets in 1942 and wasn't restored until 2014. While one cemetery from that period was destroyed during World War Two and instead of restoring the individual crosses on each grave, they have been left destroyed to highlight how, for 50 years under Soviet rule, they weren't allowed to refer to the War of Liberation.

Other cemeteries and memorials are about World War Two. This war is now referred to as having started in 1939 and called World War Two rather than The Great Patriotic War.

The crossing of the Narva River was a key step in the Soviet advance through the Baltics and eventually to Berlin. Not all Estonians were happy about this as many fought unsuccessfully against the Soviet Red Army. There are also references to other battles centuries ago, highlighting just how much conflict this area has seen.

Cemetery, left destroyed, while an independence memorial has been restored

The Narva River flows into the Baltic Sea at the beachside tourist town of Narva-Joesuu. When going inside a busy supermarket I'm overwhelmed by the amount of food options available compared to Russia. I also have to adjust from paying in roubles to now paying in euros which involves a lot less zeros to deal with. Using euros, I'm estimating that it is a little more expensive compared to Russia.

For the final time, I see Russia across the river before making my way to the Baltic Sea, where I find plenty of people enjoying the beach, reminding me of being back home in Australia.

After briefly putting my feet in the sea and finding a drinking water fountain, I make my way west until finding a quieter space to wild camp under pine trees beside the beach. After watching an orange sunset over the sea, with a few people cycling along the sand, I drift off to sleep feeling like I have gone forward in time compared to my time in Russia.

Making dinner under pine trees

In the morning, after cycling through pine forests and taking a decent short cut, I find myself in the quiet small town of Sinimae. With nothing opening until 10 am, I have to wait for the war museum to open. However, scattered outside the museum building is a collection of various metal artefacts left over from World War Two, so there is plenty to admire while waiting.

The Vaivara Sinimagede Museum focuses more on the Red Army invasion than the German one, as the Soviets caused more damage and had a longer-lasting impact with heavier fighting causing many more buildings to be destroyed and more lives to be lost. They have a short fifteen-minute film showing what happened here, along with numerous information and personal stories. Hard to imagine the devastation now as towns in this region look immaculate.

Sinimae war museum with metal items from the war scattered around it

My basic understanding of 20th century Estonian history is that it finally became its own independent country in 1920 after centuries of different countries controlling it. Then in 1940, the Soviet Union came under the pretence of protection from the Germans. However, they installed their own government and either deported unwanted people away or just murdered them. Then the Germans invaded in 1941 and did the same to other people, before the Soviets re-invaded in 1944 and stayed until 1991. Now Estonia, along with Latvia and Lithuania, are independent countries who are members of the European Union.

Further west is the city of Sillamae which reminds me of Canberra because of the wide, straight, well set out streets.

Style of buildings in Sillamae

During my ride through former communist countries, I can often tell if the city was built in the 20th century by how it looks. It will have straight streets and cement apartment blocks, instead of a combination of centuries of building styles with streets set out in unplanned ways.

After going inside the town hall for a look, I'm offered an unorganised, brief guided tour of the town hall by a local woman who happens to speak English. She tells me that Sillamae is a former closed Soviet city which was developed by the Soviet Union in 1947 to play a part in building the first Soviet atomic bomb. Many ethnic Russian people were transferred here for work, which was a common occurrence in the Baltic's where locals were forcibly moved east and replaced by Russians. Hence, I'm told that most of the current population speak and regard themselves as Russian as they or their parents were moved here.

A rare Stalin reference

In the basement, there is still a large painting of Stalin, the only reference to him on this trip outside of museums.

Because it was a closed city, this meant it didn't exist on maps or have a postal address until Estonia re-established independence in 1991. Ironically, this is where I post a few, now unneeded items home including my World Cup Fan ID, which was my visa in Russia and is no use to me except as a souvenir.

The first part of my afternoon is alongside the Baltic Sea following a signed cycling route west, sometimes on tracks between cereal paddocks and other times on quiet paved roads right next to a cliff face looking down into the sea.

Cycling route through paddocks   *Cycling beside the Baltic Sea*

This coastal route is busy with touring cyclists going both ways, with everyone I talk to cycling between St Petersburg and Tallinn, the capital of Estonia further west of here.

While chatting to a Canadian/German cycling couple of similar age to me who are on a Scandinavian loop via St Petersburg, they give me some news. They have heard that Russia enjoyed having tourists so much, they have extended the visa-free period. If you have a Fan ID you can stay till the end of the year.

I briefly thought about turning around but decided against it. However, if this rumour is true, I could visit the Russian enclave of Kaliningrad between western Lithuania and Poland instead of my original plan of going around it. I may not have a chance in the future to go to Kaliningrad and I do wonder if it's different from the rest of Russia.

A minor issue is that I mailed my Fan ID home earlier today. I still have the electronic version so this may be okay.

Eventually, I leave the Baltic Coast to begin making my way south towards Lake Peipsi. Since leaving the Baltic Coast I have seen fewer cyclists, but I am still seeing plenty of cycling signs.

I have been enjoying the variety of food, in particular bakery items, there is less reliance on plastic, and I have actually seen large recycling bins. Thankfully in a hardware store, I find a proper sized fuel source for my Trangia, so no more needing to visit pharmacies for small bottles every couple of days.

By the end of my first full day in Estonia I find myself at the resort town of Maetaguse. There is a fancy spa hotel, a paved bicycle path leading to a figure of eight bicycle track and Disc Golf course.

While cooking dinner outside the small supermarket a few locals come over. They all speak Russian and are amazed I have been cycling in Russia.

In the evening after looking around, the best place to set up my tent is on the Disc Golf course.

Camping on Disc Golf course

I'm now following Estonian cycle route 3 which, in certain sections, follows Highway 3. At times there is a cycle path beside the highway, other times there is only the highway. At certain times cycle route 3 takes a longer route just to avoid some slightly busier roads. However, all these secondary roads are better than most main roads I had to deal with in Russia.

Arriving at Lake Peipsi, it looks like I'm back at the Baltic Sea with pine trees beside a wide open waterway which stretches to the horizon. My route now follows the lakeshore through small towns initially on a highway before I'm able to divert away to the beachside town of Mustvee.

After a delicious hot lunch at the supermarket deli, my afternoon ride is relaxing, on a warm day with plenty of views of the lake while going through a few small towns with houses that have small pointy roofs.

A few times I come across a couple of large cycling map noticeboards. Each show a slightly different range of cycling routes in this region in a few colours. Some are just short, day loop rides, while there are also a few long-distance cycling routes, including one which connects with Latvia, the next country on my route.

All this cycling information is making me feel appreciated and think positively about Estonia, especially after coming from Russia with none of this. It helps

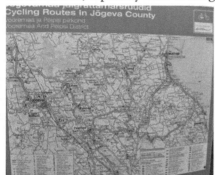

shape my route and makes me want to come back one day to explore more.

After going through the quiet town of Kallaste, I'm about to leave Lake Peipsi to head inland towards Tartu, when I come across a campground, something I never encountered in Russia. For six euros, this allows me to have a shower after three nights wild camping and to spend time patching a bicycle tube having gotten a couple of flat tyres lately in the rear tyre.

One of many large cycling maps

The actual camping is basic, just a paddock beside the lake, with some picnic tables and a shower block. There are a few car campers here and, for some reason, a trampoline, so after patching the tubes using the lake to check for leaks, my evening is spent relaxing on the trampoline.

Camping spot beside Lake Peipsi

Often, I time my arrival into cities by staying somewhere within a couple of hours of cycling to enable an arrival just before lunchtime, which allows me to then spend the afternoon seeing if there are enough places of interest to stay the night. If I feel I have seen enough then I can continue cycling in the evening. If I do stay, then I can spend the morning exploring again before leaving in the afternoon, which is exactly what I did for Estonia's second city Tartu.

The ride in involves quiet back roads through farmland as cereal crops are now ready for harvest, before following the Emajogi River, westwards to Tartu. Once I arrive at suburbia, there is a signed cycle path which leads me into the city centre via some parks. Entering many Russian cities involved going through industrial areas with traffic, so this is a pleasant change.

After crossing Emajogi River on a pedestrian bridge, I'm near the busy, permanent outdoor markets, where I find a bicycle tube. From here I make my way past a modern shopping centre to a quiet scenic town square next to the river. On the edge of the square are a few blue cycling signs to towns around Estonia.

Around Tartu's town square are cycling signs

The square is surrounded on three sides by a few multistorey buildings with numerous windows in each. The bottom level of most buildings have a different style and colour which makes it look like additional levels have been added later.

Standing out at the back of the square is a pink coloured building which is the town hall and has a helpful visitor information centre inside.

After obtaining information on plenty of things to see in Tartu, my first point of call is to visit the Estonia National Museum. To get there requires going back across the river, this time on the main pedestrian bridge directly in front of the town square. After finding a cycle path, this takes me all the way to the museum, with bicycle racks out the front.

This museum only recently moved to a large purpose-built building on an old airfield and the entrance is well designed as it feels like its funnelling me in, as the sides and high roof narrow.

As part of my entry, I'm given a key card, which, when I touch against any of the e-readers scattered around the museum, changes the information into English.

Estonian National Museum

There are also videos with a timeline showing what was happening during the 20th century, with the struggle for independence a focus. In particular it highlights how the three national colours of blue, white and black were used as a form of resistance, as the Soviets banned those colours. On display is a blue, black and white Estonian flag which was buried for decades.

This card translates information

For the first time and certainly not for the last time, I hear about the Baltic Chain, which was a peaceful protest where people in the three Baltic states of Estonia, Latvia and Lithuania joined hands together to make a human chain across the three countries on 23 August 1989. This marked fifty years since the Molotov-Ribbentrop Pact, which led to the continuous occupation of the Baltic countries until 1991.

Throughout the museum are plenty of displays explaining the communist period including various propaganda posters, items from that period and explanations on some complex issues. There are also basic examples like how hard it was obtaining a pair of jeans.

As well, the museum focuses on centuries of diverse history as modern-day Estonia has previously been ruled by many countries including Denmark, Sweden, Germany and Russia. This has caused a mixed cultural influence and a less dominant religion, so on display is a wide range of artefacts, over a wide period of time.

One room has a large semicircle wooden pictorial timeline with numerous squares having cartoons of historical events on them, surrounding a layered map of Estonia on the floor.

Pictorial timeline of Estonia

Estonia as a pawn in world events

On one horizontal row of squares are cartoons of Estonian historical events, on another row is Russian/Soviet Union, on another row world events. By lining up the squares vertically, I can compare what was happening in Estonia at similar times to other events around the world.

An example is, what was happening in Estonia during the time when the Wright brothers took their first flight, when Everest was first climbed or when man first walked on the Moon.

One particular theme is Estonia as a pawn in a larger chess battle between Germany and the Soviet Union. This is shown by a pawn piece changing flags from independence in the 1920s to Soviet occupation in the 1940s to the brief German occupation before becoming a part of the Soviet Union.

Generally Estonian events are depicted as being behind the rest of the world as they are being held back by the Soviet Union, while the rest of the world is becoming more modern with things like the internet. The latest pictures show a hopeful, more modern country joining the European Union.

The local art museum in the town square is only one euro to enter on Fridays but is worth visiting any other day. Inside are many paintings with some artists including Estonian symbols. One artist has three paintings from 1939, 1941 and 1945, all with references to the war situation at the time affecting local people. To add to its charm the building is on a lean which I'm told just happened.

Leaning art museum

Tartu is a university city which reminds me of others like Eugene in Oregon or Oxford in the UK which also have a cycling culture. Since it's summer university holidays, there is plenty of university accommodation available. Unfortunately my twenty euro dorm room doesn't have curtains so light comes in easily and there isn't air conditioning so it's hot. While opening the windows cools the room, it is noisy outside. I eventually end up putting my mattress on the floor to find a darker, cooler place to try to sleep.

In the morning, after going through some gardens and under a couple of old scenic bridges, I find the university's museum, which is located in an old church building. Most of the church is in ruin after centuries of neglect. However, there is the opportunity to walk up to the roof to a lookout but with trees at the same height, it's not the best view.

Inside the museum is both a historical display on the university's history and a few interactive exhibits explaining some of the things discovered at the university which visitors can experiment with.

The university was established in 1583 when Tartu was under Swedish rule, then shut down when Russia conquered in 1710 before being reopened by the Russians in 1802 and it became a propaganda university when the Soviet Union came. Today, one in four Estonian university students attend here.

Tartu University Museum is in the ruins of a church

My final visit in Tartu is to the depressing but informative KGB Cells Museum located in the basement of a building. As the entrance sign says:

"During the 1940s and 1950s, a prison was located in this basement where the Soviet regime held those arrested for political reasons. For hundreds of people a long road of suffering began from here."

Walking down the stairs into the basement I find a few small rooms in low light, each with different displays which help bring to life stories I have heard about before. There are prison cells, interrogation rooms and loud recorded voices of people being tortured. With plenty of information throughout the museums and many items from that period on display, it is very interesting.

The sheer number of people impacted for such a small country is hard to comprehend. A quarter of the just over 1.1 million people in Estonia in 1939 were not there after 1945, a similar statistic for Latvia and Lithuania. It's a depressing experience learning about how people suffered for 50 years, but a story which needs to be told.

Using cycle paths, I head south of Tartu before transferring to gravel roads where I'm going past a few lakes on this cold windy day. I'm feeling tired from lack of sleep last night, so my focus is just getting to my first Warmshower since leaving Russia, in the town of Otepaa. I find out as I make town, I have just missed a mountain bike race in town today.

My Warmshower host, Heini, has done plenty of cycling trips himself, having just got back from eighteen months of cycling from here to Azerbaijan, Bangkok to Indonesia, Darwin to Sydney, Chile to Brazil and Portugal back to Estonia. Heini shows me videos he recorded of his trip including in Australia, while he cooks me some nice meals including a delicious pork and rice meal for breakfast.

Sharing a meal with my host Heini

My route south of Otepaa involves an undulating paved cycle path with many people out running as the path passes by a few lakes. In other places it follows a road before eventually ending ten kilometres later at Kaariku, a resort beside the lake of the same name.

From here, I cycle on quiet roads past more rural landscapes to the twin border towns of Valga/Valka. At the railway station I see a modern orange passenger train waiting at the only current passenger rail connection between Estonia and Latvia.

I nearly go into Latvia without realising it, as the border is just marked with a few, spread out, small wooden posts. This is because both Estonia and Latvia, along with many European countries are members of the open border Schengen Area and so there isn't anyone to show my passport to. In theory, I can cycle all the way to Portugal without showing my passport depending on my route, as Heini presumably did. If I don't go via Kaliningrad, I won't have to show my passport until Croatia.

Before leaving Estonia, I visit a supermarket, by leaving my bicycle outside at a bicycle rack. Coming back outside, I find nearly a dozen cyclists have appeared. We chat for a while, but none are travelling my way.

Plenty of bikes near the border with Latvia

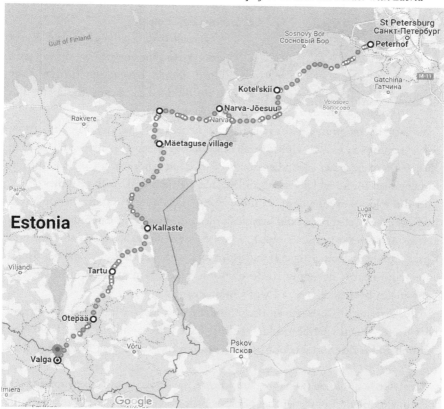

Peterhof to Valga (Google Maps)

Latvia

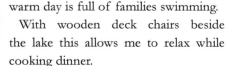

I only know I'm in Latvia because there is a large square blue European Union sign with twelve gold stars forming a circle around the Latvija name beside the road. Otherwise there are no noticeable changes.

At the Valka Visitor Information Centre, a helpful family of young adults and children show me maps of rail trail routes all over Latvia. After asking a few questions I'm able to plan a route to Riga, the capital of Latvia. However, I have to be cautious about how accurate the rail trail map is as many rail trails are still in the process of being developed.

Just south of Smiltene is a small lake surrounded by pine trees, which on this warm day is full of families swimming.

Cooking dinner by a lake

With wooden deck chairs beside the lake this allows me to relax while cooking dinner.

Once it is dark enough, I find a spot among the pine trees to set up my tent, but I should have gone further away from the lake as, during the night, I'm woken by swimmers.

So far, the recommended cycling route between Tartu and Riga has more gravel sections in Latvia, while overall roads haven't been as consistent. Unlike in Russia, there are quiet secondary roads to take but randomly a road will turn to sandy gravel for a few kilometres or become a little bumpy with potholes.

In the middle of nowhere on the way to Cesis, a lone, skinny, bare-chested mid-twenties cyclist on an old bicycle comes into view. As I catch up to him, he surprisingly speaks perfect English, so we chat away for the rest of the ride into Cesis. Charlie is from England and is looking at living in Latvia, having found some land nearby he hopes to develop into a permaculture site, just like The Crossing in Bermagui, where I was working earlier in the year.

After arriving at Cesis, we sit down under a tree in a park to share lunch and chat more. When Charlie decides he will have a nap under a tree, I bid him farewell and realise I'm envious of how more relaxed and freer he appears than me.

I feel like I should be riding on, since I only have two months to get to Turkey.

At this moment, I consider that perhaps I should have booked my return flight from Germany, instead of Istanbul. This would have meant a shorter direct ride, allowing me to either ride less or zigzag my way more. Cycling to Germany would mean travelling a similar route as the Red Army did in World War Two, seeing the overall impact. However, I'm unsure what the weather would be like in Germany in late September. This could be a route for another time, where I also see more of Estonia and visit Scandinavian countries.

I always book a return flight, as it is usually cheaper than one-way flights and adds proof to authorities that I'm leaving eventually, as I have been asked for proof on other trips. However, on previous overseas cycling trips, my flight home has been from the same airport as I arrived, so those routes have been more circular or involved train rides to end the journey. On this trip I'm cycling to a different airport.

Having an end date does provide motivation to continue cycling rather than an open trip where I can make an excuse not to cycle. However, an open trip does have more flexibility to change my route.

Post-ride, I don't regret the route I took because I would have missed out on memorable experiences. However, it's the nature of bicycle touring, I'm always thinking of alternative ideas.

Feeling rushed is reinforced when I get a flat tyre soon afterwards, where I find another small hole in my rear tyre. Thankfully, there is a decent, friendly mountain bike shop in the town square, but they don't have any suitable tyres so instead I patch the tyre from the inside using a tube patch and will see how it goes.

I'm fixing the flat in the middle of a medieval town square with a single cream-stone, red-coned castle tower in the distance. During the time it takes to fix the flat, this allows me to reflect that I'm privileged to be here and there are a lot worse places to be getting a flat tyre.

Square in Cesis with bike shop

Cesis is near the Gauja National Park which promotes cycling through it, so I begin making my way down to the Gauja River excited to cycle through the national park. Initially it looks promising with a short one-way boardwalk out to some natural rock features that have been shaped over centuries by water, with visible layers of erosion.

The cycling route starts as a nice quiet scenic ride in a valley beside the Gauja River on a dirt track while passing through a quiet forest. However, the track slowly becomes sandier and with the type of tyres I have I can't get grip so I'm beginning to slip. So instead of looking around at the scenery, my focus is on finding a sturdier path.

Cycling beside the Gauja River

Suddenly out of nowhere a light sunshower begins and gradually becomes heavier, making it an even harder, slippery, sticky ride. Thankfully, I soon come across a busy campground full of large tents and there is a picnic shelter to wait out the rain as it soon eases.

Eventually, the sandy track becomes gravel and then paved as the route leaves the river behind to head to the small town of Ligatne with a small visitor information centre closing as I arrive. My impression from the tracks cycled and seeing mostly mountain bikes in town and on brochures for this national park, is that this area is more suitable for mountain bikes, rather than my skinnier tyres, which with all my gear, doesn't travel well in sand. I'm unsure what to expect from more cycling routes in the national park.

Around Ligatne, in the side of many hills are numerous small hobbit size man-made caves with a rectangular entrance which were used as cellars. Some caves are in large exposed rock faces where I can see layers of sediment and also graffiti. There are walking paths connecting the caves, as some are high up on the hillside. In front of a group of caves is a former water-powered mill, with water still rushing through wooden channels, while nearby is a grass amphitheatre which is quiet enough for me to camp under a pine tree.

Cellars built in rocks among the hills around Ligatne

While waiting for the Ligatne Visitor Information Centre to open in the morning, I explore more of the cellar caves located on hills behind the small town. Many caves are permanently blocked off with bricks or wood.

After obtaining some information in the Ligatne Visitor Information Centre, I leave town on a terrible, sandy gravel road but once I change local councils, the pavement returns so I make it easily into Sigulda. With restaurants, cafés and plenty of tourists around, Sigulda reminds me of national park towns I have been to in North America. Sigulda is high above the Gauja River as here the river is in a deep valley, providing high scenic views on this sunny day, with two castles across the valley with differing styles and history.

From the well-kept entrance, the cream stone Sigulda Castle has high walls with some gaps that have been filled with wood. After paying two euros, I walk my bicycle over a moat leading to an archway entrance under a square tower.

Entrance to Sigulda Castle   *Inside Sigulda Castle*

Inside it is a different view, as most of the castle is in ruins with the only remains being sidewalls with empty windows. Still there is plenty of information provided to explain its history and some steps to climb.

The castle remains only take up a small part of this open green space, which provides scenic views across the Gauja River Valley to another castle just visible among trees.

There is a cable car across the river valley but it doesn't go directly to the other castle across the valley and anyway I can't take my bicycle on it, so instead I duck down a short, steep descent to cross the Gauja River before a steep climb up to the Turaida Castle.

This castle is in much better condition with a high red-bricked cone tower and an equally as high diverse collection of red-bricked buildings with a dungeon

and plenty of rooms. The Sigulda Castle is just visible between trees across the valley.

Turaida Castle has historical information, displays and mannequins and showing how people used to live here in the Middle Ages, from nobility to prisoners in the dungeon. There are still ruins but this time with short walls providing a floor plan of what it used to look like.

Dungeon in Turaida Castle

Turaida Castle, has high views across the Gauja River

Grafittied shallow cave

I have been told about a cave to visit which is back down near the river, so after descending I join a path which takes me past the cave. Rather than a cave I would describe it as a dip in the side of the deep wide canyon. It would be useless for hiding but it could be used for getting out of the sun. Just like at Ligatne there is plenty of graffiti all over the cave.

Nearby is a steep 15% zigzag brick path among trees which climbs back up to the top of the valley, to where the cable car goes. Being up high allows me to follow a signed dirt mountain bike path, with small jumps back down to the river. Here there is a cable pedestrian bridge to cross to the southern side back to near the railway station.

From Sigulda, the plan is to cycle south until meeting a rail trail near Sidgunda. During this warm afternoon I'm seeing that cereal harvest is in progress, where they are using the same modern size machinery as at home but are harvesting much smaller paddocks.

On my way to Sidgunda there are a few crossroads and somehow I make a wrong turn and end up heading west instead of south. This works out okay, it just means that tomorrow I will connect with a rail trail closer to Riga than expected. My night ends camping near a picnic ground beside a river just outside the town of Ropazi.

Initially south of Ropazi the road is busy with dump trucks, so I'm relieved when an abandoned cement railway station comes into view.

They have only just started converting former railway lines to rail trails called Greenways in Latvia, so I'm unsure what I will find. From what I can see it appears Kangari Station had a few low platforms, which are now overgrown with grass and the only development into a rail trail is that rails are gone.

As I begin cycling on this former rail route, I soon see that cars are using the route, so it is a bumpy, dirt gravel surface with rail ballast mostly removed.

After passing the former Kangari Station, I'm now cycling on an undeveloped rail trail

Former rail bridge   Rail trail finishes in an active rail yard

After crossing on a former steel rail bridge, where it appears all they have done is added a walkway across the middle of the bridge, cars are banned, so the surface is smoother. This doesn't last long as the rail trail ends unceremoniously in the presumably still active Sauriesi rail yards, where there is a railway station building and a few rail cars.

On the edge of Riga is Salaspils Memorial, located on the site of a former German Concentration Camp, surrounded by a spookily quiet forest. At the entrance is a large, long grey building, lying nearly horizontally, with one end sticking up slightly off the ground at a small angle with enough room to walk under it.

Once under the building, I'm surprised to find an open area with just a few cement slabs and in the distance spread out are half a dozen giant stone statues in different poses, representing people who went through here. Otherwise, it's an open, quiet, respectful space which opened as a memorial in 1967.

Inside the fallen overbuilding is a museum with video diaries of people who went through here. Most of the stories are distressing, as this place was built by Jews but housed political prisoners and initially children before they were forcibly separated from their parents.

Children separated from their parents

Salaspils Memorial where statues representing people prisoned here

Riga is the largest city in the Baltics. As I ride in on a cycle path beside Daugava River this confirms this, as it feels so much busier compared to my time so far in the Baltics. By following tram tracks this makes it easier to navigate into the clearly older town centre past the busy market area and under railway viaducts.

A lot of the inner city has narrow cobblestone streets, so it is a bumpy ride as I search for a visitor information centre. Google Maps suggests a few options, the first place is a restaurant with a small visitor info sign outside but inside is just half a dozen brochures in a corner so not much use.

The second option is in a smaller building but with more brochures and dedicated visitor staff who give me some valuable information. I later learn that the main info centre is in the pyramid-shaped House of Blackheads near the town hall which is only 100 metres away from the restaurant I first went to.

Freedom Monument

Martin, my Warmshower host, has organised to meet me near the Freedom Monument. This tall monolith structure is easy to find as it stands out on a bridge across the canal just north of the old town. Around the base of this monument are a few statues representing various occupations from soldiers to farmers and on top is a green lady holding three gold stars. It was opened in 1935 as a monument to the independence fight in the 1920s and remarkably was not destroyed by the Soviets, despite being threatened a few times.

While looking around, a man in his early twenties with blond hair shows up on his bicycle and introduces himself as Martin. We then cycle back to his apartment via the main markets near the main railway station. Martin collects some food while I watch the bicycles.

The next day I went to the markets to have a look through the four larger hanger sheds. There are plenty of bakery items for sale with most bread sellers using plastic bags, something supermarkets have stopped doing since arriving into the Baltics. It has been a major contrast to Russia, with supermarkets now having plenty of fresh bread baked on-site and free to choose without plastic.

Martin's apartment is small really – one room and a bathroom attached so during the day my bicycle is left locked up outside behind the gated community. Coming from a farming background it's different seeing people live in such small spaces all over Europe, something I'm having to get used to.

With plenty of time left in the day, I go for a walk around the city, starting with visiting the informative Museum of the Occupation of Latvia which, as the name suggests, focuses on Latvia being occupied between 1940 and 1991, initially by the Soviet Union, then briefly Germany before being re-occupied by the Soviet Union. It could do with more of a focus on the struggles after 1945 but still it's informative.

At times the scale is hard to comprehend because Latvia lost a third of its pre-World War Two population and its border frequently changed. Of the twelve ministers in the Latvian government, eleven were captured by the Soviets and the only one to survive captivity was the foreign minister.

Randomly in the museum, I start chatting with an Englishman about the Australian men's cricket issues, with it only being four months since Sandpapergate at Cape Town. If you're not into cricket, essentially members of our men's national team were caught cheating using sandpaper to rough up the cricket ball which is definitely not allowed.

The Museum of the Occupation of Latvia has plenty of books for sale including many in English. Since the museum is free, I decide to purchase a book. However, being on a bicycle tour I have to find a book which is a suitable size to carry while still being interesting.

With Dance Shoes in Siberian Snows is a memoir of Sandra Kalniete, a woman whose parents were separately deported from Latvia and they met in Siberia. She was born in Siberia and they were only allowed to return when she was five. Post-independence, she became a prominent politician in Latvia.

Currently, the museum is in a temporary site on the edge of the city centre, with a new building being built near the Blackheads in the city centre. Hopefully, it will become even more informative.

Riga is a bit like a smaller version of St Petersburg with a wide river and a grassed bank canal which goes around the old city centre. Having missed out on a cruise in St Petersburg, I thought it is worth experiencing one here.

This hour-long cruise around the canal and Daugava River helps inform me where many things are in Riga. The rail bridge over the wide river looks like a row of mini Sydney Harbour bridges, while also visible from the river is the white Riga Castle, the of home of the President of Latvia.

After going under the rail bridge, the Riga Castle is visible beside the Daugava River

Back at Martin's, a German cyclist has arrived to stay as well. Sebastian is on a much quicker ride than me, having cycled from Germany and he is heading to Tallinn. Martin cooks us a delicious chicken and potato meal and then all three of us cycle out to the river for a swim. After being so helpful, I'm surprised when Martin tells us that we are his first Warmshower guests.

On the ride into Riga, I went past a train carriage on display near the markets so the next morning I search for it again.

Once I find it, I learn this was the location of the Jewish ghetto during World War Two. A small block has been preserved as the Riga Ghetto and Latvian Holocaust Museum.

Location of the Riga Ghetto

I enter past a steel and barbed wire gate to a courtyard where a black with yellow roofed wooden box train car with various European city names on it, is on display. Both inside the train and on a wall behind the train is detailed information, chronicling what happened to Jewish people during World War Two.

In a couple of rooms, there is more information, with plenty of detail as it tries to individualise the people murdered. Inside one room are a hundred-odd floating lit-up kite type cubes, each with a photo and biography of a person's life before they were murdered just because they were Jewish.

One person even looks similar to how my grandmother looked when she was younger. I have no association with this as all my great-grandparents were born in Australia. Sadly, this will not be my only encounter with the Holocaust especially as I get closer to Poland.

Each box represents a murdered person including Marie

Back in the city centre is the Latvian War Museum, located in a lone medieval red-bricked cone castle tower which is surrounded by modern buildings. Just like the Riga Ghetto and Occupation Museums, it is free to visit, as each just ask for donations.

This museum has rooms dedicated to various conflicts throughout the ages with the World War One section the most informative. I learn that for a while the Daugava River was part of the Eastern Front in World War One so Riga was split in half.

With the extension of Russian Fan ID not confirmed yet I decide to visit the Russian Consulate and I'm easily let in through security. However, they don't have any fresh news as they are waiting for confirmation too. So at this stage I will stick to my original plan of spending more time in Lithuania before entering Poland, rather than making my way west towards Kaliningrad.

Across the Daugava River in the south of Riga is a railway museum near the large public library. The museum is small but has a fascinating interactive map showing the development of railway lines across Latvia. Because those who have controlled Latvia has changed a few times, there were different priorities for where rail tracks should go and what rail gauge to use, so it was a mess of a system. These days Latvia is wider east-west than north-south so most railway lines go east-west, with Riga in the middle.

Today the rail gauge in the Baltics is Russian gauge which is wider than standard gauge found in most of Europe – a deliberate decision to make it harder to invade Russia as Hitler found out. Currently there is no direct passenger rail service between Latvia and Lithuania. However, there are plans to build a modern fast rail service from Poland to Estonia, using the narrower standard gauge, so one day trains could travel from all over Europe to the Baltics.

After negotiating my way across the Daugava River using various bicycle paths, I find a quiet road beside the railway line to take me south out of Riga, when suddenly a squeaking noise begins. I have another rear flat tyre, so I decide it's time to change the tyre as I have had a few flats lately and the tyre now has a few holes in it.

The front tyre still has plenty of tread which is normal because the rear tyre normally wears out much faster due to my weight and pannier bags putting more force on it, compared to the front. Sometimes I have swapped tyres halfway through a trip, but I haven't this time.

After fixing the flat, I set off for a bicycle shop not far away, but it doesn't have the tyre type I need so I decide to catch a train back to Riga.

Latvian railway stations are similar to many Russian railway stations with low-level platforms, requiring my bicycle to be lifted up onto an old yellow and blue train with manual opening doors.

For anyone from Victoria, the colours and style of Latvian trains remind me of the old blue and yellow DERM railmotor trains which use to travel all over Victoria including places like Sea Lake but are now found at tourist railways like at Daylesford.

After crossing the Daugava River on the multiple coat hanger rail bridge, getting off the train at Riga Station requires negotiating another low platform.

In the meantime, the rear tyre is flat again, so rather than trying to fix a tube again, I begin carrying my bicycle as a bike shop is not far away. With all my bags on my bicycle it is a struggle carrying it all, so I'm stopping every 25 metres or so, to rest my arms.

This bicycle shop has a correct size tyre but not the tread I want. Therefore, I purchase another tube, fix the flat and continue searching for a suitable tyre in other bicycle shops.

Eventually I find a tyre suitable but not the same model as I have and for some reason, this tyre is light brown in colour.

For those not aware just like any other vehicle, bicycle wheels come in assorted sizes and depending on what type of cycling you're doing, you need a certain style of tread. There are also many brands of tyres each with assorted styles and levels of durability. When going off-road, a mountain bike tyre which grips more, is better suited than a smoother tyre with less resistance which is what road cyclists use.

I prefer to have a combination of both, where the middle of the tyre tread is smooth so on paved roads I fly along, with the outside tread not touching the road. On rougher surfaces I prefer to have a mountain bike tread on the outside, which allows me to have more grip, otherwise it can be a slippery ride.

While pumping up my tyre outside the friendly bicycle shop, I blow up the tube causing a loud bang, so I have to purchase another tube. By the time everything is fixed it is now 3 pm.

Smoother path for cyclists

With the bicycle shop on the north side of Riga, this requires going through the city again. With a paved on-road cycle lane next to cobblestone tram tracks this helps make it an easier ride back through the city centre and over the Daugava River again.

Once past where my flat occurred, I continue following the railway line on quiet roads with the busier highway nearby. Unfortunately, the quiet road finishes but thankfully there is a paved cycle path through the town of Olaine. It continues out of town where, beside the cycle path is a gravel road until the paved cycle path ends near a lake and the road becomes bitumen.

Eventually, the cycling signs end so I'm forced onto the highway but thankfully I soon leave the highway into the town of Ozolnieki but I'm still on a busy road.

On this warm August evening, Ozolnieki Lake is popular, there is a supermarket right next to it and regular trains are stopping across the water.

As I looking around, I soon discover that the main attraction is a wakeboard course, where people are towed around by cables instead of a speedboat. I thought, Why not give it a go, but since I have no experience with stand up wakeboarding, I try kneeboarding first. It is tough on my shoulders and I fall off a few times, while trying to hold on and turn the board correctly. My arms were still sore a week later.

Wakeboard course on Ozolnieki Lake, with a railway station behind it

While cooking dinner I find a half-empty two-litre bottle of water and went to use it for dinner. However, it tastes terrible and I realise someone has put a cigarette in it. This is a downside of trying to avoid buying water, which on this occasion, I do buy.

I considered camping near the lake, but it is still busy in the evening and street lights are everywhere, so I head into the nearby forest.

In the morning, not far away is the larger town of Jelgava which has a nice revitalised river area with a new footbridge across the river. Nearby is a memorial to Latvian independence which I'm told, during the Soviet Union occupation, was replaced with Lenin. When Latvia became independent again, the statue was added back. Since leaving Russia, the Lenin statues have all gone.

Jelgava is a railway junction town, so it has a small railway museum, where the guide is kind enough to translate information for me into English, while videos have an English option. Despite Lithuania not being far south from here, passenger trains don't travel any further south of Jelgava.

While checking online in Jelgava, I see that the Duma, the Russian Parliament has passed the Fan ID extension and Putin has signed the bill, so I can revisit Russia. Therefore, I set off in the direction of the west coast to visit Kaliningrad because I may never get the chance again and it's a shorter route to Poland.

The afternoon westerly ride is a struggle as it starts with a potholed repaired road which is bumpy, and a headwind. Thankfully the road is quiet. As the road improves the wind becomes stronger which isn't helped by the fact that the road doesn't change direction for 50 kilometres. After resting in a few towns along the way, I'm glad to make Auce, to finish the day.

However, as I check online again I discover that the Fan ID extension doesn't start until ten days after the bill is signed. So I cannot enter Russia until 14th August, ten days from now, when I plan to be near Warsaw, so I have cycled into a headwind for no reason.

I never considered waiting until the 14th because having mailed home my physical Fan ID, I only have the electronic version and I'm unsure if it will be accepted. Instead I spend the evening developing a route which should allow me to return to my original plan through Lithuania and then Poland which should keep me on schedule.

It takes a while to find a decent place to stealth camp in Auce, as people are out enjoying this Saturday evening. There are plenty of open spaces around the abandoned railway complex but none which are out of sight, out of mind.

Eventually I find a spot at the back of the sports stadium behind some trees; not my best spot but safely made it through. During the night there are a couple of thunderstorms, but they stop by the morning, so my tent is wet but I'm dry.

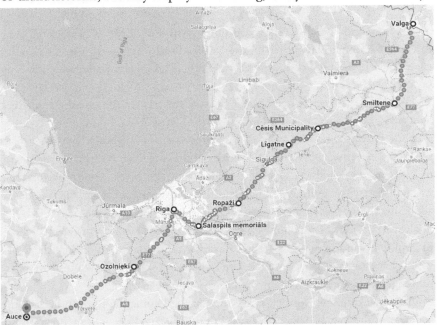

Valga to Auce (Google Maps)

Lithuania

Apart from a sign saying I'm crossing from Latvia to Lithuania, I haven't noticed any changes in landscape or shops. For a short section, the border follows the road, with a few white wooden posts with Lithuanian colours of yellow, green and red on them beside the road.

As I didn't learn much Latvian language, I haven't noticed a change to Lithuanian, especially as most

Road is briefly beside the border

people speak either Russian or English. I haven't felt like I need to learn local languages as I'm only spending a week in each country.

Naujoji the first town I come across in Lithuania, looks like I'm back in Russia with square cement buildings around an open square with a large clock cement monolith, paintings, gardens and three-sided church. After looking up the town's history online, I can see why I thought this, as Naujoji Akmenė was developed in the 1950s for a nearby cement plant for the Soviet Union.

This square reminds me of Russia

From here it is a simple cycle on good roads through small towns, each a little different.

The town of Gruzdziai has a large twin tower red-bricked church but a rarer site is an actual flushing public toilet in the town square across the road, something I take for granted in Australia.

The goal for the day is the city of Siauliai, having found an Airbnb to do some laundry, since I haven't done any since Estonia.

While waiting for my host to be ready I have a look around the long scenic pedestrian mall where on both sides are long rows of trees and a few sculptures scattered around. With it being a Sunday afternoon, it is quiet with most places closed, including museums.

A photographic museum is open, even if it is only one room of photos. The view from the roof is interesting as it shows the rows of trees in the mall even better.

Pedestrian mall in Siauliai

Since the museum has wi-fi and time zones work back with Australia, I FaceTime my parents. I learn that Kieran Hunt has died from Motor Neuron Disease. I didn't know him but I went to school for thirteen years with his daughter Jacey and it's not the first time I have been on a tour when a parent of someone I went to school with has died. As my parents are now getting older, it's something I have considered could happen to me so am grateful I can still call my parents.

This reminds me of what happened to Tim Cope during his horse journey from Mongolia to Hungary via many former Soviet Union countries. In the middle of his journey his dad died in a car crash back home in Australia, which is detailed in his book and television series, On the Trail of Genghis Khan. Tim Cope is from Australia and he has also spent time cycling in Russia, with his friend Chris, as they cycled east to Beijing. Both his journeys are inspirational.

Also staying at my Airbnb is an elderly ex-pat Lithuanian woman who lives in Chicago. She tells me she fled from the Soviet Union decades ago and still dislikes Russians. I'm not surprised to hear this, what surprises me is realising that this is the first time I have heard this from a person in the Baltics.

Roads have improved since crossing from Latvia to Lithuania, with most secondary roads being bitumen so it has been an easier quiet ride, with small towns every ten kilometres and no potholes to worry about.

The weather has cooled to mid-twenties and a few times there has been a couple of instances of short, heavy showers but

Quiet open roads in Lithuania

then the sun will come out. Thankfully, most wind has been side or tailwinds, so I have been flying along passing by farmers either harvesting or bailing hay.

In the middle of nowhere, I come across a Jewish cemetery with a large black steel gate and arch with a Star of David at the top of the arch. There is a small, newish plaque from the United States telling me it is a Jewish cemetery. Otherwise, it doesn't appear to be that well looked after, with a couple of stone remains and one headstone. It reminds me of the cemetery near Narva in Estonia which was destroyed and not repaired. I'm also coming across random roadside statues and Christian crosses often beside paddocks.

Derelict Jewish cemetery *Random roadside statues and crosses*

At a hardware store a man helps me find fuel for my Trangia stove. When we find the correct one, he lets me try it in my Trangia and then refused payment. I have had so many people refuse money from me.

After a relaxing day, I find a wild camping spot on a grass track beside the Neman River with some nice views. With the town of Vilkija high above I'm out of sight.

Just as I'm leaving in the morning a heavy shower of rain begins, which thankfully stops after ten minutes. However, there is now some puddles to dodge on the road into Kaunas. Not long after entering the suburbs of Kaunas there is a cycle path which takes me through the suburbs and over the Neris River into the city centre.

In the area between where the Neris River flows into the more dominant Nemunas River is a triangular peninsula which is where the old part of Kaunas was. A small red-bricked castle dominates the otherwise now open grass flood plain.

The castle is scenic with a walkway across the dry moat to one small cone tower with the entrance on an outside staircase. From the amount of open space around the castle and the current castle remains which include a row of smaller joining red buildings, clearly it was previously a much larger complex.

What is left of Kaunas Castle

Once inside I head down to a dungeon with photos, artwork and mannequins of prisoners but it could have more information and more accessible space.

On the surrounding floodplain are cycle paths so I join one beside the Nemunas River which allows a relaxing explore. I see a bridge to an island where the local basketball club plays in the European league against clubs like Real Madrid and Barcelona. Basketball is the favourite sport in Lithuania and is the main focus in the sports museum along with plenty of trophies and memorabilia from Lithuanian athletes.

The former Presidential residence has an excellent display on Lithuania history focusing on the period between the Declaration of Independence in 1918 and Soviet occupation in 1940. This is explained by 100 information boards each describing a significant event in that period, with each event ranked according to importance.

Kaunas was the capital during this period as nearby Vilnius, the current capital, was under Polish control during parts of this time. In 1926 Antanas Smetona, the first president of Lithuania post-independence, overthrew the then President Kazys Grinuis and became a dictator. He then fled when the Soviets arrived in 1940 and died in a suspicious fire in the USA in 1944. This is a common story in this region with countries starting as democracies after independence post-World War One but they then became dictatorships.

Hitler demanded the western Klaipeda region be returned to Germany, similar to what happened to Czechoslovakia. Lithuania appears to have resisted slightly more from being invaded by Soviets which led to worse consequences for the locals. They were really caught in the middle between neighbouring countries wanting their land.

The Great War Museum has plenty of items including numerous, slightly different models of helmets, a crashed red plane and many paintings of war on display.

It is less informative than the Latvian War Museum in Riga, but its style reminds me of a smaller version of the Australian War Memorial in Canberra. Outside the Great War Museum, is an eternal flame in front of a stone pyramid war memorial, surrounded by numerous tall poles with several types of crosses on top.

War memorial in Kaunas

My Warmshowers is with Paulius, who has made me feel so welcome including cooking me a variety of local food, sharing local information and talking about his own cycling trip in South America.

From Kaunas my plan is to cycle east to Vilnius, the current capital of Lithuania and then turn around and cycle in a south-westerly direction to my next destination of Alytus, south of Kaunas.

After I tell Paulius of my rough plans, since he is driving to Vilnius for work tomorrow, he offers instead for me to tag along and have a day of exploring the Lithuanian capital before returning to stay with him for a second night. Since this will save me time and I was only cycling that way to see Vilnius, I will take up his offer.

Paulius drops me off in Vilnius, which feels busier than Kaunas, as I make my way to my first place of interest, the Genocide Museum. This is located in a former KGB building which was used at separate times by both German and Soviet occupiers to house people for interrogations, torture and executions. This is a larger complex and has more detailed information than in the KGB cells in Tartu.

Throughout the museum, there are rooms full of information, photos and items telling numerous stories of the impact this had on people from all ages and backgrounds for decades.

Post 1945 many people hid in the woods for years as guerrilla fighters, so the Soviet Union put on display photos of numerous, executed, independent fighters as a warning to others. Many people tried to escape including a person who tried to canoe away on the Baltic Sea before being caught – one of many stories from this period.

The number of people deported after 1945 east into Russia was more than 100,000 Lithuanians, including 40,000 children. Of the people deported, 21% were farmers. I assume farmers made up a high proportion of the population, but I'm still surprised at how high a percentage it was.

Many children were deported east into Siberia.
While photos of executed resistance fighters, were
displayed as a warning.

Inside one room is a television showing a short fictional film of a man struggling while being brought in by two Soviet guards and then another guard shoots him in the back of the head. From the video, I realise I'm in the same room. It's one thing to read about people being executed but being in an actual room where it happened humanises what people went through.

The nearby quieter Jewish Museum hidden in a small house is even more depressing as 90% of Jewish people in Lithuania were murdered during the Holocaust. On display are diaries from people who were eventually murdered and information about sites nearby where mass groups of people were executed.

After leaving the depressing museums, suddenly I'm in the downtown area which is touristy with a busy shopping precinct which then leads to an open park area near the Neris River with a few old churches and a castle. I'm feeling museum fatigued and most appear to be tourist traps, so I just walk around admiring buildings from the outside.

The dominating feature is a large red-bricked tower on a dirt mound called Gediminas. Accessing the tower is via a zigzag cobblestone path up to remains of a once larger castle. With 360-degree views of Vilnius, it is mostly just multistorey buildings.

Cobblestone path up to Gediminas Tower, which is visible from street

On the way up to the railway station, I walk along a narrow cobblestone pedestrian mall on a warm day with plenty of choices of ice cream. Along the way, I go under the Gate of Dawn, a religious gate from the 16th century with Latin writing on the walls and a golden triangle eye surround by light, marking where the old town finished.

Don't bother with the railway museum in the main railway station, as it is less informative and smaller than the Latvian ones, with no English information. There are model railways, showing on a large scale where railway lines went in Lithuania, but overall it's more suitable for children with plenty of railway toys to play with.

Paulius picks me up in his car outside the railway station and we drive back via Trakai Castle. An advantage when travelling by bicycle is not having to worry about finding a car space which is reinforced at Trakai where it takes a while for Paulius to find a car park as it is busy with families enjoying this

Trakai Castle is on an island in a lake

warm sunny day. Walking towards the castle it's easy to see how touristy this place is with restaurants, souvenir shops and plenty of tourist boat rides on offer.

The red-bricked Trakai Castle is an intact castle with a few cone towers located on one of the many small islands on Lake Galve, with a wooden bridge connecting the castle to the foreshore.

After a brief look inside, I decide not to pay to go inside the castle, as it feels like a busy tourist trap and I'm a little tired from museums and attractions over the last two days. Instead, Paulius and I walk around the castle admiring the outside walls.

Before returning to Kaunas, Paulius says he needs a swim, so we find a quieter spot on the other side of the lake. On this warm day we join a few other swimmers, including ducks, in the scenic lake.

Once back at Paulius's home we end a long day with a BBQ dinner at 11 pm at night, with Paulius and his friend. We end up discussing current political issues in the region, including neighbouring Russia.

Paulius went well above as a Warmshower host, making me feel welcomed and sharing plenty of information about Lithuania and I will always be grateful for him letting me relax for a couple of days at his home.

Paulius suggests leaving Kaunas via a bridge across the Nemunas River near his home. The bridge is high above the river and presumably cars used to use it but is now only for non-motorised traffic. The bridge slopes down so I'm able to freely roll across the river to an inside horseshoe curve of the Nemunas River.

Bridge over the Nemunas River leads to a paved path through a pine forest

I'm now in a pine forest where my route involves a mixture of paved cycle paths and gravel roads.

It's a quiet ride all day except for a four kilometre section on the highway to Prienai which requires going through roadworks to cross the Nemunas River again. Once over the river I soon find another paved cycle path through more pine forests, which takes me to the fancy mineral water spa resort town of Birstonas, where suddenly cycling isn't allowed on certain paths.

I have never understood the attraction of mineral water as it tastes disgusting. However, they do have a visitor information centre which has details on a cycling route south to Alytus.

For the most part, the afternoon ride involves some gravel sections through small towns and through farmland which is okay. South of Punis, when the road turns to sandy gravel, I slowly struggle through trying to find a steady path to take.

Once in the northern part of Alytus, a cycle path beside the Nemunas River takes me under the impressive new looking rail trail bridge which crosses the Nemunas River. The challenge is finding a way up to the bridge, with seemingly the only option being to climb with my fully loaded bicycle up some pine logs stairs built into the side of where the bridge joins the hillside.

A recently rebuilt rail trail bridge at Alytus

Once up I can see a wide modern bridge with both bicycle and pedestrian lanes. It appears that the rail trail goes further north but for now, I will cross the river and search for a supermarket as I'm starving. The rail trail goes around the edge of the town centre of Alytus, but a few supermarkets are beside the trail. Along the way I pass remains of railway platforms with trees growing where trains used to stop.

On both sides of the rail trail, there are small skinny lakes, which have paved cycle paths around them. A perfect place to cook dinner but with street lights around both lakes they are not suitable to camp, so instead I go back across the rail trail bridge until finding a dark enough place to camp beside it.

In the morning, I go to see how much further the rail trail travels north.

However, it soon becomes muddy in a deep cutting. I try to keep cycling but suddenly my bicycle slips in the mud and we both go over. Thankfully, it's a soft landing, so I walk for a bit, discovering the rail is overgrown as Mother Nature has reclaimed the right of way.

Slipping in a muddy old cutting

There is a tourist information place in town and a couple of small museums with just Lithuanian language so it's hard to understand what is being talked about. However, I do learn that the rail trail bridge was demolished by fleeing Russians in 1915 and rebuilt by Germans before being demolished again in 1927 and was only rebuilt as a pedestrian/cycle bridge in 2015.

Alytus feels like a cycle-friendly town, with a few drinking water fountains and bicycle repair stands, so I thought I would check my tyre pressure using a community bicycle pump beside the rail trail. However, it just makes my tyre go flat and my own small hand pump is playing up. Thankfully, a lady sees me in trouble and offers her manual car pump which gives me enough air, even if it takes a while.

I'm in no hurry to leave Alytus because two Women's UEFA Champions League football qualifying matches are on at the local stadium in the afternoon and the evening. For the smaller nations in Europe, the champion club of each individual league competes in a four-team single round competition hosted by one country over a week. The top teams go through to the first proper round of knockout matches against clubs from better leagues like France, Germany and England.

Gintra University is from Siauliai in the north of Lithuania but for some reason are hosting football matches in the south. Therefore, on this Friday afternoon in August, there isn't a big crowd in attendance, just a few supporters from visiting clubs, presumably family and friends but still an enjoyable, relaxing experience. Neither game is close with FC Honka from Finland winning 5-nil over the Bulgarian champions NSA Sofia while the Lithuanian team wins 7-nil over EB/Streymur/Skála from the Faroe Islands.

Across the road from the stadium is a public park with a few memorials, with the main item being a large bell which is cut in half to symbolise a divided country between 1940 and 1991.

By 9 pm, as the second game finishes, it looks like a thunderstorm is imminent so instead of returning to my stealth camping spot, I find a hotel for twenty euro.

A divided country until 1991

The rain never really arrives so I probably didn't need to stay inside.

I awoke to a cloudy day with threatening rain with a plan to cross into Poland. Initially, I leave Alytus by continuing on a rail trail as it takes me nearly all the way out of town past many supermarkets before it ends, as a still-active railway line passes through the west of Alytus.

Having used this short rail trail for a couple of days I have seen how well used it is. Many locals use it to travel through town by various self-propelled methods including bicycle, scooter, rollerblades or walking.

The main road south to the border is busy so as soon as I can, I leave it to take a slightly longer, quieter route to Lazdijai. This does mean a small section of gravel road, but it is just okay to cycle on an overcast day.

I managed to get to Lazdijai just before a thunderstorm hits. By the rain radar, it looks like the rain will pass within an hour, so I wait it out by finding a restaurant which has a scenic landscape photo book showing numerous Lithuanian landscapes, while enjoying a burger. However, it is nearly three hours by the time it looks like it has cleared.

With open European borders, I don't need to stop at the border, but large abandoned customs buildings are still here. This border crossing would have been busy as it was only one of a handful between Poland and Lithuania with the Russian enclave of Kaliningrad to the north-west and Belarus to the south. Neither are members of the open European borders, so there is only a narrow border area for me to cross from Lithuania to Poland.

Auce to Sejny (Google Maps)

Poland

Having crossed into Poland, I have changed time zones and I'm now an hour further behind. Other than a brief time in Samara, since arriving I had been on the same time as Kazan, 2,000 kilometres away east of Lithuania as Russia doesn't do daylight savings.

During my ride across the border, I come across three cyclists out for a day ride and we chat for a bit before heavy rain returns, soaking me. Also out cycling, is a man with a rack on the back of his bicycle carrying a round green tub in a tin container.

Often during this trip, I would see people carrying equipment on the back of a rusty bicycle, many with homemade attachments enabling a wide range of things to be carried. This included food and many tools such as shovels and saws and I swear I once saw someone carrying a chainsaw. This reinforces to me that for some people a bicycle is their only form of transport while I'm choosing to travel this way.

A cyclist carrying gear

As I make Sejny, the first town in Poland for me, the heavy rain looks like continuing so indoor accommodation is a priority. The best option I can find is a hotel, however, with a wedding on it is a noisy night's sleep.

In the evening Adrian, my Warmshower host in Warsaw, messages me to say that every second Sunday is a legal family day in Poland where, by law, supermarkets and other businesses will be closed tomorrow. This has only recently been enacted by the Christian conservative government with plans to make it every Sunday. This explains why the supermarket is busy this Saturday evening as I head back to get supplies for tomorrow. Finding a loaf of bread for lunch and some pasta and a tin of tuna for dinner tomorrow, I don't need breakfast supplies as a buffet is included in my hotel.

For the first time on this trip, Google Maps now includes cycling routes, making it a lot easier to plan my way towards Hitler's Wolf Lair before heading to Warsaw.

I wake to a sunny dry day but with wind around, I leave Sejny in a westerly direction on a paved cycle path right beside the road. Sometimes there is a wire barrier between the cycle path and the road, other times no barrier at all. Unfortunately, a headwind

Cycle path beside the road

makes it a slow ride to Suwalki as I pass a large lake, with a nature conservation visitor centre, informing me about the local environment.

In the centre of Suwalki is the Park of the Constitution of 3 May 1791, which, on this Sunday morning, is busy with numerous markets stalls and kid's entertainment, including a pirate with his ship. With plenty of people enjoying this family day, perhaps the government is onto something. I'm also suddenly seeing a few touring cyclists.

In the park is a visitor information centre with helpful staff, including plenty of cycling related maps and information. In particular I learn of a cycling route called GreenVelo which travels around the northern and eastern parts of Poland utilising former rail lines, where possible.

Originally I was planning to continue cycling west, however, with it still being windy, I will cycle north following the GreenVelo route, which starts as a cycle path beside the road that takes me out of Suwalki.

During the ride north, I pass a different style of World War Two memorial. This one is made up of two large hands with fingers pointed up to the sky, holding a symbol made up of a combination of a large P, with its tail in the middle vertical part of a smaller w. The wrists are surrounded by barbed wire and around the base is the date of 1945. It doesn't make sense until explained to me in Warsaw.

The signed GreenVelo route takes a long windy route once the cycle path ends, so instead I have found a short cut to Przerosl. As I begin to head west this means sidewinds and rolling hills which slightly slows me down, on this quiet road.

I'm unsure what this is

In the town park in the centre of Przerosl, another local event is on with a handful of food stalls and a small concert. Performing are a group of elderly women dressed up in what I assume is a traditional dress of red pants and green vests.

As I re-join the main road heading west, thankfully the wind is calming down.

Mini concert in Przerosl

Soon visible on my right are the remains of a railway route with rails removed so I leave the highway to investigate.

The rail right of way is now an okay dirt vehicle track which I begin cycling on. It goes under a couple of cement road bridges and pass farms, until suddenly it becomes overgrown with plants. Knowing there is a road crossing, just past this point, I begin dragging my bicycle, assuming I will get through.

However, my feet start to become wet and I realise looking around that I'm now in a swamp which looks like continuing for a while. So I turn around searching for a path back to the highway but since I'm in rail cuttings with bridges high above there is no easy way to exit. I'm forced to retreat a fair way back.

Once back on the highway it is now late in the day so as soon as I spy the next town of Galwiecie, I decide to stop here. Straight away I find a park with a picnic shelter to cook dinner.

While cooking, some children come over to chat to me in Polish with some asking me to take photos of them, while others are shy. Wish I could speak Polish, so I could understand what they are saying, outside of hello and thank you.

With houses close to the park it isn't a suitable place to camp so I cycle out of town back across the highway and down a hill back to the rail route. In fading light, I can see that it is suitable to cycle, so I set off until finding a place to set my tent up in the dark.

In the morning I discover I'm near two stone rail bridges next to each other, both built with a couple of arches over a small creek. One bridge is clear of vegetation with a well-used four-wheel drive track, while the second bridge is overgrown with trees on the actual bridge. I soon spot, painted on the bridge, a couple of bicycle symbols with a red rectangle mark underneath, informing me I'm on a cycle route.

Two former rail bridges, one overgrown, one a cycling route

This rail trail continues for a short while until just before meeting the highway again, as rails still exist on the abandoned railway line, I have to return to the highway. After going under twin cement rail bridges, I follow the abandoned railway into the town of Goldup.

I'm in town before 8 am so I have to wait until 9 am for the visitor information centre to open. This does give me a chance to explore the park square in the centre of town with a lake in the middle. I also meet a middle-aged Canadian female cyclist, who is heading the same way as me and we would interact a couple of times during this morning cycle on the GreenVelo.

Once out of town the GreenVelo route returns to being a rail trail as it travels through a few cuttings surrounded by forests, while going under cement bridges. Along the way are a few rest stations with picnic tables, shelters and bicycle racks.

Bridges over the former railway line   *A few bike rest stations on this trail*

Stopping at one rest station for morning tea allows me to chat with some of the many cyclists I'm encountering on the trail, with most going the other way.

The rail trail surface is gravel which at times is a little rough but manageable as it becomes slightly worse the further west you go towards Wegorzewo, while

Most of rail trail passes by farms

the landscape is becoming more open farmland with crops and dairy farms.

The rail trail ends in the town of Wegorzewo as west of here the rails are still in place. However, a path beside a scenic canal takes me into the centre of town, with plenty of people out enjoying the sunny day with numerous small boats and cycle paths around the port area. It's a perfect spot for lunch, as I chat to a few more cyclists and everyday tourists.

On the way out of town is the abandoned railway station which I have been told is a museum but when I get there, it's closed. There are a couple of small rail work vehicles which I assume are used for tourist purposes on this closed rail.

With rails still here, the GreenVelo route is a paved path beside the main road with a row of trees separating me from the road as I head west.

Eventually Lake Marmy comes into view with yachts on the water. While admiring the GreenVelo map at an information shelter, a Polish cyclist stops for a chat as he explains to me where the GreenVelo goes.

Abandoned Wegorzewo station   *Map of GreenVelo route*

It continues a fair way west along the northern border of Poland, while in the other direction it travels south along the eastern border region of Poland, a potential route in the future.

The reason for going this way first in Poland is to visit Hitler's Wolf's Lair, the location of the failed assassination attempt in 1944. From here I will have to leave the GreenVelo behind as its route is north of the Wolf's Lair.

Despite leaving the GreenVelo, initially I'm still encountering a few cyclists on a quiet road as the lake gradually disappears as a forest blocks my view.

Before leaving the lake, there is a complex of abandoned World War Two German bunkers on both sides of the road. On the side away from the lake is the popular Mamerki Bunker Museum which is in two sites. Firstly, I pay to walk around a bunker with not much information, as it is more about seeing the large cement bunkers which are cold and dark inside with plenty of people exploring.

A short walk along is a museum building with too many information boards covering the whole of World War Two, along with a few war items including small planes.

Across the road, among trees on the lake side are a few abandoned cement bunkers. With not much daylight getting through the trees it's a spookily quiet location, especially as there are fewer people around, no staff and no information.

Some bunkers are in worse condition than others, with some having large cracks in them as the forest is slowly reclaiming the area with trees growing in between gaps.

The bunkers that are open require a torch to see inside, but all I see are bare dusty rooms. While on the sides of some bunkers are numerous steel rectangular bars sticking out, making a ladder. It's easy climbing reminding me of climbing a silo back on the farm. Once at the top, I find a flat roof area which is easy to then walk across as the bunker still looks in good condition.

Nature is reclaiming the bunkers   *Climbing a bunker*

My route to Wolf's Lair is easy, relaxing cycling through a couple of small towns, a mixture of forest and farmland. As the forest becomes thicker, an abandoned railway line becomes visible as I follow it until the entrance to a busy place.

After paying the entrance fee, I'm allowed to bring my bicycle inside, where I find a busy place with people being led around by tour guides. Near the entrance is a large map showing the numerous numbered cement bunkers squeezed in a surprisingly compact site.

The first site I search for is where the assassination attempt on Hitler happened on 20 July 1944. All that is left is the cement foundations of the building, with a small bronze plaque marking the site.

Overall, this site is in worse condition than the bunkers earlier in the day with many buildings just piles of rubble. This is because many were blown up when the Germans fled. The buildings which weren't blown up, often have long cracks from the ground to the ceiling so there are many no entry signs due to the danger of rocks falling, but plenty of people ignore this directive.

Many cement slabs which should be falling over, appear to be held up by numerous long tree limbs, while new trees are growing back in places between any gaps in the rubble.

There are a couple of intact rooms with some photos and brief information but I left feeling that it could do with more work to make it a more impressive site for independent visitors as I didn't find it as informative as I hoped. There was more information at the earlier bunkers near Lake Marmy but it's still worth seeing if you're passing by.

While working on this book I read that this may be changing soon with more information being provided. This site has only been open for visitors since the 1990s after communism fell so it had been left derelict for 50 years.

There are many cracks in the bunkers and some cement slabs are being held up by sticks

Today has reinforced that once again, often places I have heard about previously are less impressive once finally visited, and it's often the unknown places which are more memorable.

The town of Ketrzyn is nearby with a decent visitor information centre and a few things to see in town but with rain predicted tomorrow, I will start heading south towards Warsaw.

Eventually, on dusk I arrive at the small lakeside town of Swieta Lipka, with a few restaurants on one side of the road and a large gated salmon-pink coloured church with twin towers, golden sun symbols and clocks on the outside, making up half the town. With a religious service on when I arrive, I have a quick look inside but for me it is just another fancy church with religious artwork on the roof and back wall. Behind the church is a lake, a perfect quiet spot to camp among pine trees.

Behind the large church in Swieta Lipka, is a lake which is a suitable camping spot

As predicted heavy rain begins in the morning so my ride becomes about cycling as quickly as I can rather than enjoying the scenic lake beside me.

The rain eases by the time I make Mragowo. It's a scenic town with cobblestone streets and cycle paths beside another lake. The museum is closed but I still enjoyed seeing the town.

My afternoon ride is on a secondary road through numerous small towns. Clouds return as I make Szczytno, a busy town with a large clock tower dominating the main roundabout in the gap between twin lakes.

On the edge of the city, I come across a large Walmart type store called Kaufland for the first time. It is busy with shoppers, which made more sense later in the day when I learn tomorrow is a public holiday. Kaufland sells not only food but also clothing, hardware supplies and much more.

However, I can't find a decent visitor centre, despite searching for a while, as I'm now out of paper maps. I have reverted back to using Maps.me which I'm now getting used to using. Finding a quiet road for 30 kilometres through a pine forest, which avoids the main road to Wielbark, I'm expecting this road to become gravel, but it stays paved the whole time so it's a quiet relaxing cycle with no traffic to worry about.

I have found so far in Poland that I have been enjoying cycling more than spending time in towns because of decent, quiet, secondary roads, whereas in Russia, towns were my focus, because roads were terrible.

Wielbark is a busier town than I expected, however, my initial focus is on collecting supplies since tomorrow is a public holiday called Armed Forces Day, the Polish equivalent of Anzac Day in Australia. I'm expecting the majority of businesses to be closed tomorrow.

Cooking dinner in Wielbark

I'm not sure where I'm sleeping yet, so in the meantime I have found a picnic table to cook dinner in the public park, with plenty of children out enjoying themselves in the nearby skate park. Having not found any decent place to camp, I cycle out of town in the dark, eventually finding a spot in the pine forest to set up my tent.

In the morning, while randomly on the way to Przasnysz from Chorzele, a paved cycle path appears beside a quiet road for 30 kilometres. The amount of traffic doesn't justify the cycle path, it doesn't look like it has been developed from a rail trail and it isn't the shortest route between the two towns anyway.

Unplanned, I have timed my arrival into Przasnysz just before a military parade is due to begin in the town square. This town's open square has just a small two storey town hall in the middle so there is plenty of space for various men and women to march in, dressed in various military uniforms which I assume are from throughout the 20th century, along with half a dozen horse riders dressed in uniforms. I recognise World War One and Two era uniforms, along with what looks like modern uniforms.

Speeches are given which, since it is naturally in Polish, I don't really understand but still appreciated seeing the day. A larger parade is on in Warsaw and I assume many more parades are being held across Poland today.

Armed Forces Day is on 15th August each year. I thought it would have to do with fighting Germans but it is actually when Poland defeated Soviet Russia in 1920, confirming Polish borders after being re-established as a country after World War One. When the Communist Party came to power after World War Two, the day was banned as naturally, the Soviet Union didn't want a defeat to them celebrated. Therefore, it only became a commemoration again in 1992.

Military parade in Przasnysz on Armed Forces Day

Over the past few days, I have seen numerous Catholic crosses in random places, sometimes in towns but often in the middle of nowhere. All have had many streamers tied from the top of the cross down to the fence that surrounds it. I have been told it is to do with a Catholic religious holiday also on 15th August called Assumption of Mary, something to do with Jesus's mother.

For Assumption of Mary

The rest of my day is about cycling as close to Warsaw as I can, so I fly along going through small towns and a couple of larger ones. After crossing the wide Narew River on a dam wall, I enter suburban Warsaw, where a community event is on in a churchyard, with performers and some markets on.

From here, I'm close to central Warsaw, where I assume Adrian, my Warmshower host's home is, so I thought about making his home tonight. However, while checking messages online, I see Adrian has sent a message saying he has recently moved a fair way out in the western suburbs, far away from my current location. It's now too late in the day to make his place tonight so instead I search for a place to camp. It doesn't take me long to find a small forest park not far from the Wisla River.

I'm a little annoyed that Adrian didn't tell me earlier he has moved, because I asked him to host me based on his original location, which is within walking distance of the city centre.

It's easy navigating in the morning on a brick-paved flood levee embankment beside the Wisla River. I could have stayed on this all the way into the centre of Warsaw but with me needing a shower and some clean clothes, my priority is making my way to the west side of Warsaw to my Warmshower host Adrian's home.

However, my iPhone battery is low which is a hindrance for figuring out exactly where Adrian's home is, so I'm searching every café I can find to see if they have a power plug to charge it.

Eventually, I find a coffee chain to charge my iPhone, allowing me to get online to confirm Adrian's address.

I sometimes struggle with finding a specific address in cities because, having grown up on a farm surrounded by small country towns rather than numbers or even street names, I know a location by who lives there or used to live there.

So, when people give me their address with multiple numbers, I get confused trying to understand what order the numbers mean. If people live in a multilevel apartment block, they often have multiple numbers including one number for street address, one for the apartment block, one for the floor and one for the door and I'm sure other numbers as well.

An extra challenge is that often these apartment blocks all look the same, especially in former communist countries, so people can't give me a specific detail to look for.

It takes me a while to figure out where exactly Adrian's apartment is because of the multiple numbers in his address and all the tall white apartment blocks which look the same. Adrian is no help as he is at work. I end up going back to a shop nearby which has wi-fi to search for his address on Google Maps a couple of times. It doesn't help that I have to get through a coded gate first before finding the entrance to his apartment.

At one stage, I thought he had given me a dodgy number especially after he gave me a different address last night, and remembering how I experienced non-existent apartments in Russia. I eventually find his apartment in one of a few surrounding multilevel tower blocks, with a community playground in the inner courtyard. Thankfully the key is where Adrian told me, so once inside my first priority is to refresh myself with a bath and do some laundry. I haven't had a wash since my first night in Poland, while it's even longer since doing laundry.

Sejny to Warsaw

With it now only early afternoon, I leave my bags here and cycle into Warsaw to get my bearings for tomorrow's rest day.

Warsaw has many popular paved cycling paths throughout the city, which are mostly excellent – just occasionally I have to be aware of driveways, power poles, bus shelters and metro works. Often cycling paths are separated from pedestrian paths and in some places, signs say not to cycle on roads and instead use the cycle path.

After taking a break from museums during my initial cycling in Poland, I return to them in Warsaw. I would recommend coming on a Thursday, as both the informative Jewish Museum and the Gestapo Prison are free to visit.

Outside the Gestapo Prison was a tree which survived the German bombings in World War Two and after the war, many plaques dedicated to people who died at the hands of the Gestapo were placed on it. This tree died in 1984 so it was replaced with a fake tree, which still today, has the plaques around the main trunk.

I go to lock my bicycle up outside but I'm soon told to move as I have accidentally lock it to a part of the prisons memorial, so I find somewhere else to lock it up.

Inside the former prison are numerous types of information on the conditions imposed by the Germans when Warsaw was occupied. Included is a poster showing how much food people got depending on what nationality or religion you were classified as, for example, if you were German you got 100% meat ration, while Czechs got 86%, Poles 36% and if you were Jewish you got nothing. Once again, there are plenty of information panels with biographies and photos of so many people who died, each having individual stories.

Replica tree with plaques

Meat rations in Warsaw   *Biographies of Gestapo victims*

Compared to the Baltics and further south in Hungary, Serbia and Bulgaria I don't recall coming across references to the communist era in Poland. This doesn't mean they don't exist, I just noticed World War Two was more prominent here, especially because of the Holocaust and the Warsaw Uprising.

The larger, newer, Jewish Museum only opened in the last five years in a park near the sixty-year-old Warsaw Ghetto Memorial. This time there are plenty of bicycle racks, jam-packed full of bicycles as inside the museum is also a library. The museum starts out as an overview of centuries of Jewish history in Poland but becomes more detailed as you move through to the 20th century, where the horrors of the Holocaust become the focus.

Throughout the museum are numerous items, photos and individual stories. At times, it is overwhelming especially as the museum is closing soon so I'm trying to see as much as I can.

The most reflective for me is a section where you walk into a replica of streets in 1930s Warsaw, showing people living their normal lives before the Germans came. In the next darker room, you're suddenly transferred to the horrors of the Holocaust.

At its peak, more than 7,000 people a day were being deported from the Warsaw Ghetto to the nearby death

A replica of a Warsaw street in the 1930s

camp of Treblinka, located in the countryside east of Warsaw.

After all this misery I just go for a cycle with no real plan other than to get ideas on what to see for tomorrow's rest day.

I end up going through the old central part of town seeing some interesting castles before eventually I'm in the royal gardens south of the city. Signs are saying I must walk my bicycle through this popular garden late in the day.

With the gardens located in the south-east of Warsaw and Adrian's home way out in the north-western suburbs, it takes a while to get back via a loop route rather than through the city.

When I finally get back, I meet Adrian, as I spend some time chatting with a nice man, whose pregnant wife Anna is away staying with her parents. Adrian explains how he is part of a group of Warmshower host in Warsaw who communicate with each other to help find a host for cyclists passing through if someone cannot host. Somehow, we begin talking about the new Polish government which he admires, which sounds more conservative than Australia.

He also explains he now lives way out in the suburbs in a block of apartments. These apartment blocks remind me of similar ones in Russia just newer, with not much space, as my bicycle is stored on the balcony.

On my day off my bicycle after using a combination of bus and tram, I find my way into the old part of Warsaw. I discover a long pedestrian mall near the river with plenty of interesting buildings to see and plenty of free walking tours on offer.

Randomly I decide to go on an orange umbrella free tour with Eric around the old part of town. It starts near the large salmon-pink coloured former royal palace which is high above the Wisla River as Eric explains some basic history about Warsaw.

Many people live in apartments like this

In a European context, Warsaw is a young city, only becoming the capital when the King Sigismund III Vasa moved here in 1596 from the much older Krakow, causing a rivalry which still exists today.

Orange Umbrella tour in Warsaw

I already know a little about events in Warsaw during World War Two including that this city was the site of a massive Jewish ghetto with its own uprising in 1943 and a larger Warsaw Uprising in 1944. Eric explains, by giving real-life examples, what impact both events still have on Warsaw today, especially as the Germans destroyed Warsaw as a reprisal for the second uprising. Rebuilding is still going on today where many buildings, which appear to have centuries of history, have in fact only been rebuilt within the last few decades.

Eric guides us into the old town square which feels very touristy as he explains it is mostly used by tourists. More interesting to me is the surrounding multistorey buildings which were destroyed, and have been rebuilt with the same pre-World War Two outside façades but with modern buildings inside. This means if the inside has been enlarged with modern expanded rooms, they may have uneven windows next to each other because the outside isn't allowed to change.

The old town square is surrounded by the remains of a larger red-bricked castle wall with cone towers, some of which can still be walked through.

Outside the castle wall, is the remains of a moat and also a statue of a young child wearing a helmet and carrying a gun. This is a memorial to children who helped in the Warsaw Uprising, with children mostly running errands, as war affects everyone.

Children memorial

While walking along the main pedestrian mall the topic of Poland using its own currency of zloty rather than euros comes up. Eric explains with Poland's history of losing independence to neighbouring countries, this makes them still concerned today about losing independence, so having their own currency is important.

Just like in Australia, they have a World War One memorial. It originally opened in the 1920s under a wing of the Saxon Palace, but the palace was then destroyed by the Germans after the Warsaw Uprising.

Today the only remains of the palace is a small balcony held up by two rows of three archways with the eight columns holding up the roof. Each column has dates of various battles over centuries of conflict in Poland including those from more than a thousand years ago. Under the balcony is a tomb of an unknown soldier and an eternal flame, which is guarded by two soldiers who ceremonially change guard on the hour.

Behind the tomb is a large garden with statues and water fountains leftover from when the palace existed.

World War One memorial under the remains of a wing of the Saxon Palace

Since I enjoyed my first tour with Eric I thought, why not go on another tour after lunch, this time focusing more on the Uprising and the ghetto. We visit numerous locations where many people were executed on the street; at each location is a large 3D cross coming out of the plaque. Written on each cross is the date of each execution and an estimation of the number of people shot, while often bullet holes are still in the surrounding walls.

People were shot here

Above one of the executions, on the side of an apartment tower block is a colourful mural, showing how the city has revitalised but has not forgotten the people who died.

One of many sites we look at is a former bank building used to help organise part of the uprising. The outside of the building has been left looking derelict from the uprising period, while a symbol of the uprising is still visible on the outside.

This symbol is Kotwica, the Polish word for anchor, made by the combination of the letter P and W with the P sticking up from the middle of the W It has a few meanings but came to mean fighting for Poland. This is the same symbol on the war memorial I saw on my first day in Poland.

A mural is above a memorial

Where the Jewish ghetto walls were, is often marked on the ground with words and dates making it clear it's about the ghetto. At one former entrance, there is further information with a map showing where all of the ghetto was, which took up a few blocks.

I learnt a lot about Polish history on both walks, but clearly there is more to learn.

I finish my Warsaw exploration by visiting the popular Uprising Museum which focuses on the general Warsaw Uprising in 1944. I walk inside to find plenty of information, but it's not long before I'm confused about which direction I should be walking for it to make logical sense to

Where the Ghetto's wall was

understand what happened. Individual information makes sense, but I feel like I'm jumping all over the place, with information next to unrelated documentation or from different periods of time. I'm still learning a lot, just not in order.

There are some similarities to what happened to people in the Baltics especially to those who helped the Red Army, some of whom were persecuted once the fighting stopped and communism took over.

From Warsaw, my plan is to follow the Wisla River to Oswiecim via Krakow, because in some places there is supposed to be a dedicated bicycle route which follows the Wisla River mostly using levee banks. Eventually the idea is to make it into a continuous long-distance cycle route which travels the length of Poland as the Wisla River does.

As for navigation, I have found cycling-based paper maps in visitor information centres in various towns in Poland, while Google Maps shows cycle paths in Poland so it's easy navigating.

Leaving Warsaw on a high levee bank

After finally crossing the Wisla River to the eastern side of Warsaw, I find a cycle path which leads to a high levee bank beside the highway as I cycle south out of Warsaw. Unfortunately, the levee bank randomly ends so I'm forced back on the busy highway, which isn't enjoyable, especially when going around roadworks with no road shoulder.

Eventually, side road options become available which thankfully are quieter as I'm now zigzagging my way south, initially through outer suburbs of Warsaw. During the day while on a narrow road with a few cars, suddenly I hear and then see a loud car hooning towards me travelling really fast. It then overtakes into my lane forcing me to jump off the road. It's just like being back in Russia.

Camping in a pine forest

Gradually the houses begin to spread out and soon I'm cycling through small towns and passing by apple orchards. By the end of the day, I'm on quiet back roads cycling through pine forests so I just find a spot off the road to camp. It's a quiet night with just a few mosquitoes to deal with.

My Sunday morning is peaceful as I'm passing through a few scenic towns with nothing open; in between towns is a green rural landscape. I'm mostly using grey-bricked cycle paths either on top of the levee bank or down below next to the levee on the side away from the Wisla.

As I approach Kazimierz Dolny, I see a few tourist boats in the river and a large castle visible up the hillside on my left. As I get closer the number of people increases dramatically as the levee bank is now full of pedestrians, causing me to slow down to walking pace.

Kazimierz Dolny isn't a large place, but the town square is packed, with plenty of busy restaurants, souvenir shops, a visitor information centre and a large drinking water fountain under a wooden shelter in the middle of the square. In front of the drinking fountain, a karate performance is on, while many of the walls of the surrounding cream buildings have sculptures of people on them.

Approaching Kazimierz Dolny   *Main square in Kazimierz Dolny*

The tourist office informs me about a natural gorge not far away, which requires cycling up away from the river. It's not obvious where it is until I come across a busy café, where there are signs to the gorge behind it.

It's a deep, natural erosion channel gorge with tree roots visible inside the gorge and because of the changing vegetation above it, the light changes as I travel through. It's popular so it's safer for me to walk my bicycle through the gorge, which allows a closer inspection.

Eroded gorge

The other end of the gorge connects with a paved road which descends back to town passing two different castles on a hill. After stopping to go for an explore, I'm told I have to walk down the hill to get a ticket to then walk back up again to enter the castle.

The main cream-coloured stone castle is missing its roof but still has high walls, a metal gate and archways to walk under. There are a few rooms to visit with open, clear windows providing views of the surrounding landscape but there is barely any historical information.

The main castle with the smaller round castle above

View from the round cream castle looking back to Kazimierz Dolny

Further up the hill is a round cream castle which looks like it belongs in a chess game. On the outside a wooden staircase curves around halfway up before there are more stairs inside which take me to the top for my highest point of the day.

From here, I can see the other castle, the whole of Kazimierz Dolny, my levee bank route to here and it looks like the levee bank continues further south.

To get back down to town requires negotiating a steep cobblestone road with not much grip causing me to nearly slip a couple of times. I'm nearly safely down until suddenly my bike slides into the edge of a stone wall, causing a small hole in the outside centre of my right pannier bag. Using some tent repair tape, I'm able to plug the hole.

Having arrived into Kazimierz Dolny on a levee bank, I assume I can keep cycling further south on the same levee bank because Maps.me shows a dotted line continuing. However, the levee bank soon runs out but nearby is an okay looking dry four-wheel drive track. However, it soon becomes a hilly rough track with plenty of potholes and short steep sections, so I'm relieved once I find a path which allows me to return to a road.

The rest of my afternoon is through small towns and forested landscape. I end my day as it started, camping in a forest just off the road, where owls keep me awake during the night.

In the morning, it's a mixed bag of cycling using either levee banks or gentle hilly roads as I snake my way through small farming villages and pass barking dogs while crossing the Wisla River a few times on small car ferries.

Just like in other former communist countries, there is a contrast between towns which were clearly built in communist times with wide straight streets and flatter landscape, compared to older towns which have narrow, windy cobblestone streets with market squares and castles which are often located on a hill overlooking the river.

Sandomierz is an old town, located on a hill with scenic medieval gates leading to an open town square with a large red-bricked town hall dominating it. On this Monday, it is noticeably quieter compared to yesterday, with many things closed.

Across the road is the visitor information centre which has a decent cycling map which will be useful for the rest of my time in Poland. Having barely seen any touring cyclists since leaving the GreenVelo, I'm pleasantly surprised in Sandomierz to meet a German touring cyclist. We exchange experiences, but find he is travelling a different way.

Later in the day, after going through more small towns and another ferry crossing, I enter the new looking city of Tarnobrzeg with wide straight streets and plenty of modern buildings and shops. My bicycle is making a small creaking noise. I have tried cleaning and lubricating the chain but it's still making a noise so I find a bicycle shop to see if they can help. However, they are disinterested and make no effort to help me. Maybe there is a language issue, so I keep cycling. With Tarnobrzeg being a new city there are plenty of bicycle lanes mostly beside roads. One takes me out of town and around a large lake and past a campground until randomly ending beside a busy highway.

Unlike the previous few evenings where there was the option to camp in a forest, all I'm cycling through this evening is small towns and cornfields with nowhere suitable to camp.

In fading light, I arrive at the small town of Gorki, where behind a row of houses is a football pitch with a small wooden plank grandstand. It's not the best spot but it will have to do as I haven't seen or found any better options online. I start cooking dinner while waiting for darkness when hopefully the locals leave the nearby playground.

After setting up my tent in the dark I drift off to sleep assuming now that everyone has gone home it will be a quiet night sleep. Unfortunately, not long after settling in, dogs notice me, with barking coming from a few surrounding houses. This is annoying but not unusual.

However, when one small dog starts running around my tent barking, this is irritating and even when I try to chase it away, it just comes back, so I search for another spot. I find a spot around the corner of a building to move my tent to and thankfully the barking eases, but still it's not the best night sleep as this new spot has more street lights.

I awoke to quietness, so I pack up and leave Gorki for an easy direct cycle to Szczucin. After looking around, including seeing an abandoned railway station, I make my way north to the Wisla River where a signed cycle path on a levee bank begins.

Shortly after joining the levee bank is a bicycle rest stop station with a shelter, picnic table, a large map, bicycle tools and recycling bins. From the large map, I can see this cycling route will take me all the way to Niepołomice, more than 120 kilometres away. During today's ride I saw a few more similar cyclist rest stops.

Every so often on this levee bank, there are signs in assorted colours but mostly orange, informing how far to the next town.

I'm mostly passing through green farmland, with plenty of paddocks in crop, while every so often there are cows on the trail. The day started sunny, but over time clouds have appeared, thankfully without rain, while mountains are starting to appear in the distance.

A few bicycle rest stop station are beside this signed levee bank cycle route

A consistent view all day

For most of the day, I'm on this levee bank cycle route beside the Wisla River, except when I have to cross the tributary Dunajec River. This requires using a free ferry a few kilometres south of the Wisla River. Once I'm across the Dunajec, the cycle route takes a long loop ride back alongside the Dunajec to where it flows into the Wisla.

To save time I re-join a road which takes a short cut saving seven kilometres but I soon realise after having to constantly check my map for turns, it is easier to stay on the levee bank route even if it is a slightly slower ride.

When I was in Russia, I would have loved the option to use a levee bank route especially when following the Volga. Even the past few days using quiet roads through small towns has been relaxing and it was what I had wished it had been like in Russia.

At times, the levee bank will take long horseshoe bends where I can see across the flood plain to where I have just cycled from. It reminds me of being on trains when climbing in the mountains but I'm not climbing.

Near the end of the day, this levee bank is starting to feel a little repetitive, especially as there aren't any towns to break up the day as the banks go around towns. So later in the day, I plug into some podcasts to motivate myself.

Throughout the day the levee bank surface has been mostly paved but for some reason, five kilometres from Niepołomice the signed cycle route leaves the levee bank which continues as a gravel path. I decide to stay on the levee bank until going under a road bridge where there is a cycle path into the town centre, as once again, the town is not on the river.

Niepołomice market square is busy with teenagers being teenagers. After exploring around a small quiet city, I make my way to my Warmshowers with Misha on the way out of town.

Misha is in his early twenties and is a perfect host, making me feel welcome in a proper two storey house, where three generations are living. Misha's English is fine, but his grandfather only speaks Polish, so it is interesting as Misha translates between all of us. I know some Polish words but because I'm only planning to be here for just over two weeks I haven't learnt as much compared to Russia.

Misha helps me do some bicycle maintenance which fixes the creaking sound as we clean the chain thoroughly and we share a delicious meal. In hindsight I should have taken up his offer to do laundry but with a two-night stay already organised with another Warmshower host in Krakow, I thought I would get it done there.

After dinner, Misha shows me around town by car, as I share some Australian songs like True Blue. In the morning, he shows me a route out of town as he cycles to work.

Niepołomice is a satellite town of Krakow so it's mostly suburban cycling between the two. Thankfully, I'm able to use a cycle path for most of my route to Krakow. My first stop of the day is Oscar Schindler's factory which is now a museum, with a line building up outside before it opens at 10 am.

I expected it to focus on Schindler rescuing Jews just like the book and film but instead the museum focuses on Krakow during the German occupation in World War Two with only a small mention of Schindler.

Inside is a small replica of Plaszow concentration camp, helping give a visible perspective of the horrors of the Holocaust. There are many stories including how university staff tried to reinstate the university during the occupation which caused many professors to be arrested and sent to concentration camps. It is an interesting museum, with similar information to what I learnt in Warsaw.

Replica of Plaszow concentration camp

Once over the river and past a large castle, suddenly the number of people

becomes overwhelming in the street as I enter the largest square seen on this trip. It feels larger than Red Square in Moscow except for the fact that there is a long multistorey rectangular shopping market in the middle with a veranda right around it with numerous archways.

On a tour in the main square in Krakow

Barbakan Gate

Straight away there are many people offering various tours, while the information centre is focused on selling tours than local information. I can't find an information booklet on Krakow, or maps for locations outside of Krakow but I can buy plenty of souvenirs, with many shops inside the market selling tourist junk, while there are plenty of fancy restaurants. It feels more touristy than Warsaw, which is more like Canberra in that it was a small place until the capital was moved there, while Krakow was the historical capital.

After enjoying free guided walking tours in Warsaw and being told there are some in Krakow, I search for one that fits my schedule. I learn of one starting near the well-kept red-bricked Barbakan Gate in the northern part of the old city.

This two-and-a-half hour afternoon tour is popular as we are split into two groups and I can walk my bicycle for most of it, seeing many buildings while learning about Krakow's history. As this was the capital of Poland for many centuries, it was a target for various armies from as far away as Mongolia which is why medieval walls were built right around the city.

Today the outer wall is mostly gone and for the most part is now a circular park which goes around the city centre. I just have to avoid the numerous pedestrians on this paved path.

Around this path are many historical information panels, including explaining how often Krakow was occupied by other countries including Prussia, Russia, Austria and Germany.

Our guide talks about how Polish independence was developed by slowly building Polish pride up until proclaiming independence in 1918. There is less focus on World War Two as Krakow was occupied but not destroyed.

The Wawel Royal Castle dominates the southern part of the city with its own walls still intact, as this was where Polish kings were buried like Westminster in London. This is the only place I can't take my bicycle on the walk so I leave it locked up at the bottom of a long row of stairs at the entrance, next to a few other bicycles.

Since the city is so old there are often buildings with combinations of different periods of time so certain parts of buildings look out of place.

This is evident in the grounds of Wawel Castle with wings of churches often added throughout history, each with their own style. This site is busy but still has space to walk around and see views of the Wisla River down below.

My bike locked to stairs outside Wawel Castle, while there are a mixture of styles inside

Once again, my Warmshower host messages me to say his home is located out in the suburbs but thankfully in the direction towards Oswiecim.

However, when I arrive I discover that he isn't here. Instead I'm greeted by a young German lady (whose name I didn't record) who explains she is also staying, having spent a year cycling in places like India and Iran and is on her way home. She shows me a tiny granny flat beside a family home. This flat is one room with a small kitchen and bathroom, open to any cyclist to sleep on the floor.

Also staying is Simon and Anne-Marie from Quebec City, who are around my age and on a similar length tour also ending in Turkey, having started in Denmark. However, they are running out of time, so they are catching a bus to Vienna to get ahead of their tour.

While having a free place to sleep is appreciated especially in a tourist city, it's a different Warmshower experience. It feels more as if I'm staying at a hostel or campground rather than a person's home, especially as I only met him once in person. He did however, provide some cycling information by WhatsApp.

A couple of times when in busy cycling routes or tourist hotspots I have stayed with Warmshower hosts who host often, where it has felt like they are offering out of habit and I'm just another cyclist passing through.

When staying with people who have never or rarely host, they are often more excited I'm staying. With many not having experience with cycle touring themselves, I can share my experiences to encourage them to tour.

On my day off my bicycle, after a suggestion by a relative, I visit Wieliczka Salt Mine, using public transport.

As a railfan, I try to experience and learn about local services while I'm travelling but I often make mistakes with using public transport. In the case with Krakow, I accidentally buy two all-day bus tickets having thought I made a mistake when trying to purchase the first ticket. This does make up for other times when I may have accidentally fare evaded. When I change to a train to take me out to Wieliczka the conductor tells me that the bus ticket doesn't include the train ticket.

Wieliczka Salt was mined for centuries until 2007 as salt used to be a precious resource. In the 1700s the Austrian-Hungarian Empire developed it into a tourist attraction, while the mine was still running.

Today it is a busy tourist site with people lining up early for guided tours with many language options available. Somehow, the English line is short, so I managed to get in, in reasonable time with many flights of wooden stairs to descend as the stairs go around in a square.

This mine has numerous underground chambers including many set up as Catholic churches, with many religious services still held here each Sunday. There are many religious carved sculptures including The Last Supper and the Polish Pope, John Paul II.

Sculpture of Polish Pope, John Paul II, among many religious chambers

Most mining infrastructure is still here on display except for the horses who have been removed. When the mine operated, horses were kept underground their whole lives working in the mine.

Halfway through the tour, there is a restaurant where the guides tell us to take a break and re-join any tour when you're ready. Somehow I accidentally end up on a French guided tour and by the time I work this out it's too late to turn back so I just admire objects on display while trying to recognise French words. The site is worth a visit if you're in the area but terribly busy so arrive as early as you can.

I'm off to Auschwitz tomorrow. I'm not sure what to expect, as so far on this trip I have already seen so much suffering and death.

I'm looking forward to finally cycling in some mountains on the weekend but with a rainy weekend predicted I may be delayed. I have been lucky with the weather so far in Poland, as it has been sunny and around 30 degrees each day.

It's now day 81 of my 120 day trip so I am now two-thirds of the way through my tour. I'm not sure if this means I only have a short time left or plenty of time.

I awoke to discover that back in Australia we have just changed Prime Minister again, with Scott Morrison becoming the seventh Prime Minister in eleven years after a party vote. On the day I'm off to Auschwitz, our new treasurer is Josh Frydenberg, whose mother escaped the Holocaust as a toddler.

I had to pre-book a few days earlier as there are limited spaces for individuals to visit Auschwitz. So I leave the outskirts of Krakow just after 7 am, allowing plenty of time to get there.

After cycling on windy roads and crossing the Wisla River to the north, I re-join, for the last time, a levee bank route beside the river which takes me nearly all the way to Oswiecim. The surface of this cycle path varies with the majority being paved, especially close to Oswiecim.

Oswiecim is the name of the city where the Auschwitz Concentration Camp was located. The old town is on the eastern side of the Sola River and the camp was on the western side near the railway station. The Sola River flows into the Wisla River just north of Oswiecim and once I'm back south across the Wisla, I'm able to join a cycle path beside the Sola to head south towards Auschwitz.

After collecting food from a supermarket, I continue on the cycle path. It is now beside a road with no real signs of the concentration camp, until a brick wall with barbed wire on top comes into view across the road. Then after a right turn, I'm cycling beside a former railway line before the entrance to a car park appears on my right.

Around the car park, it suddenly becomes extremely busy with numerous large buses and hundreds of people lining up for tickets. I could be out the front of any tourist attraction except the mood is subdued and fewer children are around.

Having arrived early for my free pre-booked tour I can see by the number of people lining up I have no hope of

So many tourist buses

joining an earlier tour. Instead I make my way across the active railway line to Auschwitz II, more commonly known as Birkenau, which is free to enter any time during the day.

Straightaway the infamous large, wide, red-bricked gate comes into view, with a railway line through the middle gate. The weather is now becoming overcast, matching the mood of this sombre place.

I'm directed around the side of the main gate, where in front of a barbed wire fence is a bicycle rack.

Bicycle rack outside Birkenau

After locking up my bicycle, I get my first view of a large complex stretching out in front of me to the horizon – the scale of the site surprises me, as I didn't expect it to be this large.

With most barbed wire fences still here, it looks like I'm in the third Jurassic Park film, when they return to an abandoned island with structures rotting away.

The first noticeable thing after walking in is the single cattle rail car which I recall from an Australian documentary, and that it was donated by Frank Lowy. He is a wealthy Australian, who as a teenager, survived the horrors of being a Jew in Europe, while his father Hugo died here.

Rail car donated by Lowy family   *Most fences are still here at Birkenau*

Remains of a gas chamber

Past the train I walk the same route, which for many people, after coming by train was their final walk, directly to a gas chamber.

I'm surprised how small each of the gas chambers were, especially compared to the size of the whole Birkenau complex. I was expecting them to have taken up the majority of the camp, but they were hidden out the back. All the chambers I see have been demolished but the brick foundations below ground are still visible. Its unimaginable that people were being gassed here day after day.

Away from the gas chambers, some buildings are still standing. Inside a large building is information showing what happened to people who were not destined to be gassed straight away. These people were dehumanised by having their clothes taken away, their hair shaved off and given the infamous striped uniform.

Most wooden buildings are gone with just the brick chimney sticking up among foundation remains, making it even scarier. Some of the huts which are still standing and open for visitors, show where people who weren't gassed straight away lived in cramped conditions. Packed inside these huts are multitiered wooden bunk beds, with just wood to sleep on, while there is a chimney in the middle of the hut. I can't imagine living here for years in a place of suffering.

Many huts have only chimney remains, while others allow me to visit inside

I could keep describing Birkenau, but most people understand how cruel a place it was. After an hour and a half, I have barely covered half the camp but it's time for my guided tour back at Auschwitz 1.

There is a free shuttle bus between Birkenau and Auschwitz 1, so I leave my bicycle here all afternoon. After lining up and going through security we are given an earpiece and meet our guide before being led through the infamous Arbeit Macht Frei gate.

The sheer number of people both murdered and imprisoned on this site is hard to comprehend even when we see rooms full of dead people's hair and personal equipment like shoes and luggage with names still on them. One room has numerous artificial legs, leftover from disabled victims.

Rooms full of items including artificial legs and luggage with names on them

It wasn't an enjoyable tour as it felt like the guide just told us information from a repetitive script, while moving us quickly through in a large group. I didn't like having to use an earpiece to hear her and we were not allowed to wander around by ourselves. Still it's worth visiting to see evil at its worse.

After the short tour, our guide takes us by shuttle bus to Birkenau, where she explains what certain buildings were used for. However, the tour ends early as a thunderstorm begins so everyone seek shelter in the tower of the main gate.

It's both fascinating and depressing to see how organised it was. Why couldn't the Nazi party use their organisational skills for good.

I don't feel I learnt as much at Auschwitz 1, compared to Birkenau. So if you can't get an Auschwitz guided tour, I recommend just walking around Birkenau at your own pace, as there are plenty of information panels and fewer people.

Glad I went beforehand to Birkenau, as the rain doesn't ease so I find a hotel in the modern town across the water. Because of the weather I don't look around Oswiecim but I'm also feeling sad after visiting Birkenau.

In the morning with rain around until 10 am, I spend time trying to understand why Australia has changed Prime Minister again, so I don't leave my motel until my checkout at 11 am.

As I'm now leaving the Wisla River behind, the landscape is becoming mountainous especially as I'm taking back roads with a few short climbs. There are also occasional spits of rain on this cold, overcast day.

By midafternoon, I cycle into Wadowice, which I soon learn is the birthplace of Pope John Paul II. Therefore there are plenty of pilgrims in town and museums dedicated to him. This is not something I cared for. It just happened to be on my route.

Throughout the rest of the day, it gradually becomes cooler with occasional light rain so I'm feeling like I'm cycling with blinkers on, just wanting to find a warm dry place.

With worse weather predicted for tomorrow, I find a cheap hotel lodge near the town of Makow Podhalaski with no one else staying here other than the elderly hosts. This lodge isn't in the best condition, but it is quiet, has a kitchen and wi-fi, so I have all I need to keep me dry as the next day it rained all day. When I did ride into town for some supplies, I became soaked.

I do speak by WhatsApp to David Manuca who works for Football Federation Australia about my ride in Russia during the World Cup. He was looking at making his own book on people's FIFA World Cup experience, which hasn't been published yet.

Outside of watching a couple of films on my iPhone, most of my day is spent working out where to enter Slovakia. My plan is to enter via the alpine tourist town of Zakopane into the Tatar Mountains with the expectation of some scenic alpine cycling. I won't be visiting the Slovakian capital of Bratislava, as it is further west than my planned route to enter Hungary just north of Budapest.

A few people still use horses

In the morning, the rain has cleared but it's still a cold overcast day as I'm trying to avoid highway cycling. For the most part I'm using secondary roads with some small hills to negotiate but there is one dirt track with a few puddles to get through as I pass a man with a horse and long wooden cart.

Once I'm back on a semi-busy road I begin a long slow climb towards Zakopane, until randomly near Czarny Dunajec while looking on Maps.me, I notice that a rail trail is nearby, so I go for a look.

It's paved, so I will begin cycling on to see where it goes. It soon takes me to a steel rail bridge, where beside the rail trail is a pointy alpine shelter with picnic tables and a map showing that the rail trail continues into Slovakia as the border is close by.

After looking at the map I make a snap decision – instead of spending the afternoon climbing with cars on a cold and cloudy day to Zakopane, with presumably less scenic views of mountains due to the weather, why not enjoy a rail trail into Slovakia.

This will mean exiting Poland a day early and a total change of route in Slovakia, causing me to miss out on seeing the Tatar Mountains, as I will be further west than planned. However, this will save time as it should be a slightly less mountainous route.

Warsaw to Slovakia border (Google Maps)

Slovakia

Rail trail bridge

Rest station at the border

After crossing Dunajec River on a former steel rail bridge which is in great condition and passing a derelict former railway station, the remote border soon appears with just a picnic shelter here.

The border area has a wooden picnic shelter beside the rail trail with an information panel. I assume by the pictures it is on bicycle safety, as I don't understand Polish or Slovakian. It is only possible to cross countries on a rail trail because of open European borders so if I had to show my passport then I doubt this rail trail would exist.

The border is marked with a white cement post which has an S on one side and a P on the other, along with 1920 on both sides; I assume this was the year the border was established. It is easy to tell exactly where the border goes because vegetation has been cleared.

Later when looking at Google Maps, the green rail trail looks like it just ends at the border, since Slovakia doesn't show bicycle routes while Poland does. This is possibly the reason why I didn't notice this rail trail when planning my route all day yesterday. It does show up as a pink cycle route on Maps.me but this requires zooming in more to notice cycling routes.

Once into Slovakia the trail gradually descends for thirteen kilometres, providing scenic open views of green hills even on an overcast day, as I'm going under a few, long covered wooden bridges. This reminds me of descending on rail trails in the Rockies, but this time with a better surface. This is a highlight of the trip, so no regrets with changing my route.

I'm not the only person cycling this rail trail with a few day cyclists around, as I chat to one couple while stopping to look at an info panel beside the trail. This shows the mountains in the distance which I should have been able to see if it had been a clear day.

There are a few long covered wooden bridges to go under as I descend on this rail trail

After crossing the Orava River I'm in the town of Trstena, where I have to leave the rail trail as from here the railway line still exists as it travels south beside the Orava River.

Usually, I try to spend all my local money before leaving a country but since I have left Poland early, I still have 20 spare Polish Złoty, so I head to a bank to change it to euros. I'm surprised when I'm told I need my passport to do so when I entered Slovakia without showing my passport.

I carry a photocopy of my passport in my wallet, which is usually accepted for ID purposes, but the teller wants to see my passport to change money. I haven't used my passport since leaving Russia a month ago so now I have to search inside my pannier bags.

My theory for separating my passport from my wallet is if I lose one, I will still have the other. I have never had an issue with anyone going through my pannier bags and anyway, if they opened the bag, they would have to go through smelly clothes to find my passport.

The local bicycle shop gives me a cycling map of the region, but none of the routes is like the rail trail. Instead they are more suited for mountain bikes as they are a mixture of farm tracks and deteriorating paved roads which run parallel to the main roads but on a higher elevation, requiring the crossing of numerous small hills.

The cycling route I follow looks okay as it takes me away from the Orava Valley with a climb over a hill before cycling beside Lake Orava.

Later in the day, it is a struggle finding a decent place to camp as all flat surfaces are taken up by buildings. I'm passing a couple of paid campgrounds, but they are all beside the main road, so I don't see the point of being kept awake by traffic.

Once I leave the lake behind, I'm now travelling on tracks which are on the hillside of the Hrustinka Valley with a few small creeks to negotiate. I'm going up and down like a roller coaster, while down below in the valley is the main road.

Camping and cycling through the Hrustinka Valley

None of the small towns I'm passing through have suitable places to camp, so I just keep going. Eventually, as it becomes dark, I find a spot between farm paddocks just off a track, dodging cow paddies while setting my tent up in the dark.

In the morning, while continuing on this deteriorating track on the side of this shallow valley, I'm concentrating on dodging puddles when around a corner there is a rare sight, a flock of sheep with no fences or shepherd in sight. I have seen more cows on this tour.

After a second breakfast at the small town of Hrustin, I now must climb out of the Hrustinka Valley because if I continue following this valley, the tracks will eventually run out.

After a short climb on a quiet road over a small mountain range and then an even longer descent with a couple of switchbacks, I arrive into Oravsky Podzamok, a small town beside the Orava River. This is the same river I left yesterday when climbing away from Trstena as the recommended cycle route involved two climbs instead of just following the shorter valley, but this avoided the highway.

In Oravsky Podzamok I notice on top of a small hill is a cream castle, with a black tiled roof. The visitor centre at the bottom in town informs me that there are guided tours of the castle with an English tour of 90 minutes duration starting soon. While waiting for the tour to start I find an Airbnb in the city of Martin down the valley, which will allow me to do laundry, having not done it properly since Warsaw twelve days ago.

After locking my bicycle up, I walk up the hill to a large closed wooden gate, with about twenty people waiting. When the gate opens, a couple of guards dressed in brown and holding sceptres walk out, followed by a couple of young guides.

Only half a dozen people are on the English tour, as we go through the gate and walk through a long, round roofed, man-made tunnel, with a couple of wooden horse carriages on display. Our guide explains how this tunnel entrance is a key feature for the defence of the castle as it is easy to block off.

On the other side of Orava Castle entrance, is a tunnel to access the castle

Once through the tunnel, we are now in an open square with high walls. Higher still are the main rooms of the castle. In the square is an orange and white building which appears to have been added more recently.

I'm enjoying learning about the numerous ways this 13th century castle's defences were designed and who controlled the castle over the centuries. In the rooms higher up are assorted items on display including machines used to torture people, along with royal shields and artwork on the walls.

We can't go all the way to the top part of the castle as it is still in disrepair, due to fighting between Germans and the Soviet Union soldiers near the end of World War Two. However, since the castle is so high, there are still decent views of the river valley down below.

Inside the castle is a stretch machine to torture people

Once back on my bicycle, my route is all beside the Orava River, where I'm passing through a few small scenic mountainous-looking towns. Initially there are secondary road options, some of which are dirt tracks, with some involving short steep climbs compared to the flatter highway. Eventually, the highway is the only realistic choice. There is the option of dotted lines on Maps.me but I have no idea if they actually exist and if they do, it will be slow climbing up and down on dirt tracks.

Once on this busy highway it actually has a decent road shoulder, something even on open roads I haven't found very often on this trip. Even when it becomes a narrow gorge, it still has enough room to fit in the Orava River, a railway line and a highway while still having a decent road shoulder on this scenic ride. A couple of times a passenger train goes past but I never consider taking the train.

Slovakia is generally mountainous so once out of the valley any flat spaces have been taken up with houses and industry. As I enter a built-up area, suddenly the amount of traffic becomes worse while I'm trying to negotiate my way to the centre of Martin. After visiting a busy Kaufland, I find a cycle path beside the road to take me into the town centre past a few parks.

Later in the day, I learn tomorrow is a public holiday – a celebration of an unsuccessful uprising against German occupiers on 29th August 1944. Public holidays are great for learning about a country's history and culture but frustrating as things can be closed, like supermarkets.

With my Airbnb host not getting home until after 8 pm, after having a look around town and visiting a busy supermarket, there isn't much to do except wait in the pedestrian mall as dusk begins.

Randomly a man in his fifties comes up to me and starts chatting to me in broken English. It's a normal conversation with him asking me questions about Australia, cycling, where I have come from and going, while I ask about Slovakia and Martin. So far this feels like many other chats I have had over the years while touring, until suddenly he starts making sexual references and getting closer to me and then basically propositioning me for sex. Straight away I say no and leave to collect my bicycle and he thankfully leaves me alone.

To make it an even worse night, my Airbnb is beside a busy noisy road and my host hasn't made me feel very welcome and is annoyed when I ask to do laundry.

If anyone is from Martin I apologise, I'm sure it's a nice place but in the morning, I just want to leave. Thankfully, I have found what looks like a quiet route for the first 30 kilometres by using doglegs roads which cross a railway line a few times while going through small towns to avoid the highway. However, the first part out of Martin is a dotted line on Maps.me beside the railway line so I'm unsure if I can cycle this way.

Thankfully, it is an okay track to cycle, sometimes beside the railway line, other times beside a channel. At one stage I end up in an old abandoned airport runway with people flying model planes on this public holiday. From here, it's easy, relaxing cycling through small towns crossing the railway line a few times.

Just before joining the highway there is a service station, with some delicious chocolate twists, my cycling treat in Europe. They are much cheaper and more common than in Australia, often only around $1 Australian when they are $4 back home and not as decent quality.

From here, the secondary roads run out because a climb begins. It's not particularly high, just steep in places and since I haven't done climbs like this on this trip, my body isn't used to it. The highway is quiet, presumably because of the public holiday but I never saw anything special happening except that it feels quiet with most shops closed.

Just after, the highpoint of the day is the town of Kremnica with another interesting church and a monument in the open town square. This monument reminds me of the Millennium Bell in Veliky Novgorod with sculptures of people all around it but this one is much skinnier. Many of the surrounding multistorey buildings in the square are either cafés or museums, with most open today.

The tall, skinny, white church with green roof looks more like a castle surrounded by two small round well kept medieval walls, with steps to get inside the gate to the gardens. Inside there are information leaflets in many languages to help explain the history of the church and town.

From the top part of the church tower, I can walk right around a balcony providing 360 degree views. I can clearly see that Kremnica is surrounded by mountains and I can just make out the valleys where I have cycled from and where I will be heading.

Monument in Kremnica and a view from the church tower

From Kremnica I roll downhill at a gentle pace for nearly thirteen kilometres without pedalling or needing to brake except for a short 200 metre section. Not having been in any mountains until Slovakia, I have missed being able to just roll along admiring the scenery until the road flattens out as I arrive at a T-intersection.

From here, I have two choices: either turn right and follow the Hron River using secondary roads beside a freeway, taking me out of the mountains as it flows into the Danube, or I can turn left to cycle to Zvolen and then will have to do some small climbs on quiet roads to head south to the Danube.

I will take the quieter route, mostly because I like the name of Zvolen. My route is easy using secondary roads which often cross either the Hron River, the railway line or the freeway.

It's noticeably quiet as I arrive at Zvolen to find a wide long pedestrian mall with a few playgrounds, statues and drinking water fountains. A kebab shop is still open and this time I order just chips and kebab meat separately. I have found in Europe, instead of the Halal Snack Pack we get in Australia with just those ingredients, here in Europe they include salad in the box. After looking at maps, I see references to a castle on a hill on the other side of the Slatina River called Pustý Hrad. However, once across the river, I discover that the rear path up to the castle is too steep for a bicycle. So, after a short time walking my bicycle up away from barking dogs and around a single horizontal pole gate, I find a short path off the track which feels safe enough to leave my bicycle locked to a tree.

As I begin walking up, I'm hoping that Maps.me is accurate, as this forest track has no signs and no one else is around as it takes a zigzag route. Thankfully, an hour later as sunset is imminent, the trees disappear as I arrive at the top of a hill to find various stone castle ruins on top of a mountain. The views of the surrounding mountains and Zvolen in a spread-out valley below are scenic, with large gaps where rivers flow through mountain ranges all around me.

I'm not alone, as a few people are also looking around, while a handful of teenagers are here with food. Presumably they are planning to spend the evening here.

There are many information panels on the history of the castle as it is spread out with a couple of areas to see. Some parts of the stone ruins are in better condition than others, with plenty of stone walls. There also appears to be recent new additions of wooden carved statues of people scattered around.

It would have been a tough place to conquer as it's steep all around; even building this castle would have been hard. I could spend longer here but as it is now nearly dark, I better start walking down.

This time I descended via the front side of the castle in fading light which has more short zigzags to negotiate. It's dark by the time I return to my bicycle to camp in the forest below.

New looking wooden statues among the remains of Pustý Hrad

As I drift off to sleep, I'm listening to an ABC conversation podcast about a man who escaped Czechoslovakia during the failed 1968 revolution. Other than Turkey, every country I visited on this trip for more than a day had been under communist rule post-World War Two.

However, during my time in Slovakia I haven't noticed any references to communism. I suspect since I haven't been here very long and because I'm not visiting the capital Bratislava, I may be missing communist references.

In the morning, after visiting the tourist office and while waiting until 10 am for Zvolen Castle museum to open, I visit a forestry museum which, for some reason, along with forest information has pictorials of many European cities in the 1800s.

However, after cycling up to the Zvolen Castle I discover it's closed for a music festival for tomorrow, so I missed learning more about Zvolen and Slovakian history. In a park near the castle is a camouflage colour replica of an armoured train used in the Slovakian Uprising which was commemorated yesterday, not that I saw anything happening.

From Zvolen my cycling map suggests a route with no road in the middle, so I assume I will get through. Once I find a way out of Zvolen the initial cycling is a slow relaxing climb through a forest beside a creek on a quiet road for ten kilometres.

For the last kilometre it becomes steeper on the first of four climbs today. After going under a stone archway on a sunny, not a cloud in the sky day, the road ends at a bus stop past the small town of Kralova.

There doesn't appear to be a route from here except for a dotted line on Maps.me. Therefore, on my iPhone, I turn my GPS on and set off on a faint track passing farmhouses with barking dogs thankfully behind a high fence. In front of me is a tree line with a tiny gap to walk my bicycle.

End of the road

Once among the trees, the path narrows over a small hill requiring my bicycle to be walked for a short section.

It isn't too long before I leave the trees behind as a dirt track returns and I'm now between paddocks full of hay bales. Soon after this, the bitumen returns and becomes a quick descent to the town of Sasa.

Sneaking my way through farmland

The rest of the afternoon involves some small, slow climbs on quiet roads through a forest with some double-digit gradient climbs before quicker descents as I slowly make my way towards the Hungarian border.

Every so often I'm passing through small towns and occasionally there are views of various farms and mountains in the distance. It appears to be sowing season, with a few tractors around today.

I have missed this type of hilly cycling on this trip, it has been a relatively flatter trip overall compared to previous trips.

To Sahy

Near the end of the day I'm beside the Ipoly River, which in places is the border between Slovakia and Hungary, but at other random places the border is two kilometres further south as this small river takes a meandering route.

By the evening, after visiting the border town of Sahy, I see a track between paddocks leading to the distant Ipoly River. At the end of this track is an open grass embankment which is a perfect hidden place to set my tent up.

Farewell Slovakia, I hardly knew you. With only a month until Turkey, my route must be more direct, meaning I will be spending only a short amount of time in each country.

Hopefully one day I can return to see the Slovakian mountains properly and I can learn more about the country as I didn't learn much.

Southern Slovakian landscape   Camping beside a levee bank

Hungary

In the morning, it's a short ride to Hungary, on a rough quiet road to a T-intersection where there are just small wooden posts to mark the border. For the next 30 kilometres the Ipoly River is just out of sight on my right and is the border until it flows into the Danube.

After seeing the disappointingly small Ipoly River, I'm concerned that the Danube River will be disappointing. However, as soon as it comes into view, I can see it is a wide, noble river worth seeing, reminding me of the Volga.

A cycling route called EuroVelo 6 follows the length of the Danube from its source in Germany to where it flows into the Black Sea in Romania. It's a popular cycling route so hopefully I may encounter cyclists going the same way as me, but this may mean I'm treated as less of a novelty by locals.

As soon as I join a paved cycle path beside the Danube, I begin to encounter numerous touring cyclists for the first time since being on the GreenVelo in Poland. I also see the first of many large white cruise ships on the Danube, the type often seen advertised on television in Australia as European holiday cruises.

Cycle path beside the Danube

Across the Danube, a castle on a hill begins to appear, so once I find a ferry at Nagymaros, I cross the river to investigate.

This time it is an easy climb up to Visegrad Castle on a paved road with leaves noticeably starting to change on this last day of August. The car park below the castle is busy with a couple of cafés, tourist shops and some picnic tables for me to make a sandwich.

The actual castle is built on a dirt mound, with the stone sections of the castle becoming narrower as the layers build up. After paying an entrance fee I can walk around the whole castle, using a few connecting stairs. Some parts of the castle are in reasonable condition, while others, especially the stone walls, look like they require refurbishment. On display are animal trophies collected over the years, furniture from when royalty used this castle and a crown and sceptre.

There is some information around the castle, but it could be more informative or even have an option of a guided tour.

Visegrad Castle

View from Visegrad Castle, while there is a collection of items inside

More memorable is the views of the Danube from the castle on a beautiful sunny day. From this high point, I can see the river in both directions as it curves its way around hills and there appears to be an island downstream in the middle of the river.

After a quick descent I'm back to river level and I continue following the Danube as the river becomes narrower. From here the Danube splits nearly evenly for a bit, with a long skinny island called Szentendrei in the middle before the two rivers re-join just before Budapest.

I cross to Szentendrei Island using the only bridge to explore an island which has a combination of towns and open spaces to see. Eventually, I'm near the most southern ferry on the eastern side of the Szentendrei Island. However, instead of crossing tonight, I will find a spot to wild camp on the island which will enable me to be within twenty kilometres of Budapest in the morning. The island keeps going further south but with no towns or ferries to exit the island, it's less developed with plenty of open spaces and rows of trees. This makes it easy to find a spot to set my tent up in the dark.

After a terrible sleep due to pain in the stomach, I take a ferry which is guided across the river by an attached tugboat. From here I'm in suburban Budapest where I utilise cycle lanes and quiet roads beside a railway line to get me into central Budapest.

My first task in Budapest is to find a bicycle shop as my front tyre has done every kilometre on this trip and some previously before that, so it needs replacing. I'm also hoping to change my front cassette.

The first shop has a suitable tyre but doesn't have a suitable front cassette so after changing the tyre I cycle to another bicycle shop which doesn't have what I need. However, they ring another nearby bicycle shop to check if they do and then the lady gives me directions to that bicycle shop. Nearly every bicycle shop on this trip has been so helpful with most refusing payment for minor jobs.

This isn't a minor job, so I have to leave my bicycle at the third shop for the rest of the day, while they replace the chain, middle front cassette and rear cassette. I should now be all set for the rest of the ride, even if the chain could have lasted longer. More than likely it would have needed to be replaced before Turkey anyway, so it makes sense to do it all now when I have time.

Despite sending numerous Warmshower requests, I have had no luck at all in Budapest in finding a place to stay. From reading many Warmshower host profiles they get numerous requests, with a couple of hosts specifically saying they will not host people cycling beside the Danube. Instead I have organised an Airbnb with Brigi who let me check in early to a large apartment not far from the third bicycle shop.

Finding myself in an old-looking apartment block, with a small open courtyard with balconies inside on each level, my apartment is surprisingly large with a few bedrooms. Brigi explains that often groups of people stay here but I have it all to myself for the next two nights.

As for exploring Budapest, there is really two cities, the flatter Pest side which I'm staying in which has a proper city centre including the scenic parliament. The Buda side is hilly, has a large castle and looks like it was more the aristocracy side. Budapest feels similarly touristy to Krakow with information stalls and numerous spruikers trying to sell me attractions. As always, I try to choose a few places of interest to see rather than trying to see everything, as I could spend a week here and not see everything.

Back home in Australia, I'm known for not wearing shoes, just something I have always done. However, on a bicycle tour, I spend all day wearing shoes so when I'm off my bicycle I prefer to give my feet a break.

When the national museum has a cloakroom, I check in my bag and my shoes and go barefoot in the museum. For the first hour, no one cares, until one staff member threatens to kick me out if I don't walk back to the cloakroom and put my shoes on.

Despite this I enjoy spending the afternoon at the Hungarian National Museum as it travels through centuries of history, showing different cultural styles and mentioning numerous historical figures. It starts out with focusing mostly on royalty but gradually changes as communism takes over after World War Two.

The most interesting fact is seeing how the Hungarian borders have changed so often. Not much of the country has stayed Hungarian the whole time – even Budapest was once part of the Ottoman Empire for nearly two centuries. Modern-day Hungary is a lot smaller than at its full might.

The popular Terror Museum focuses on the communist years, in a former secret police building. On the outside of the Terror Museum are numerous round plaques with a photo, name and date of death of a person who died during this period.

I arrive early in the morning having been told the day before you need plenty of time to get through. It takes me two hours to get through as it is much larger than similar former secret police museums I have been to so far.

The Terror Museum, with photos of victims on the outside

The main focus is the ten years after the end of World War Two which led to the failed 1956 protest and then execution of the Prime Minister and others in 1958. They were so close to ridding themselves of communism in the 1950s, but it was not to be for another 30 years. On show are numerous propaganda videos from that period, showing how communism would improve their lives. If it hadn't been so terrible for the locals, you would think it silly the methods they used to try to influence people.

The Hungarian Parliament building beside the Danube is an impressive Gothic cream building with red roof, with a single large dome in the middle of a long multistorey building. It isn't that old, as it was only started to be built in the late 1800s and was completed in 1904.

On the side of the parliament building away from the river, is a large square with similar tall buildings surrounding it on four sides and a tram line going through the middle of the square. This was the scene of the 26th October 1956 protest which turned deadly when Soviet and Hungarian forces opened fire on unarmed protesters, with many soldiers firing from the surrounding rooftops.

Within the square is what looks like a subway entrance but instead, it is an underground memorial to the 1956 uprising held in a small room. Information, videos and photos help to inform me what happened, along with a list of names of people who died and a burnt Hungarian flag.

There is a busy parliament tour which shows off the building features rather than concentrating on the parliamentary system. This tour is popular, so you have to pre-book and I managed to find an English tour later in the day.

It is a quick 45-minute tour with a large group of a gold coloured buildings with numerous golden arches throughout the building and paintings on the ceiling. The upper chamber of the Hungarian Parliament building has been unused since 1946 because, with a one-party state, there was no need for a second chamber, and it hasn't been revived since.

Hungarian Parliament	*Hungarian flag from the revolution*

Inside the gold coloured Hungarian Parliament

While walking outside the parliament building alongside the Danube, I come across a plaque saying this was where, late in World War Two under German occupation, Jews were shot in the back of the head and dumped in the river.

People were executed here

After looking up from the plaque beside the edge of the river, I spy dozens of metal shoe sculptures symbolising where the people were shot and then thrown in the river. Naturally, this helps humanise the situation. Reading a plaque you can dismiss this but not when you see evidence of where humans were executed.

Nearby is a controversial memorial to the Holocaust, with protest signs attached because the memorial doesn't mention that Hungarians assisted in deporting Jews to be murdered in concentration camps. Instead it just blames the Germans.

There are plenty of different coloured bridges across the Danube to the hilly Buda side with a few large castles Having seen plenty of castles already on this tour, I don't need to see another one especially as it is crowded with long lines.

So I keep walking further around with no plan except to just see what I can find. There are some quieter sections up a few stairs on the outside part of the castle which provides views of many fancy looking buildings on both sides of the Danube.

World War One exhibit

Further along back down beside the Danube I stumble on an interesting exhibition focusing on World War One and the Austrian-Hungarian royal family. Since the assassination of Archduke Franz Ferdinand and his wife Sophie was the trigger for starting World War One, focusing on both makes sense.

Many of the displays provide a different perspective on the war, from soldiers on the front line, to generals making decisions, to nurses and doctors in hospitals. The major focus is on the family connections between most of the European royal families whose countries were fighting each other.

Budapest has felt claustrophobic with not a lot of open spaces and so many tourists.

From here I will head south following the Danube to Croatia, so I will not get a chance to see much of Hungary, as my focus at this stage is following the Danube.

Before leaving Budapest, I search for a decent cycling map. Thankfully there is a dedicated map shop. They have a few cycling maps including a thick cycling booklet for the whole EuroVelo 6 cycling route between Budapest and Belgrade in Serbia. However, this booklet is too heavy for me to carry so I go without a decent map.

Light rain begins as I leave using cycle paths where available beside the Danube. There are some EuroVelo signs in places, but I keep losing the exact route. I'm soon crossing an anabranch of the Danube onto Csepel Island, which is similar to Szentendrei Island, in that it is in the middle of the Danube. However, the northern part of this island is more developed as it feels like I'm cycling through suburbia. It doesn't help that the EuroVelo route is taking a few doglegs, so I'm having to constantly check where I am, while occasional cold showers of rain appear.

Once I'm beside the anabranch on the eastern side of Csepel Island, the road has a few puddles to avoid on the way to the town of Rackeve.

Rackeve has a small visitor information centre where I find a decent single page cycling map showing the whole EuroVelo 6 route in Hungary. This map shows that in some places there is a choice to cycle on either side of the Danube especially when it comes to the route south out of Hungary. I can either cross into Croatia on the western side of the Danube or Serbia on the eastern side. Since after a day or two in Croatia I will end up in Serbia anyway, I will probably take the option to briefly visit Croatia.

South of Rackeve, the weather and the towns have cleared, while the road is now beside a levee bank beside the anabranch. For some reason which doesn't make sense, houses are on the river side of the levee bank.

Leaving Csepel Island involves cycling on top of a levee bank past fisherman and caravans until arriving at a narrow lock. After using a narrow walkway which requires my bicycle to be walked across the lock, I'm back beside the Danube.

Levee bank cycling on Csepel Island

Even with a bicycle map I'm still getting lost a few times as EuroVelo signs are not consistently at every turn and my new map isn't detailed enough. At one stage I'm unsure if a track beside the river is the cycling route or just a random track. After investigating a short section, I realise it isn't the correct route, so I go a little further away from the river until finding the correct signed route.

However, sometimes even the well-signed route is just a bumpy grass-covered levee bank which is hard and slow to cycle on. I'm suddenly also dealing with a few bugs flying into my face.

Later in the day, I begin searching for a way to leave the levee bank, soon finding a road to take me away from the Danube to the town of Szalk-Szentmarton.

EuroVelo 6 route on grass levee bank

After obtaining supplies at the local grocery store, I search for a place to camp. Finding a quiet local sports ground, with just picnic tables and a mowed football pitch I decide to camp here.

Throughout the night, I'm woken a few times by loud thunderstorms which sound like they are going right around my tent.

There is light rain in the morning as I set off to get back on the EuroVelo 6 route. Unfortunately this involves a busy road with trucks to Dunavecse as heavy rain returns so I'm not feeling safe or visible.

Thankfully joining a levee bank which goes around town helps reduce my stress levels before heading into Dunavecse to get out of the rain and find hot food. Also trying to stay dry is a mid-twenties German cycling couple who are sheltering in a bus shelter with their gear spread all over it.

For some reason, after a short break I keep cycling but by the next town of Apostag, I'm over the rain. Thankfully, a library is open which allows me to relax while charging my iPhone. After an hour it looks like the rain is easing, so I decide to continue cycling. Sadly I'm wrong as light rain continues to fall for half an hour until it finally eases as I arrive into Solt.

From here a paved path is right beside the highway through the town of Harta and then onto Dunapataj, which then becomes a cycle path through town.

Beside these cycle paths, I'm starting to notice more detailed green and yellow EuroVelo cycling signs, not only informing me about towns nearby but also places of interest along the way including accommodation and food options. Writing is in Hungarian but with many symbols, it's easy to understand what they each mean.

Outside a grocery store in Dunapataj it seems like there are more bicycles than people inside. All bicycles appear to be owned by locals as I haven't seen as many touring cyclists south of Budapest. It appears that the EuroVelo 6 route is more popular between Germany and Budapest.

From here the route is back on the road as it takes a longer, more relaxing loop road closer to the Danube through small towns instead of the more direct highway.

Cycling signs on the EuroVelo route   *So many bicycles outside a grocery store*

I have no idea what this is

While passing through the town of Ordas I see a strange statue in a tree. From a closer inspection it's a carving in an oak tree stump, with the head of a man at the top and below him is a horse with just its head and front legs, both figures are painted in white. The whole thing is covered with a wooden roof which looks like a bow of a boat and the carved-out part of the tree reminds me of a canoe. However, without any explanation, I have no idea what it represents.

While writing this book, I looked it up online and apparently it is to do with Prince Ferenc Rákóczi II, who rested under this oak tree in 1704 during his unsuccessful campaign of Hungarian independence from the Austrian-Hungarian Empire. Prince Ferenc Rákóczi II is a national hero but I don't recall hearing his name while in Hungary.

I'm running low on methylated spirits, so I leave the EuroVelo route to duck into the larger town of Kalocsa away from the river. I find fuel and dinner supplies easily, only in Russia was it hard to find fuel for my stove. I didn't need any in Turkey, as I had enough so I'm not sure about the situation there since my stove is alcohol-based.

Re-joining the EuroVelo 6 is easy using a quiet, scenic tree-lined road back to the river, now on a gravel levee bank route with decent views of the river.

After a clear afternoon, by the time I make the edge of the town of Fajsz, rain is looking imminent. Thankfully, there is a picnic shelter beside the ferry dock to cook under as heavy thunderstorms begin.

This shelter isn't the best with a leaking roof and no sides, so once dinner is eaten, I make my way across the road to a pub with a dining room to relax in for a few hours and I have a brief chat with locals. Thankfully, rain clears by 10 pm so I make my way back to the levee bank to wild camp in the dark. I can see lightning in the distance but c1an't hear thunder and during the night the stars come out. Thankfully the weather is forecast to be sunnier for the next week.

In the morning, the levee bank is covered in fog but thankfully no rain as my morning ride is nearly all on a relaxing paved levee bank surrounded by grass to the city of Baja. I just have to watch out for the occasional car and a flock of sheep.

With the sun now out, I cycle in on a levee bank beside a canal and pass an outdoor market into the town square.

Camping on levee bank

At the visitor centre they have information brochures to guide me around town for a quick look but of more interest to me is a forest tourist railway across the Danube so I thought, why not go for an afternoon train ride.

Crossing the Danube is easy with a separate path on the bridge but once back on land the cycle path disappears, and I'm surprised how narrow and busy the road is. It doesn't help that right next to the road is a high railway embankment, so there is no room to get off the road. The amount of traffic is a shock compared to the past few days of levee bank cycle paths and quiet roads. After eight kilometres, I'm grateful to leave this highway and I hope never to have to do that again.

The Gemenc Forest Railway is a narrow-gauge railway which, as the name suggests, was built to take logs from the forest but now is a tourist railway with guided tours through the forest.

Gemenc State Forest Railway

The actual green train has open carriages with a canopy and bicycle symbols on the train so presumably I can take my bicycle on board, but I didn't.

The train ride is okay but with me not understanding Hungarian I'm not learning much. Thankfully one fellow passenger speaks some English and is kind enough to translate a few words for me to get the gist of it. At the end of the line for an hour we are allowed to walk around to visit a couple of bird hides beside wetlands before returning. Maybe if I spoke Hungarian, I may have enjoyed this more, but I didn't find it that interesting.

I'm now on the opposite side of the Danube to the EuroVelo 6 route but I'm not cycling back on that highway again.

Instead, on Maps.me there appears to be a levee bank route on this side of the Danube which will connect with quiet roads until I can use a ferry to re-join the EuroVelo 6 route.

After cycling through a lumberyard which is still used, crossing the normal railway line and the highway, I join a paved levee bank which takes me to the small town of Bata. South of here, there is a three kilometre middle section which is a dotted line on Maps.me but I'm assuming since it has been okay so far in Hungary, I should be fine.

It starts as a paved levee bank but suddenly turns into a farm track but with it only being three kilometres until a road returns, I decide to continue rather than backtrack onto a highway.

Following a faint track

Unfortunately, the track soon becomes a wet paddock track before gradually disappearing altogether before a rough cleared area looks like a path, so I keep going.

Eventually, I come across a crossroad where straight ahead it looks like a faint path keeps going but Maps.me suggest I should turn right and head north to an actual road. It's behind a locked farm gate and I have no idea if this road exists anyway. In hindsight, I should have explored in the opposite direction towards the Danube to see if it was any better as there is a dotted line track beside the river. However, while thinking about which way to go suddenly heavy rain begins so I make the dumb decision to continue straight ahead, hoping to get to the next town quickly.

Soon the track disappears altogether with just numerous trees and shrubs in the way. I begin lifting and dragging my bicycle through trees and shrubs as a cliff face is now on my right and a billabong is on my left.

I soon realise it makes no sense to keep going forward, so I try climbing with my bicycle up the steep cliff face. This is a struggle as I drag my bicycle up before abandoning it halfway up to see if there is a way out. Once at the top I discover a high fence and private property so no way to get out. It is even harder trying to get my bicycle back down without dropping it.

Once back down I leave my bicycle to see if I can cross the billabong with no idea if it will lead anywhere as I'm hoping there is a track beside the Danube. It's a slow muddy walk as I search for a route among trees which will allow me to get through without getting stuck in the mud or stepping in puddles. Eventually, I'm relieved to see a track with vehicle marks beside the river so I return to collect my bicycle and drag it through trees and puddles to a muddy track.

Other than being soaking wet, I'm okay and I'm hoping my bicycle is too. I'm more just annoyed with myself for ignoring the obvious that it wasn't a route. I'm assuming this mud track will take me into the small town of Dunaszekcso but there is no guarantee.

Thankfully, this track does connect through to Dunaszekcso but due to the delay with getting through, I have missed the last ferry of the day to cross the Danube to re-join EuroVelo 6.

I will now have to use the highway which I have been trying to avoid and caused me to take the short cut in the first place.

The highway is quiet in the evening and at one stage I pass a hostel but it is closed. So, I continue via a cycle path into Mohacs arriving in the dark. Being dirty I would appreciate a shower and after a quick online search, I find an apartment for sixteen euros.

The host lets me pay in euros as I still have spare from Slovakia. This will also allow me to work on a job application.

Mohacs has a long pedestrian mall to explore and some museums with a few people in the morning doing so. Randomly while looking around town I stumble on the Busóudvar Cultural Centre.

A cycle path into Mohacs on dusk

People dressed up in sheep clothing to frighten the Turks away

Where I learn about a local resistance to Ottoman conquest in the 1500s when the locals dressed up literally in sheep clothing and wore wooden masks with horns to look like devils while carrying burning sticks to frighten the Turks away. This is celebrated with a Busóudvar festival each February for six days, with people dressing up in the frightening outfits. This museum has life-size mannequins dressed up with a light show showing piles of sticks being burnt and visitors can dress up as well. It is an interesting, unique museum.

I could now cross on a ferry to the eastern side of the Danube and cycle directly into Serbia from here. However, I will stay on this side, which will allow me to visit Croatia for the first time, if only for a couple of days before entering Serbia.

Before leaving Hungary, I take a side road to visit Mohácsi Nemzeti Emlékhel, a battle site where the Hungarian King Louis II died along with thousands of others in a 1526 battle against the Ottoman Empire.

It is an interesting memorial with two parts, firstly a white round glass museum explaining the battle in detail including a fifteen-minute video. I'm alone for the English version but there are plenty of people for the Hungarian version. The staff put the English version on for me and presumably can offer other languages.

Outside is the memorial which is made up of numerous skinny, tall, individual wooden-carved statues which are spread out over a large site. I'm not sure if this is deliberate but these statues make a spiral shape. Each statue represents human remains found on this site.

Memorial to 1526 battle of Mohacs

In retrospect, I feel like I got to know touristy Budapest but not much more of Hungary besides the countryside beside the Danube.

I haven't needed to use my passport to cross a border since leaving Russia. This will now change, as Croatia is not part of the Schengen open European border and neither is Serbia, Bulgaria or Turkey.

As I approach Croatia a large border fence is visible with an observation tower behind the fence in a cornfield.

I'm let through very easily as the border guard is more interested in where I have cycled from than any customs questions.

My first border fence since Russia

Saly to Mohacs

Croatia

After crossing the border, I notice three changes, firstly all the small blue water fountain taps are now fire hydrants, so I have been forced to buy water again after not needing to since the Baltics. Secondly, cycling signs are slightly different and I haven't found a cycling map yet.

Thirdly, the number of flying ants has noticeably increased. I previously noticed them occasionally in the afternoon, usually while cycling on levee banks, but in Croatia they are everywhere, even on main roads and in towns, constantly flying into me and landing on me. Thankfully, they don't bite, it's more they just get down my shirt. The second day in Croatia they were not as bad, so it may have just been a weather issue.

My afternoon route involves a few doglegs through farmland and small towns until arriving into the town of Belje.

Once in Belje I'm not sure where to sleep. Originally I thought about camping at the football ground, but it is being used in the afternoon and anyway, houses are close by. My plan is to cycle to the city of Osijek to see what options I can find there.

A mobile butcher

On a cycle path on the way out of town as I'm about to cross a small river, I see a track leading off to my left beside the river, so I join the track and head off to see what I can find.

This track follows a curvy river which feels like a billabong, many people are fishing and there are a few simple shelters with nothing underneath spread out along the river, and for some reason there are some straw artwork statues. I have accidentally found a perfectly quiet spot away from the road with no one caring that I'm sleeping here.

Camping by a billabong

It's a quick morning cycle using a bicycle path beside the road to Osijek. Just before crossing a river the bicycle path ducks away from the road to join a path beside the northern bank of the Drava River. Beside the river is the dirt mound remains of a star style fort with grass on top and plenty of brick oval arches around the base. Across the river appears to be a larger, more intact castle.

The quiet northern bank of the Drava River is less developed with a few parks and swimming pools to cycle past before crossing on a pedestrian bridge to the southern side to the city centre.

After crossing some tram tracks, I arrive at a busy pedestrian mall as the city is slowly waking itself up. While waiting for the visitor information centre to open, I find wi-fi and see that Jaiwei, who I had met in Saransk in Russia more than two months ago, is now in Croatia too.

After messaging each other, we arrange to meet again in the town of Vukovar not far down the road, but I will need to leave Osijek soon. Before leaving I visit the busy markets for some fresh fruit and there is enough time to briefly visit the castle I originally observed across the river.

From the outside, Tvrda Fortress still looks like a castle with high grass-topped walls, a tower and castle-style entrances with a moat.

However, inside the fortress are more modern buildings with red-tiled roofs and a town square in the middle. Rather than feeling like a tourist site, the buildings appear to be used for regular life as I see teenagers leaving

Tvrda Fortress has dirt mound walls

a school. It's quiet around the outside walls so I'm able to freely walk on top.

To get to Vukovar, instead of following the longer dogleg EuroVelo 6 route, I have found a short cut using back roads away from a river so hopefully, I can get through.

The short cut is initially fine except for the last section which in places becomes a muddy farm track through cornfields causing my bicycle to become full of mud.

Once back on the road I'm cycling through industrial parts of Vukovar, as I pass a war memorial with a modern-looking tank on display, so I stop and go for a closer look. There isn't much detail, but I presume it has something to do with the Yugoslavian Wars in the 1990s.

After missing a turn requiring a U-turn, I finally find my way down to the Danube with an open riverside area for pedestrians including a short-paved cycle path which takes me close to the town centre. Finding a busy pedestrian mall during this lunchtime and a modern shopping centre, I wait for Jaiwei to arrive.

Meeting Jaiwei again

As I wait I begin to feel my back is a little sore. I suspect this is due to rushing to get here through the mud.

Eventually, I see a touring cyclist coming towards me but Jaiwei doesn't recognise me initially until I pull him up. We then spend some time chatting about each other's experiences since previously meeting in Saransk in Russia more than two months ago.

He has gone via Georgia and Turkey and from here he will be now heading west towards Spain and then plans to visit South America.

Jaiwei did eventually make it to Spain via Germany and then flew to North America and cycled across the USA and down to Mexico before flying home to China in March 2019.

Jaiwei gives me his Serbian SIM card, the first time since Russia I will have mobile internet. For the most part, I have been able to find public wi-fi easily enough since leaving Russia. For some reason Jaiwei doesn't want the Hungarian paper cycling map, instead he is relying on his iPhone for navigation.

After Jaiwei leaves in a hurry, seemingly not stopping to look around town, I decide to have a look around Vukovar. I find a museum in a large building beside the Danube which presumably must have been an important residence. Along with plenty of local history and artefacts, they have a room focusing on the Croatian War of Independence in the early 1990s.

It's harrowing stuff with videos showing the devastation on people and places, of a war during my lifetime. I don't know a lot about the conflict, and I imagine Serbia will tell a different story. As part of any bicycle trip, I try to learn about historical events and often post-trip I will learn even more.

From Vukovar, I'm back on the EuroVelo 6 route following the Danube but only occasionally is it visible, while often along the way the road dips down to towns and then I have to climb back up again. At random places, I'm going past a few bicycle stations with a map, bicycle stand, tools and bicycle pump.

While cycling beside cornfields another touring cyclist comes towards me. This older Swiss man is on his way home from cycling in the Stans in Central Asia. I offer him my cycling map of Hungary which he gratefully accepts.

Bicycle repair station beside the Danube

By the time I arrive in Iloke the last town on the Danube in Croatia, my back is killing me so a soft bed to sleep in is preferable, which will hopefully relax my back. After searching around town my best option is a hotel beside the Danube with views of Serbia across the river.

Normally I prefer to find accommodation with a kitchen, but this one doesn't have one, despite being the most expensive stay of the trip. It cost me $63 Australian, so cheap for Australian standards but expensive for Eastern Europe, although this does include breakfast. Since I have already purchased some sausages, I end up cooking them using my stove in the gardens outside the hotel, as darkness falls over the Danube.

During the evening I email a few physiotherapists and osteopaths in Novi Sad in Serbia, to see if I can get an appointment tomorrow.

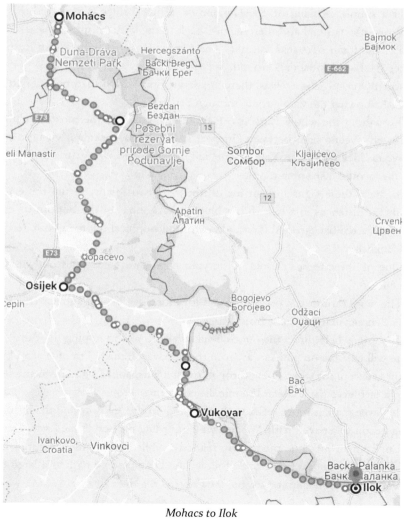

Mohacs to Ilok

Serbia

Serbia had the most informative EuroVelo 6 cycling signs

After a simple crossing of the Danube on a high bridge, I briefly show my passport, it's stamped and then handed back to me with no questions asked as I enter the town of Backa Palanka. The Cyrillic alphabet is back, but in most places the Latin alphabet is around.

Most noticeably for cyclists, there is a large EuroVelo 6 map noticeboard in English showing the whole route through Serbia.

Throughout the whole EuroVelo 6 route in Serbia, are the most numerous, consistent cycling signs between Hungary and Bulgaria, making navigation easy. I have no idea what EuroVelo 6 signs are like in Germany, Austria or Slovakia but they would take some topping.

Normally these signs inform me of the next two towns on the route with kilometre distances in white with a blue background. On the bottom of each sign with a red background is an individual philosophical quote in both Serbian and English.

"One of three things should be on your bike, your hand, your butt or your bike lock."

"The word "tomorrow" was invented for indecisive people and for children" (Ivan Sergejevitch Turgeniv, from Russia)

These signs help direct me out of Backa Palanka as I'm hoping the EuroVelo route will take me on paths away from the highway. Initially I'm on a semi-busy highway except for when going through small towns, until a sign directs me away onto a dirt levee bank which I'm initially concerned about.

The levee bank is more relaxing than cycling on the highway and thankfully it soon becomes a paved path. While having morning tea beside the levee, I assist an Englishman with pumping up his rear tyre, while he gives me directions into Novi Sad. The last section closely follows the Danube on a path as a large fort on a small hill gradually comes into view across the river.

Levee bank into Novi Sad, where Petrovaradin Fortress is across the Danube

Accessing the city centre is easy as a series of small town squares are connected by pedestrian malls from the river to the town hall. I'm passing various multistorey, traditional European looking buildings as well. At the visitor centre, they have a pamphlet telling me about a EuroVelo 6 app and a free one-page map showing the Danube cycle route in Serbia. Both will make navigation easier from now on.

Map of EuroVelo 6 in Serbia

One physiotherapist in Novi Sad has replied to me with an appointment to treat my back. However, since she feels her English is poor, she has organised her ex-husband to come along and translate.

Her English is fine, but her ex-husband speaks more comfortably. I had been hoping to get a physical service on my back, but she just gives me a script and her ex-husband walks me to a chemist to help order some pain medication. I appreciate the effort they both went to and I'm hoping the tablets will help.

After a short explore around Novi Sad on this quiet Saturday afternoon I make my way across the river to Petrovaradin Fortress.

Leaving my bicycle down below, I walk up to the top where, on the riverside of the fort, there are fancy restaurants with people dressed in formal attire.

Away from the restaurants there is plenty of space to walk around the high straight walls above the river below and to look around the former fortress.

Compared to the front of the fort, the back side away from the river is more an abandoned star fortress which is larger than the one in Osijek. There are a few rows of high stone embankments with grass on top, with a normal road going through the middle of the fort.

I could staying the night in Novi Sad but if I cycle a few more hours tonight this should allow me to arrive into Belgrade by lunchtime tomorrow. Being Sunday, this will enable me to visit some museums before most are closed on Monday.

Petrovaradin Fortress with restaurants at the front, while the rear is abandoned

Not long after leaving Novi Sad suddenly I'm in the middle of a crowded local carnival in Srmeski Karlovci with jumping castles, local concerts and plenty of market stalls.

The most popular item for sale is a very sugary pastry treat, which is dough wrapped around a rolling pin-sized object and baked. The thin roll pastry is then dipped in your choice of various ingredients including sugar, chocolate, breadcrumbs and cinnamon. It's delicious but not the best for my health.

A rolled pasty treat

Since the carnival is crowded and noisy, I'm feeling claustrophobic, so I soon leave. According to the EuroVelo 6 route I'm supposed to start climbing away from the Danube.

However, I decide to follow a track beside the railway line as it looks like this avoids a climb. It soon becomes sandy and eventually runs out as I'm now among railway construction and I'm unsure exactly where I am.

Using GPS on my iPhone, I find a path up a hill to get back up to a road. This is my third alternative route idea which hasn't worked in the past week. Maybe I should stick with the EuroVelo route.

As daylight is disappearing, I'm struggling to find a decent place to camp as all the small towns I'm passing through don't have anywhere suitable and I'm away from the Danube. Eventually in the dark, I manage to find a rough track between cornfields to camp on the edge of a town.

After a quiet, relaxing night, I set off cycling through farming areas, with nothing memorable except for a half-paved road. Because the paved section is on my left, for a small time I'm cycling back on the left side of the road, it's just like being back in Australia.

Camping between corn fields

Eventually, suburban Belgrade begins, but thankfully I'm able to avoid most of it by making my way down to a cycle path beside the Danube. It's a simple ride using a cement cycle path. I just have to be careful of the pedestrians, in particular young children as this riverside area is busy on this Sunday morning.

The bridge crossing of the Sava River into Belgrade proper is easy with dedicated bicycle lanes, plenty of signs and there is even a lift to allow bicycles to get from the bridge down to the riverside.

I have only booked one night at an Airbnb apartment, as many museums are closed on Monday, which is common in Europe.

So, this afternoon is about visiting any interesting places which will be closed

Sign on a bridge into Belgrade

tomorrow; even then some are closing by 2 pm today. On Sunday's in Belgrade many museums are free to enter.

The Military Museum has plenty of Serbian military history throughout the ages but what is noticeably absent is any obvious references to the breakup of Yugoslavia in the 1990s. A vastly different perspective from my brief time in Croatia. From my limited knowledge, I understand Serbia was the chief antagonist.

The museum is in a small section of the large Belgrade Fort, which dominates the headland at the point where the Sava River flows into the Danube. Since most of the fort is free to visit any time, I hope to return tomorrow for a longer explore.

Military museum in the Belgrade Fortress

The most interesting and popular is the Tesla Museum. I'm required to line up outside and be guided around in a large group at a specific time. This works fine as the guide is excellent as he shows some of Tesla's inventions, with some still working as he demonstrates.

Since I have found more to see during Sunday afternoons explore, I book another night in my Airbnb apartment.

I have been cycling every day since Budapest a week ago, so a rest day will do me good, especially as my back is still sore and the tablets aren't helping. In the evening, I find a massage parlour near my apartment, which has helped my back.

Since I'm having a day off, why not see if I can get my shoes repaired as they are starting to fall apart. I easily find a shoe repair shop and I'm told they can fix my shoes today. I only have one pair of shoes, so I will be spending all day walking around barefoot and unlike in Hungary, no one appears to care or notice.

Most of my day is spent on two free guided walking tours, both are two hours long and start at the Republic Square, where a kilometre-long busy pedestrian mall connects with the Belgrade Fortress.

The first tour focuses on 20th century history including communist times as my guide uses large building façades to explain what Belgrade was like during the communist era. Most of what he describes is familiar to me from my time in former Soviet Union countries, as Yugoslavia was a mini Soviet Union.

Just like in Russia there are a few large scenic churches including the large domed Church of Saint Sava, which is still being built but mostly looks completed with plenty of religious artwork on the ceiling in the rooms I could access.

Our guide points out a bombed multistorey building which was home to the local radio-television station, which has been left as it was, to highlight the impact of the NATO bombings on Belgrade. This is the only reference to the Yugoslavian Wars I saw while in Serbia, certainly nothing about anything Serbia may have done to other countries.

Saint Mark's church   Colourful buildings   Bombed building left as it was

The second walking tour with a different guide focuses on the old part of the city including the large Belgrade Fortress which is now a free public park. The fortress is mostly still intact with a mixture of older stone buildings and newer red-bricked buildings, which have been expanded over the centuries.

It's a large complex to explore with many places to walk around, moats to cross, various different styles of entrances, many high castle walls and buildings, including towers, still in excellent condition. Inside the fortress, there are plenty of war vehicles on display, clay tennis courts between walls and plenty for kids to see including a dinosaur museum, with life-size dinosaurs on display.

From the fortress are views of the Danube and Sava rivers down below with plenty of stairs to negotiate to an open park area with remains of more former buildings in the flood plain confluence of both rivers. The Belgrade Fortress was one of the most scenic locations on the trip which is even more special because it feels like this is a space for everyone rather than just a tourist attraction.

Sporting facilities among the Belgrade Fortress

Riverside of the Belgrade Fortress

I have been pleasantly surprised by how much I enjoyed Belgrade, as I had no real idea what to expect when I came and I'm glad I had a rest day here smelling the roses.

For the next few days, I'm hoping the ride will be scenic as I go through the Derdap National Park with twenty tunnels to go through as the Danube flows through the scenic Iron Gates Gorge.

On my way out of Belgrade on a large bridge over the Danube, I see two touring cyclists ahead of me. Despite being on a popular EuroVelo route I haven't seen many touring cyclists since Budapest. I soon catch them as we join a rough narrow dirt levee bank, which is overgrown with grass.

Anna and Will are both from the USA but are living in Germany and have been following the Danube from Germany over the past three weeks. Despite the rough levee bank the morning flies along as we chat about both our respective bicycle trips.

Sadly, I have to bid Will and Anna farewell in Pancevo because I'm hoping to make the last ferry of

Will and Anna on dirt levee bank

the day across the Danube to Ram, which is further than where they are aiming to cycle today.

On a breezy day, I'm making good time passing through small towns on a semi-busy road. Soon there is an option of either a levee bank route beside the Danube with a questionable surface or continuing on the shorter road. With my aim to catch the 5:30 pm ferry I take the road.

After lunch when both routes briefly re-join in the town of Kovin, I realise I have enough time to risk the levee bank option. Initially I'm on a paved road next to a levee bank before it becomes a dirt four-wheel drive track and the levee bank is a similar surface. Despite the rough surface, it's quite relaxing cycling, passing by wetlands, with the only traffic to worry about from a small sand mine.

As the route returns to the road, I meet an older woman in Dubovac who is on a credit card bicycle tour, meaning she isn't carrying any camping gear. Her accommodation needs are more restricted, so she is stopping here because there isn't any indoor accommodation for a while. Because I have a tent, I can continue without needing to worry as much about where I'm sleeping.

After crossing a canal, another grass levee bank option becomes available, which takes me past fishermen to a ferry terminal beside a hotel. Having made great time, I have an hour to relax here.

Just before the ferry is about to leave, who should show up but Will and Anna who have decided to continue further on today.

We cross the Danube just before sunset as the water has a reflective glow

On the ferry with Will and Anna

as Ram Castle and the small attached town comes into view.

Anna and Will inform me about a paid campground nearby so I decide to go with them. We cycle up out of Ram and cycle for half an hour during dusk, as Anna directs us to a small campground, for only my second and last paid campground of the trip.

Crossing the Danube to Ram

After finding sparse facilities on my previous European camping experiences, I'm surprised to find a shower, picnic tables and a camp kitchen. It's also quiet and at night there aren't lights on all night, two reasons I normally avoid campgrounds.

Paying to camp, with decent facilities

Will and Anna have individual tents, so they are not a couple as they explain more about following the Danube in Germany and Austria, while we cook our respective meals. When they get to Romania in a couple of days, they are planning to catch a bus back to Germany.

Today is a day I have been looking forward to because I will go through the Iron Gate Gorge. I would have liked to cycle with Anna and Will, but they are having a short day, while I need to travel further as the days are starting to run out until my flight home.

After climbing up from the campground to a small dam wall, I realise I have left my utensils at the camp kitchen. It's a quick return, where Anna and Will are in no hurry as their tents are still up.

Initially, it's just like any other day beside the Danube, with a mixture of decent surface levee banks, quiet roads and paved cycle paths beside the road. Sometimes I'm beside the Danube, other times I briefly drift away before returning as the river becomes wider with Romania now across the water. Along the way I'm passing through a few small towns with long riverside parks on this relaxing sunny day.

After visiting a delicious bakery in Golubacki, the cycle path disappears as the road starts to follow the river in a deep gorge, with a small section where the gorge is overhanging the road. I assume this is the start of Iron Gates Gorge. Just around the corner is a large stone castle with numerous different towers built on a side of the gorge. As I get closer the river provides a scenic reflection of the castle.

Road is often close to the Danube near the start of the Iron Gate Gorge

Reflective Golubacki Castle

However, the water doesn't look that inviting with what looks like green algae and I have been told not to swim in the river. Golubacki Castle is under renovation, so it isn't open for visitors except on Sundays at the moment. A brand-new looking visitor centre is open, where I learn that the castle has changed hands many times over the centuries.

On the hillside the castle is built on, is a new road tunnel which goes under the castle. Once I'm through to the other side, the road stays reasonably flat especially at the start, with the river often at the same height as this quiet road. On both sides of the gorge are numerous hills with different natural features to admire, so I'm hardly noticing the kilometres going by because the scenery is so distracting.

For most of my ride in the Iron Gate Gorge I'm at water level

Three Serbian cyclists follow me for a while and we briefly chat in broken English. They are doing a loop of the gorge area as there are two EuroVelo 6 routes, one on each side of the Danube and this continues through Bulgaria until the Danube is just in Romania. The Romanian side has a similar road occasionally visible across the river.

After the small town of Dobra, out of nowhere the road suddenly begins to climb for a short distance above the river and then I go through the first of twelve tunnels. Most are short with daylight visible from both ends except for a couple which are 250 metres long. A few times I'm going through tunnels close together where I can see the next tunnel while going through a tunnel.

One of the longer tunnels has a button to enable flashing lights to inform cars that a cyclist is in the tunnel. Once after no traffic for a while, a truck and a few cars suddenly showed up, otherwise I'm feeling safe going through tunnels.

A sign for cyclists to inform other road users that a cyclist is in the tunnel

Except for one longer climb near Boljetin with an even longer descent, it's a simple ride into the small town of Donji Milanovac. They do have a tourist information centre but as the guide says, there is not much going on and the supermarket is disappointingly small.

Serbian supermarkets are more like Russia with less fresh fruit, meat and bakery items compared to the more varied choices I have had since leaving Russia. However, actual bakeries have been delightful.

In the middle of the gorge there isn't much flat ground for camping, so I have found an Airbnb fifteen kilometres down the road. Leaving Donji Milanovac the road scenically hugs the shoreline with most houses beside the road built on terraces, including my Airbnb guesthouse.

My terraced multilevel wooden accommodation has plenty of rooms, each with their own balconies providing scenic views of the Danube, with a couple of long white cruise ships going past.

Leaving Donji Milanovac

My terraced accommodation, with breakfast by the Danube included

While eating my delicious egg-based breakfast cooked by my Airbnb hosts I'm admiring the scenic gorge and considering what I will see today on the second half of the ride through the Iron Gates Gorge.

I set off on another sunny day cycling at river level as the scenery is even more spectacular as the gorge narrows. Eventually I have no choice but to begin a long climb through the final two tunnels, while down below a few speedboats are travelling through the gorge. However, they all appear to be departing from the lower Romanian side, so they are not accessible to me. Often while I have been climbing, the Romanian side is flatter but there have been sections which would involve climbing too.

Road is beside the gorge for most of the time before a climb begins

I pace myself up the climb and there are plenty of opportunities to stop and look at the view. Once up to the high point of the day, there are spectacular views of the river and surroundings and I can see faces have been carved into high long rock faces on the side of the gorge.

Apart from Slovakia, this trip has been relatively flat, so the climbing has been enjoyable, especially as I have been actually crosses a scenic mountain range, rather than just going up and down for the sake of it.

After quickly descending, I meet the three Serbian cyclists again, one of whom gives me a packet of biscuits. Once out of the gorge the landscape becomes noticeably drier and the temperature increases.

Carvings in the rock face and a railway line are both on the Romanian side

As the Iron Gates Dam approaches, I can see on the Romanian side that a railway line now follows the river below the highway, but I never see a train.

At Iron Gate Dam One, I could cross into Romania but with it looking more industrial on the Romanian side and the fact that I will only be crossing back into Serbia half a day ride later downstream, I don't feel like it is worth it.

Just after the dam there is a small area of Roman remains called Diana. A 2,000-year-old fort which has been abandoned since 596 with plenty of stone ruins, red-bricked squared columns and red-bricked archways is still here. It could do with more information, as even the one information sign I find is fading, while no one else is around.

Roman remains called Diana

The rest of my day isn't as spectacular as it's now flat to Kladovo, the largest town of the day, with industry visible on both sides of the river.

Once again in Serbia the supermarket is disappointing but there are many restaurants in town, so I try the Serbian national dish called Pljeskavica, which is a semi-spicy meat patty covered in cheese and a red sauce. It's okay to eat but would be better on a cooler day.

While the local markets have plenty of red veggies including chillies but no fruit for sale.

Pljeskavica

The EuroVelo 6 route from here follows the river on a longer loop but with it not looking anything special, instead I will climb directly over a small hill, saving twenty kilometres.

The rest of my afternoon involves cycling through small towns near the river before eventually a road beside the river begins which passes by many small homes with people out fishing on their private jetties. This road has a varied surface, is paved at the start and end but in between is gravel or stones but with little traffic it is a relaxing ride.

Near the end of the day with no plan of where I'm sleeping, I end up at Milosevo Football Ground on the edge of a small town. A social match is on, so I watch the game before chatting mostly through Google Translate with locals.

The football club's president then offers for me to sleep in the wooden clubhouse with a sloping roof so that's what I do. It's a quiet night on my mattress inside a small room surrounded by photos and trophies of the club's history. This reminds me of a similar offer in Wales in 2013 when I stayed at Undy Athletic clubhouse.

Sleeping inside Milosevo football clubhouse

Before crossing into Bulgaria, I still have plenty of spare Serbian Dinar, so I purchase a heap of food, discovering that the local bakery has a version of a meat pie. I had been meaning to try it but haven't had the chance, turns out it's a delicious soft pastry meat pie.

Apart from the Baltics which all use the euro currency, every time I have changed countries I have had to change currency. I usually try to spend all my local currency rather than losing out when exchanging money. It's always hard to judge how much to get out at an ATM, I either get too much out at the start or find I am going back a few times and then in the end often have spare money or not enough for a final purchase.

Ilok to Ram (Google Maps)

Sometimes shops will let me use all my loose change and then use my debit card for the rest of the purchase.

Just before crossing the border in the middle of nowhere, I ring my parents. It's amazing how I get better reception in countries which appear to be economically worse off than back home in Australia. Being smaller in size does help.

The final cycling sign quote on the EuroVelo 6 route as I leave Serbia is "You are leaving Serbia. Don't cry because it's over - smile because it happened. We wish your bike to have tires always full of air, to transfer your dreams to roads and paths. Have a nice rolling in Bulgaria" These motivational cycling signs did not exist elsewhere except Serbia.

While I was in Serbia, some university friends organised a charity run from Wangaratta to Melbourne over five days, raising money for Motor Neuron Disease as one of the runner's mother has died from it. As well, since the father of a former classmate from thirteen years of school lost his battle a month ago, I decided to make a donation of an Australian dollar for every kilometre I cycle on the same days they were running.

Since I was cycling along the Danube, I expected it to be a fast cycle. Normally I don't care how far I cycle but over those five days, I cycled 499 kilometres.

I enjoyed the EuroVelo 6 cycling route the most in Serbia, but I am curious as to what cycling will be like elsewhere in Serbia. I hope to come back one day to see more of the country and I would like to learn more and get a different perspective of the conflicts when Yugoslavia broke up by visiting neighbouring countries.

Serbia has felt like what I expected Eastern Europe to be like and feels closer to Russia.

It's still not as undeveloped as Russia and I will see what Bulgaria and Turkey are like for my last twenty days of this trip.

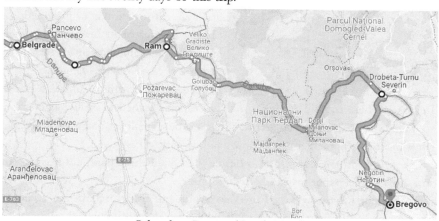

Belgrade to Bregovo (Google Maps)

Bulgaria

At the border there are signs about not taking certain food like citrus into Bulgaria but after the customs officer has a quick glance in my bag, I'm waved through. He is more interested in my ride than questioning me about my intentions or what food I'm carrying.

The Bulgarian currency rate is similar to Australia, so I won't get notes with thousands on them but are only worth 10 Australian dollars. Instead I will get twelve Bulgarian Lev, so I won't have to do currency conversion calculations every time I purchase something.

Initially the EuroVelo 6 route in Bulgaria takes a longer northern horseshoe loop route beside the Danube, so instead I will take a short cut to Vidin to re-join the EuroVelo route there. I'm glad I stocked up on food in Serbia, as I can't find the centre part of the town of Bregovo and somehow I find myself on the opposite side of town. Luckily, this is the correct side for the direct road to Vidin.

After an incredibly quiet ride traffic-wise I arrive into Gamzovo, which feels like a ghost town, as it is noticeably quiet and bland. This was common in Bulgaria, with many towns much quieter compared to the rest of my European experiences, while large cities are still busy.

The last city for me on the Danube is Vidin, which is quiet and there isn't much to see. Even the castle is quiet.

This smooth-sided stone cream castle which appears to have had a red brick top layer added later, looks in reasonable condition. Unlike in Serbia I have to pay a modest entry fee but there isn't any information at all provided, so I have no idea of its history. Still there are some nice buildings inside the castle and okay views of the Danube.

Vidin castle

Just like many other European cities, I can see where the old city was in Vidin, especially the old walls. The stone south gate still exists with an archway that maybe a small car could get through, while most of the former wall is now a public park.

The visitor information centre is beside the Danube in a park, but it is closed so I don't have a paper map to help direct me.

From Vidin, I'm back on the EuroVelo 6 route but unlike in Serbia, there aren't bicycle signs so I'm guessing my route while passing through small towns on a reasonably warm day.

Thankfully on this warm day I'm passing by a few decorated stone water fountains, with water constantly flowing out of them, presumably from a spring. Since people are stopping by the side of the road to fill up their bottles, I assume the water is okay to drink and I keep using them in Bulgaria.

I assume this water is safe to drink

At one stage, a quiet road beside the Danube looks like a promising place to camp but I keep seeing houses all along the route so there is nowhere sensible to stealth camp. Eventually I decide to stop in Arcar, my last town near the Danube.

Arcar doesn't look like it's in great shape with a few derelict buildings. However, unlike in Serbia, it is easier to find decent recycling bins. Often together are a few different coloured large bins, each with pictures of what items should go in each.

Colour coded recycling bins

Arcar is away from the Danube with a levee bank visible in the distance on the edge of town and there is a football pitch, but this time without a clubhouse. Past the football pitch towards the Danube is a shrubby area with plenty of space to set up my tent in the dark.

The obvious difference in Bulgaria, are the numerous death posters which are everywhere and are often found in groups. I have seen them all over bus shelters, on the outside of homes, power poles and any other spare spaces. Each A4 sized poster has the person's photo, their name, their date of birth and death and what I assume is information about the person as apart from dates it's all in Cyrillic.

Numerous death posters, found all over the place

From looking more closely I can see a wide range of ages of the people who have died, with the saddest being children. Unlike Australia, where there are notices for someone who died in the last week, many of these posters are of people who died years ago. A few times I saw people replacing fading ones with the exact same poster. I'm told this started during the communist era.

I have been following the Danube since Hungary and today I will leave it behind to start the long climb to Sofia, the capital of Bulgaria. I'm estimating it will take me two and a half days, not because I'm climbing particularly high, rather it's just that Sofia is that far south of me and I will be taking an indirect route to avoid highways and steeper routes.

As I leave the Danube behind, I see the only cycling sign I saw during my brief

time on the EuroVelo 6 route in Bulgaria. This route keeps going further for a while until the Danube flows into the Black Sea in Romania.

EuroVelo 6 sign in Bulgaria

After a short climb, the landscape changes as it becomes less dry with spots of greenery, but there is still a dry heat and a mountain range is beginning to appear in the distance. While resting beside road works before the longest climb of the day, I suddenly feel a sharp pain as something has bitten me on my left ring finger. I assume it's a wasp as it's still alive.

It stings but I'm more concerned about if I get an allergic reaction because I have had one bad reaction to an insect sting once on my foot. In that instance, eventually my skin went pink and I began to struggle to breathe requiring a doctor's visit. Since then I have had no allergic reaction to a few insect stings, but I still carry antihistamine. I search for my small first-aid kit which I have hardly used on this trip and then take a couple of antihistamine tablets.

After fifteen minutes, with no reaction just a sore finger, I begin climbing on a terrible, all gravel, rocky road surface but with no traffic to worry about. At the end of the road is a closed road sign so that's why I didn't see a car.

The only city I pass through today is called Montana, which is not related to the US state, as it's actually the new name of this city. It is set out with straight roads, cement buildings and large public spaces, just like many other communist-era cities on this trip. There isn't anything special about Montana, I'm just grateful to visit some okay supermarkets even if they have less fresh bread options than the same branded supermarkets in other countries. Sorry for going on about food but as a hungry cyclist, food is one way I judge a country.

My route for the afternoon involves following a railway line on a quiet road when suddenly, at one town, the traffic increases dramatically with constant groups of six or so semitrailer trucks all following each other in varied directions. I'm unsure why as it doesn't look like a busy road on my map or a route between large cities. So when I learn there is an interesting site called God's Bridge away from the busy road I begin climbing gently up on a rough track.

At the top there are some small castle type stone ruins, while of more interest is down below, where there is a large open cave with a natural bridge to explore. I'm able to walk right down under the bridge and around it to a damp area. Randomly there are some picnic tables with pizza ovens but sadly all downstairs so my bicycle can't come. As it is now 6 pm and no one else is around I decide to camp here while admiring the sunset and the surrounding hills.

God's Bridge

Awoke to a fog over a mountain in the distance

Thankfully, I don't have to backtrack from God's Bridge; instead my route to the city of Vratsa is initially via a dirt road. As I get closer, a large mountain range comes into view behind the city.

Once in Vratsa, there are plenty of green spaces in what feels like an edge of a mountainous city with steep roofs to keep the snow off. I'm also starting to see a few large statues, which, along with the Cyrillic alphabet and many cement communist era buildings, reminds me of Russia.

Large statues in Vratsa

My route up this mountain range will involve following the Iskar River and a railway line mostly using a secondary road which looks like a quiet gradual way up to Sofia. This is the type of route I prefer to follow.

On the edge of a mountain range

Initially, there is some freeway cycling with a steep descent on a busy road with a decent shoulder. At one stage, I'm travelling at approximately 70 kilometres per hour, when randomly my large Nalgene bottle falls out of its holder onto the freeway. I slam on my brakes and scramble to pick it up with cars racing past. Thankfully, apart from severing the connection loop between lid and bottle, my Nalgene bottle is fine.

Once off the freeway, it turns out to be a perfect route, with little traffic on a great surface. There is one small section at the start when I take a dirt track to avoid the freeway but once back on a road the freeway takes a different route which also takes away the traffic.

The rest of the afternoon is a cycling highlight of the trip which involves

Colourful Iskar Gorge

gradually climbing on a quiet road with occasional downhill sections breaking up the climb on this sunny day. There are a few short tunnels to go through especially at the start, while the railway line and this road are constantly crossing the Iskar River to find a decent route. During the climb, five passenger trains go past but no freight trains. There are plenty of distracting mountainous natural features, with many geological layers visible in Iskar Gorge, along with many trees having a yellow and green tinge. Along the way there are many terraced houses in the small towns I'm stopping in every so often for a snack.

Climbing through Iskar River Gorge

After a relaxing ride just before the gorge finishes, I find an Airbnb with Jim, an Englishman, housesitting just off the main route. This allows me to relax and do some laundry before arriving in Sofia tomorrow.

It's easy climbing out of the gorge in the morning as it becomes flatter and the suburbs of Sofia begin. By using a farm paddock track between two railway lines, I find a quieter way into Sofia.

Once in Sofia, I'm suddenly stopped by various armed forces marching in front of me. Turns out 17th September is Sofia Day, a religious holiday celebrating Sofia, as the city is named after a church. I have accidentally managed to find myself another public holiday. Because of this many people are around, some museums are free to enter and there is a peaceful political protest march on, with security around. The protest is mostly around the Alexander Statue which commemorates Russia winning a war against the Ottoman Empire in 1878, which led to Bulgaria re-establishing independence.

Scattered around Sofia are four visitor information centres with basic information. It would be better if there was one dedicated centre with more information, as the small centres are more about selling tours or just a minor part of a bookshop. I do at least now have a map of Sofia.

Marching over a yellow brick road   *Chessboards are popular in parks*

Sofia, the capital of Bulgaria, is an interesting experience and surprisingly I learn more about the ancient Roman history of the city rather than more modern history. I never considered Bulgaria as having an association with the Roman Empire, until I read earlier this year Ghost Empire by Richard Fidler, an Australian, who is also the main host of the excellent ABC Conversations podcast. He explains that the Roman Empire, which extended into modern-day Turkey, split between east and west in the 3rd century AD Constantinople, the modern-day Istanbul, was the capital of the Eastern Roman Empire until the Ottomans conquered it along with Bulgaria.

In Sofia, they have uncovered many Roman era buildings during subway construction and I'm freely allowed to enter rooms, with knee-high wall remains. This site looks well looked after, even if most sites are out in the elements, while others are behind glass. These uncovered sites are made of layers of stones and square tiles both in cement so presumably from different periods of construction. There are information panels in both Bulgarian and English which is a big help.

In a courtyard surrounded by modern buildings is St George Church Rotunda, the oldest in Sofia. This 4th century Roman era church is a single cone red-bricked building with stone ruins out the front. It's a lot smaller and older compared to other churches on this trip.

Found Roman remains under the street   *4th century St George Church Rotunda*

The Regional History Museum surrounded by gardens is fascinating, showing how Bulgaria became an independent country again in 1878. To achieve this, they had to import a royal family, who ruled until 1946, when communism came to Bulgaria. The communist era appears to have been erased from history as it isn't mentioned.

Mosaics often have chipped off pieces

There are a few churches in the city and under one church is an underground Basilica with Roman-era mosaics on the walls and the floors along with other artefacts to see inside. Many mosaics have random sections chipped off so imagination is required to see the whole picture.

I'm staying at a bicycle shop, as they are the only Warmshower hosts to reply in Sofia. This is my first Warmshower stay since Poland, as many requests have gone unanswered. Since I have been on a popular cycling route for the past few weeks, I assume the few hosts available get plenty of requests.

When I arrive at the bicycle shop, they are surprised I'm here as they have no idea I'm coming. They let me stay as they explain they offer a couch in the basement of the shop surrounded by bicycle gear. This means I have to leave my bicycle outside during the day. It was safe but not ideal while I walk around town. I found out later Jaiwei had stayed here too.

They also run free bicycle tours of the city, so in the evening I go on one. It's a different experience to a walking tour; I see more of the city but perhaps miss some walking spots, but this does allow me to cycle through scenic gardens around Sofia. I'm told that the numerous yellow brick roads in Sofia inspired the Wizard of Oz.

While trying to sleep in the bicycle shop, I'm hampered by a small couch which I just don't quite fit in, the shop smells of cigarettes and the neighbours are noisy.

In the morning, since I feel I have seen all I want to see, I decide to leave Sofia. By leaving now this will allow more time to get to Turkey.

I'm not rushing off straight away, instead I slowly make my way out of the city via the Museum of Socialist Art. This museum is located way out of the city, requiring some searching to find it among apartment blocks. I am not sure if this is a deliberate decision to forget communism or not.

After paying an entry fee, outside on display are numerous statues from the communist era including a Lenin statue and a red star which used to be prominent in Sofia. The museum is smaller than expected but still interesting, especially as a few pieces of thoughtful modern artwork is included which shows communism in a bad light.

The most vivid art piece is a sculpture of a man who was trying to cross into Austria from Hungary, being killed by a guard dog, with blood pouring out of his head while two guards watch.

Inside are posters from the communist era and insightful artwork reflecting on that era. The most memorable is of a screenshot of a computer screen with a communist-era photo with a choice to delete files with the words. "Are you sure you want to permanently delete all your history prior to 10.11.1989? Yes or No". This sums up the communist era during my whole tour with some places just wanting to forget the period, while others want to highlight it as a lesson of history.

Star from communist days

Reflective Artwork on communist era

Heading east from Sofia I have two choices – in both cases this will involve crossing hills twice. The only difference is that the slightly shorter route is beside a freeway, so it makes more sense to take the quieter, longer route.

After getting through an industrial part of Sofia and taking a dirt track through corn paddocks with mountains in the distance, it quietens down. The climbs are okay, nothing serious, I just pace myself up with barely any traffic to worry about with a few small towns along the way. The last gradual climb is longer with an open landscape except for a few more trees around the top before a quick descent as the small hilly scenic town of Smolsko comes into view.

Afternoon climbing

In the centre of Smolsko, men are sitting in cafés playing cards and smoking. However, instead of chatting straight away, my priority is to find an open grocery store and somewhere to sleep before perhaps returning. Once again, there are a couple of small general stores in Smolsko with mostly just packaged food available, reminding me of general stores in Russia.

Before cooking dinner, I search for a quiet spot to stealth camp, finding what I hope is a hidden place close to town past a cemetery. Rather than setting up now, I return to town and I will return to set my tent up once it is dark enough. Most times when I'm wild camping I try to find a suitable spot or even a plan B to camp during daylight hours. I then leave to cook dinner somewhere else and return once it's dark enough.

While cooking a tin tuna pasta dinner in the park in the centre of Smolsko, an elderly man comes over and offers for me to sleep in his townhouse across

Swetson on the right with his friend

the road. He looks harmless so I finish cooking my meal and take up his offer.

I find a modern home as I explain my trip to Swetson and his friend, while Swetson talks about his own experiences in visiting Australia. They insist I drink vodka which, once again, burns my throat so I drink as slowly as I can, so as not to get a refill. I begin to eat my pasta but Swetson insists I eat his hot chicken soup, despite him not eating much himself.

Swetson's friend (I didn't record his name) comes back over in the morning to give me some apples. He originally wants to give me a kilo worth, but I explain I can't possibly carry them all.

During the foggy morning, I pass another sign in both Bulgarian and English with a book symbol telling me there is a library nearby. I have seen these signs often in Bulgaria but I'm yet to find a library so I head into town to see if I can find one but once again, I can't. I could have asked but it

Signs for a library

has become a matter of pride to see if I can find one without help; I never did.

Throughout the day there are a few small climbs in a mini alpine landscape as I'm passing small towns in between hills. A gradual sunny downhill ride in the afternoon takes me through more towns as it becomes a more open landscape.

By 4:30 pm, I'm in Stroevo, the last town before entering the large city of Plovdiv. I consider stopping here and cycling into Plovdiv tomorrow as I have found a football ground on the edge of town to camp at. While looking around the football pitch I can hear that it's near a busy road. Since I will just be waiting around for it to become dark, it makes more sense to keep cycling to Plovdiv tonight, even if I have no idea where I will be sleeping.

Initially, Plovdiv is a busy, not particularly interesting city, until I cross the main river on a covered pedestrian bridge with shops. Suddenly it's quieter with a pedestrian mall leading to a small open area next to a red and white spotted mosque. Nearby is a decent visitor information centre which is about to close at 6 pm. After ducking inside, I'm informed about a free guided walking tour starting at 6 pm.

It's a popular tour including a few Australians as apparently Plovdiv is a tourist hotspot I have never heard of. Our guide focuses on a few periods of history, in particular the Roman Empire because many Roman remains have only been rediscovered in the 20th century.

These remains include a Roman Chariot Stadium buried under the main pedestrian mall and nearby is a horseshoe-shaped Roman Theatre. Both were lost to history for 1,750 years. The theatre has been fully uncovered and is now used for concerts, while the stadium is still under the main street but with one end open. This allows the horseshoe-shaped steps at one end of the stadium to be visible and accessed.

Roman Stadium is under the street

On the street level is a model of the stadium which lines up with the pedestrian mall, showing how large the stadium was, with rows of terrace seating on each side which still stretches for 500 metres under what is now the main pedestrian mall. At one end there was also an aqueduct which has been lost to history.

A model of the Roman stadium   We also visit the old town part of the city off to the side away from the city centre, with plenty of cobblestone roads and many stairs to negotiate, while walking my bicycle past many 19th century buildings in fading light. These wooden buildings come in a range of styles of architecture and in an assortment of colours including salmon-pink, brown and white. Most buildings have balconies protruding out, with various shaped windows with shutters and artwork surrounding the windows. Clearly people were competing with each other for the fanciest building.

Colourful 19th century buildings in Plovdiv

While on the tour, I book an excellent Airbnb, with just a small room, which is all I need. In the morning, I go for a further explore to see more of what my guide told us about last night, learning more about the history of Plovdiv and Bulgaria.

I start with exploring inside some of the 19th century buildings from last night, some of which are now a museum. Learning more about the successful 1878 Bulgarian War of Independence against the Ottomans, along with seeing artwork and information on individual houses was worth the time.

The main interest for me is to walk down the stairs on the small part of the Roman Stadium which has been uncovered and restored only in the past decade. Down below is a short 3D film of the stadium's history, showing what they assumed it looked like during Roman times when it was being used for athletic events and chariot races.

Down in the open end of the Roman stadium, while a mosque is above

When walking through the white stone archway entrance which comes out in the middle part of the horseshoe curve stairs, this allows me to imagine I'm participating in a chariot race, especially as there is a mural in front of me allowing a perspective of the stadium stretching out in front of me.

Alas the Roman Theatre is closed for a concert, but I can still see from the outside the white stone horseshoe-shaped theatre steps and a few random columns and statues behind the stage. As it was built in a hillside, I can see more of the city stretching out behind the stage.

The Roman Theatre

The archaeological museum has plenty of Roman items on display including coins, statues, decorated vases and mosaics. Many of the statues are missing certain parts, usually either the head, feet or hands, which makes them look older. Mosaics are often missing pieces too, which requires using my imagination.

Artefacts in archaeological museum in Plovdiv

I hadn't heard off Plovdiv before, so it was a pleasant surprise. Especially as it is a reasonably sized place to explore with some tourism but not a ridiculous number of tourists.

My afternoon ride isn't inspiring with an open flat landscape while cycling in a slight headwind. I'm on joining roads between towns as I cross a more direct freeway four times. Sometimes I am going under the freeway through small tunnels as I snake my way along, with a mountain range just visible south of me.

On these secondary roads, I come across a rural situation I'm used to back home, seeing people chasing cows. However, it must be harder with no fences on any of the paddocks I'm cycling past.

Making it feel even more monotonous is that most small towns are feeling the same with the majority of houses made of red tiles and red bricks. Many houses look like they have seen better days, with plenty of rubbish around, sometimes with horses chained up outside.

The condition of houses makes me assume that Bulgaria is the poorest country I went to on this trip. No other country has as much rubbish directly outside houses but thankfully the roads are much better than in Russia.

This was a rare time during my trip where I thought that this may not be the safest place to stop or leave my bicycle just from judging the houses. This makes no sense especially as people I have met have all been friendly.

While stopping in one town, suddenly I'm soon surrounded by a friendly group of children. As my Bulgarian is terrible, I'm not sure what they are talking about, but some want me to take a photo of them.

I realise while chatting to the children that gradually people's skin colour has become darker since leaving Slovakia. When cycling it can take longer to notice the change in countries ethnicity, compared to when travelling by train or plane. It's only when I go through photos that it becomes more noticeable.

In Russia, other than travelling World Cup fans, the lack of diversity was noticeable, even in cities. The only time I noticed diversity was around Kazan, where some people had a central Asian appearance.

I don't have any plans for where to finish cycling today so I just keep going as shadows are becoming longer. Eventually I find a long skinny park with a playground and park benches, in the small town of Tsenovo to cook dinner. While walking around town waiting for it to become dark enough to set up my tent, I encounter two seemingly wild horses in town. Eventually, I find a spot among trees to stealth camp, where I hear dogs barking for most of the night.

The first stop on hopefully my last full day in Bulgaria is the city of Dimitrovgrad. The name is familiar to me, having stayed in a Russian city with the same name, and it turns out there are three cities with this name, the third being in Serbia. They are all named after the first communist leader of Bulgaria, Georgi Dimitrov. The Bulgarian city was the first one named, despite being the youngest as it was established in 1947 as a planned communist city, while the other two were existing cities renamed later.

It is easy to tell this is a new city by how it is set out in a grid with straight roads and wide-open spaces for pedestrians.

In the city centre, there are gardens to explore, plenty of statues and a water fountain in the middle of the city but it's quiet with only a few people around.

With many plain buildings made of cement, it feels quite different to Plovdiv yesterday, reminding me not only of Russia but also of communist era cities in the Baltics and Poland.

Central Dimitrovgrad

Dimitrovgrad History Museum actually talks about the communist era. Since the city didn't exist before then they really can't talk about anything else. While most communist-era museums on this trip have focused on the struggles under communism, this one is more positive, while not shying away from talking about struggles.

With an English audio guide provided it is easy to learn about how the city was established with many topics discussed. On display are plenty of photos and stories, along with a few actual items from the period.

During the communist era in Bulgaria after World War Two, they set up volunteer workgroups using young people to do large-scale jobs like building roads and railway lines. Many people look back at that time as a positive experience.

After a delicious crepes snack, my route leaving Dimitrovgrad involves some short, steep sections as I cycle south on a longer, quieter horseshoe route to avoid the main road to Haskovo.

Straight away, I can tell Haskovo is an older city because the streets aren't straight, and buildings are more varied in style. With narrow laneways leading to random streets it's much easier to get lost and it feels a little claustrophobic.

One museum is full of Roman items, including a few statues and a coin collection. Did you know that the word "soldier" comes from a coin called "solidus" which was paid to armies.

After heading south on a busy two-lane freeway, once I turn off it becomes a quiet route on the foothills of a more southern mountain range called Rhodope. I'm passing through rough-looking small towns with red-bricked and red-tiled houses all looking the same, often with stone fences around each house.

A common style of house

While stopping at a café I happened to get online to discover I have been offered some outdoor education work taking school students on a ten-day bicycle trip back in Australia in late November. After recently hearing back that I wasn't

Camping by a dam

successful in a full-time role I applied for, I had been considering cycling past Istanbul. However, with work confirmed, I will keep the same departure date. By the time I got to Istanbul, I was glad I was flying home.

I end my day wild camping beside a dam outside the small town of Tankovo, where thankfully the mosquitoes don't appear.

It's an enjoyable morning with a hilly downhill ride through orchards on the way to Mezek, where I can see a medieval fortress up a hill.

After climbing up past the tennis courts, I find an okay fortress to visit but it looks close to ruins with small stone walls. This fortress provides decent views of the dry hilly landscape, while around the castle on display are a few games but I'm too early to see them in action.

Artwork on the road

Back down in town, the lady in the general store explains how to get to a rare intact Thracian Tomb in a cave in a hill, by taking a side road up a gentler hill than the fortress. On the actual road up is a group of drawings of Greek mythological figures, which at a certain distance, makes them look three-dimensional.

No one is around the tomb entrance despite it being advertised as being opened by now. After waiting a bit, as I'm about to leave a man shows up to open it. Another visitor has showed up and he offers to explain its significance, as otherwise it wouldn't have made much sense. It isn't that impressive anyway, just a long passageway built out of stone blocks to a small room.

Just before the Greek border, randomly there is a cycle lane just on my side of this quiet secondary road which leads me into Greece beside the freeway. This is strange after not seeing any other cycling infrastructure anywhere else in Bulgaria.

Random cycling lane

Bulgaria felt the closest to Russia, with a similar Cyrillic alphabet, the amount of rubbish and both trying to forget their communist history. Just like in Russia, I enjoyed the cities more than the countryside, except for the enjoyable climb to Sofia.

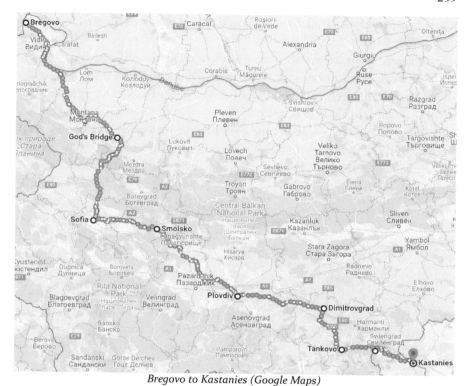

Bregovo to Kastanies (Google Maps)

Greece

So far on this trip border crossings have been very quick, with officers more interested in my cycling than any customs issues. After handing over my passport I'm expecting them to stamp it and hand it back to me straight away as has been happening at previous borders.

However, for some reason, it's taking a little longer and while I'm waiting, a busload of tourists are let through ahead of me. I'm confused as I'm not offered any explanation or asked any questions.

Eventually I see they are going through every page in my passport. I suspect they can't find the correct stamp saying I had left Hungary, my last Schengen country, as I'm now back in the Schengen Zone, with euros as the currency.

As an Australian, I can spend 90 days out of 180 days in Schengen Zone countries without a visa, so I assume they are working out how long I have been in the Schengen Zone. Since I entered my first Schengen country of Estonia less than 60 days ago and have spent sixteen days out of the Schengen Zone since Hungary, I'm well within the visa-free limit.

Eventually, after what feels like twenty minutes, my passport is returned with no explanation and I'm free to enter Greece. I will only be in Greece for a few hours because it looks a quieter route than the main one from Bulgaria to Turkey just north of here.

In Bulgaria, I snaked my way along using secondary roads, taking a longer route through small towns with some small climbs instead of taking a more direct freeway. In Greece, I join a quiet freeway which I'm looking at leaving as soon as possible to visit Greek towns.

Not long into Greece, a lone touring cyclist comes into view with a Polish flag sticking up from the rear of his bicycle. Having not seen a touring cyclist during my whole time in Bulgaria, I'm interested in talking to a fellow traveller.

Meeting a Polish cyclist

Thankfully, he speaks English well as he explains how he has cycled from Poland and is heading to southern Greece, while I talk about my time cycling in Poland. Somehow, we end up talking about his time working in Saudi Arabia, which he didn't enjoy due to working conditions. We never exchange names.

After an hour and a half of nonstop chatting, we have crossed this small north-eastern bubble of Greece on this quiet but quick freeway. Since this freeway has mostly been on top of an open hilly landscape I have missed going through small towns, as they are all down below around the river border just north of me.

Normally I prefer taking a small town route which is what I plan to do in Turkey, but it was nice to cycle with someone for a while.

I now need to leave the freeway and my cycling friend to cross into Turkey as there are only two roads which cross from Greece to Turkey. The other crossing is well south of here and a longer ride. I have heard that the city of Edirne in Turkey is interesting to see.

Before crossing the border, my route takes me to Kastanies, the only town I will be going through in Greece. Straight away the obvious difference to Bulgaria is the modern white houses with clean streets. This is a similar experience to when I crossed from Russia to Estonia, in both instances it felt like I have gone forward in time and wealth. Once in Turkey, it felt like I went back in time again.

I still have some euros left over from Slovakia, which I use at a supermarket, as restaurants appear to be closed in the middle of the day. After seeing a small railway station on the edge of town, my time in Greece is up. Two hours after entering Greece, I leave for Turkey.

Turkey

On the edge of Kastanies is the Turkish border which has a vastly different atmosphere compared to previous border crossings. The Turkish border guards are armed with high-powered guns, which is intimidating. A lengthy line of cars are waiting to get into Turkey, so I assume this may take a while. However, the guards wave me through to the front of the line, where cars are being thoroughly searched. I'm asked to open my pannier bags, but it is only a quick glance inside before I'm told to move on.

As an Australian, I need a visa to enter Turkey, the first time I have needed a visa since Russia. Thankfully, it's an electronic visa so before leaving home I applied for a three-month tourist visa. It is a simple online process, I just paid a small fee and entered an estimated date of arrival. In my case I put 1st September as I assumed that would be the earliest I would arrive. In return, I'm emailed a three-month window to be in Turkey from September to the end of November which works fine with my flight home from Istanbul on 2nd October.

However, without a physical Turkish visa in my passport, the officer asks me if I have permission to enter Turkey. I quickly show him my electronic visa on my iPhone, which I assume he will scan the barcode or take a photo of, but he only has a glance at it and lets me into Turkey.

All this takes less time than earlier in the day when I crossed into Greece. On the Turkish side, it is much quieter which surprises me as I expected more people would be trying to get into Greece.

Once away from the border it is noticeably busier than Greece with numerous people selling food by the roadside, just like in Russia.

After crossing a bridge, I arrive in the city of Edirne where suddenly the amount of people becomes overwhelming, especially in the pedestrian mall. With so many people it feels like I'm exiting a packed football stadium or a peak hour train station. It doesn't help that many people are trying to sell things using loud voices and music is being played, a contrast from quiet Greece.

Busy Edirne

While it is now harder to find wi-fi, I eventually find that ING bank has it but I need to use my Russian SIM card to get online to contact my Warmshower host to let them know I will be over soon.

With wi-fi hard to find in Turkey, a couple of times I visited mobile phone shops to try to get a local SIM card, but none could find a SIM I'm allowed to purchase as a tourist. At one shop, staff spent half an hour trying to help me, also giving me a cup of tea, while they smoked in the store.

One of two main mosques in Edirne

Ceiling of a mosque's courtyard

I can't find a tourist info centre to help me find things to see in Edirne, so I just start looking around with two large mosques standing out. The mosques in Turkey are different in style to the ones I saw in Russia, more cream in colour instead of white and with more of an Arabic influence. Straightaway I can see how each mosque has a few small towers attached to them which I soon learn are called minarets.

Entering the mosques requires taking my shoes off, something I'm comfortable with. Taking photos inside the main chamber is discouraged but it is fine in the outer courtyard. Some people are praying but most are just looking around at the Islamic artwork including the high dome ceiling.

Surrounding the courtyard are inward-facing verandas, with numerous red and white striped decorated archways and the ceilings are covered in Islamic artwork including Arabic letters and symbols. In the middle of the courtyard is an open roof area with a fountain to wash your feet.

The nearby Turkish and Islamic Art Museum is informative as it explains how the mosques were designed and what significance certain aspects of a mosque are for.

Just like churches initially, I find mosques are interesting to admire but over time most begin to look similar with the same dominate cream colours, similar Arabic religious artwork, the same courtyard style to wash your feet and an inside prayer area. The main difference is the slight variations of size and extra additions like having more minarets, which usually depended on who was paying for the mosque to be built. In a way, it looks like walking into McDonald's or any other franchise, all with slight differences but selling the same familiar thing.

The two mosques in Edirne look the same as they were both designed by Mimar Sinan. He improved the style of his buildings over time, so the younger mosque is regarded as an improvement. He also designed numerous buildings around the Ottoman Empire, including an old stone bridge on the western entrance to the city, where I briefly meet two German cyclists.

From here, I follow the small Tunca River on a levee bank as I make my way to my Warmshower host's home in the suburbs on the eastern edge of town, my way out of Edirne tomorrow.

While searching online using my host's wi-fi I can't get onto a few websites including Wikipedia and Booking.com. I have managed to find a few Anzac Cove guided tours but so far, all I'm finding are tours which all leave in the afternoon from the nearest town of

Touring cyclist crossing the old bridge

Eceabat, as this allows for people to do a day trip from Istanbul. I will see how I'm travelling before deciding on what tour to do.

My Warmshower host Özgür and his housemate Enes are nice friendly people of similar age to me. We share a meal and chat for a while in the evening using a mixture of English and Turkish with the help of Google Translate. However, by 11 pm, I'm ready for bed so I head to my room, but they are still up until 2 am while I'm trying to sleep.

In the morning, they are still asleep when I want to go at 9 am so I write a WhatsApp message and leave. Later I receive a reply saying they had only woken up at midday. In Europe, I struggled with how late many people stay up and then sleep in, as I like to get to sleep earlier because I'm normally woken up by the sun.

Once out of suburbia I'm able to join a secondary road which initially is a dirt farm track but slowly becomes sandy. Thankfully, this only lasts for a brief time until meeting a bitumen road.

It's harvest time so there are many harvesters with caterpillar front wheels, presumably harvesting irrigated crops as there is plenty of mud around. Grain is being collected in small, open bin trailers with large wheels, driven behind a small tractor.

Plenty of tractors and trailers

In previous countries, it was common to see locals using bicycles as everyday modes of transport, where I often admired the wide range of items hanging off them. Since crossing into Turkey, bicycles have nearly vanished from the local population, along with bicycle infrastructure including bicycle stands outside supermarkets.

A cyclist is a rare site in Turkey

I have seen more motorcycles so they may have replaced bicycles but not all. When I do see an elderly man on a bicycle, we stop for a chat and then he takes me to a café for a cup of tea and he talks about his cycling experiences in Turkey.

It appears to be more common in Turkey for dogs to be unleashed with a few aggressively chasing me. This continues for my whole ride south to Gallipoli. During one short climb, a pack of dogs chase me for a bit which is a little frightening and a good motivator when climbing. Thankfully once I was far enough away from the dogs, they leave me alone.

Despite being near the Evros River which is the border with Greece, my route south becomes hilly with short climbs. As I leave the river behind to cross to the wide yet shallow Ergene River Valley, it becomes hillier before flattening out.

The actual Ergene River is narrow but is surrounded by a marshy landscape, so in the 15th century, a nearly 1,400-metre-long stone bridge with 174 arches was built to cross it. Luckily, it was built wide enough for cars to pass each other to what now is the city of Uzunkopru. This bridge is the symbol of Uzunkopru, with a statue in town dedicated to the bridge.

The long Uzunkopru bridge is the symbol of the town

On a small stone covered road

After a kebab lunch with friendly inquisitive staff, it's now warm and my route becomes hillier as I'm passing through small towns on varied road surfaces. Sometimes it is bitumen, other times gravel and sometimes the road is covered in small stones, which doesn't offer any grip. Traffic is only farm trucks so it's much more relaxing than Russia.

The further south I travel the more open the landscape becomes as I'm passing through mostly farmland without fence or trees, with plenty of harvest stubble being burnt off in preparation for sowing. As I edit this in autumn 2020 back in Australia, burning off is being done on farms around me and the smell takes me back to Turkey.

This being my first full day in Turkey, I begin to notice in towns numerous men sitting in cafés drinking tea, smoking and playing card games. The men are friendly, but it feels like a boy's club, as it's rare to see any women at these establishments. Throughout my time in rural Turkey, when I saw older women, they are likely to have their hair covered.

These cafés are useful for getting a cool drink; I just need to avoid smokers as unfortunately Turkey appears to have the most relaxed smoking rules of all the countries I visited on this trip. It's worse than Russia as smoking inside appears normal in many businesses, with people having no consideration that I might not want to be around it.

I'm also starting to hear the Islamic prayer call being broadcast five times a day on loudspeakers, usually from one tall skinny minaret tower next to a small mosque in each town. Locals appear to just accept this noise as normal like bells in a church, with most not stopping what they are doing, just going about their daily lives.

Personally, it sounds like a cat being strangled especially at 4 am and I find it to be annoying, in my face noise pollution, especially when I'm trying to sleep. I can accept people needing religion but prefer for it not to be so prominent, instead it should be kept inside for people who want to hear it.

Just before dusk, I see a water trough which looks like it is from a spring just like in Bulgaria. However, the water doesn't look as inviting, more like a stock trough, so I don't fill my bottles.

The small farming town of Begendik reminds me of farming communities back home, with grain being cleaned, presumably from the recent harvest.

Harvest is on in Turkey

Nearby is a reasonably quiet spot behind the football clubhouse to camp.

As I'm about to head to bed, I hear drifting across the paddocks Islamic prayers from towns in the distance, which I can't even see lights from. Individual prayers appear to start at slightly different times, like they are competing against each other or someone needs to get a new watch. Because it so far away it sounds soothing like thunder in the distance, rather than directly on top of me.

Camping behind the football pitch

During the night I suddenly desperately need to go. I frantically search for my toilet paper and shovel and then race out to the recently ploughed paddock behind the football ground to add some manure, while unchained dogs are barking nearby.

After a couple more events during the night, I realise that Turkey has literally given me the shits. I haven't felt sick in any other country during this trip.

In Bulgaria, I was able to drink from water springs, just like locals with no problems but I suspect Turkish water isn't as good or maybe something else has affected me. I will now switch to bottled water, not something I like doing but I hope this fixes the problem.

It doesn't help that in Turkey most public toilets require payment, which is usually to an older woman who gives me only two pieces of toilet paper, as there isn't any toilet paper available inside these grubby toilets. When you have diarrhoea, you need more than two pieces.

Thankfully, I carry some spare toilet paper but over the next few days, my supply decreases. I'm also carrying a small folding shovel which is useful especially when away from towns. It comes on quickly, so a couple of times I have added some manure to paddocks.

Path dead ends in between barriers

I stopped in Begendik last night to avoid arriving in the city of Kesan, so I set off in the morning as it gradually becomes busier. Thankfully, there is a path to cycle on beside the freeway but unfortunately this path soon ends between two silver freeway barriers as an on-ramp joins the freeway.

After lifting my bicycle over a barrier, I'm on the freeway but thankfully soon there is an exit into Kesan as I search for a toilet and a SIM card. I find a dirty, paid toilet but have no luck with a SIM card as friendly staff can't work out a way for me to buy one as a tourist.

After a brief look around busy Kesan, I find a side route to take me south. However, the route soon turns to dirt before improving as the road returns towards the freeway and ducks under it to join a decent secondary road. Eventually, there is no option but to return to the freeway as a mountain range is in front of me and there isn't a secondary road option. Just before joining the freeway on the side of the road, farmers are drying a crop, it's a black seed but I'm not sure exactly what it is.

Drying a crop beside the road   *Climbing up Korudağ Rakım Pass*

Despite suffering from diarrhoea, I can climb in the heat easily as the freeway has a wide shoulder for me to cycle on and even if the traffic includes semitrailers, it is still relatively quiet. Halfway up I stop at a small restaurant to empty my bowels again and refresh myself with lemonade as I'm feeling dehydrated

Once over Korudağ Rakım Pass, as I begin descending quickly, the Aegean Sea becomes visible. I stop for a moment and contemplate that the last time I saw a sea was in Estonia, two months ago and I have unintentionally cycled a continuous route all the way since the Baltic Sea. This is unusual for me as on previous trips I probably would have taken a train somewhere along the way.

After descending to nearly sea level, I'm now at the top of a narrow part of the start of the Gallipoli Peninsula with the Dardanelles Strait not far away on my left. With only one major road connecting the Gallipoli Peninsula with the rest of Turkey, there is no alternative but for me to be on this busy, noisy freeway on a warm day. Thankfully, there is a decent roadside shoulder to cycle on, so I plug in some podcasts to block out the noise.

At one stage there appears to be a road beside the freeway with a few buildings dotted along including a roadside café to get a cool drink. However, this road is rough and slow, so it is easier and quicker to return to the freeway.

After a while, I leave the freeway near the town of Guneyli as the freeway takes a more direct easterly route to Eceabat, which is the main town on the eastern side of Gallipoli Peninsula where Anzac Cove guided tours depart from.

Instead, my route now follows the hilly middle part of the Gallipoli Peninsula, and at times I can see the Dardanelles and the Aegean Sea, sometimes both at the same time. However, I never actually visit a beach because while it would be a quick ride down, it would be a steep ride to get back up. I will wait until Anzac Cove.

The road conditions change frequently, from good bitumen to bituminised stones to gravel. On a flat surface, this would be okay but when trying to climb numerous short steep sections it is a struggle as I'm feeling fatigued and I need to stop a couple of times to defecate.

Every so often is a small town, with each having a couple of small general stores with similar pre-packaged food just like Russia.

Hilly road through the middle of Gallipoli Peninsula

In the evening while collecting dinner supplies in Degirmenduzu, a couple of cafés are full of local men drinking tea and chatting but once again no women are around. A couple of the locals speak some English and are used to encountering Australians as I'm now close to Anzac Cove.

Eventually in this undulating landscape, I find a reasonably flat, recently harvested paddock to camp. The weather is predicted to cool off tomorrow.

Road sign for Anzac Cove

In 1915 with the deadlock on the Western Front, the British authorities under the leadership of Winston Churchill came up with the idea of a backdoor route knocking out the Ottoman Empire from World War One by conquering Constantinople. This would open up a route through to the Black Sea to assist Russia.

Firstly, they had to get through the Dardanelles Strait, a narrow inlet between the Gallipoli Peninsula and Asia. However, warships couldn't get through due to Ottoman guns and sea mines. Therefore, the Australian and New Zealand Army Corps (ANZAC) who hadn't seen any action yet, were tasked on 25th April 1915 with a landing at dawn on the west side of the Gallipoli Peninsula and crossing it, while the main force of British and French landed on the bottom of the peninsula at Cape Helles.

Neither landing was particularly successful with both getting stuck only a short way in because of Ottoman resistance and the terrain. By December 1915, nothing more substantial had been achieved despite many battles and another failed landing at nearby Suvla Bay. Compared to the shambles of the landing, everyone was successfully evacuated, including my great-grandfather.

Despite it being an unsuccessful invasion, Gallipoli has become the most famous war site for Australians. April 25 is the national war Memorial Day in Australia with military marches and memorial services, including dawn services in Australia and overseas. Thousands of Australians and New Zealanders gather at Anzac Cove at dawn on 25th April each year, with this service broadcast back to Australia.

After a windy night I awake to an overcast day, and thankfully it's a tailwind so I set off knowing Anzac Cove is only two hours ride away.

Unfortunately, as soon as I set off, I notice my rear tyre is flat, the first one since replacing my rear tyre in Latvia. While I'm changing the tyre in the chilly wind, another two minor diarrhoea events happen. Once everything is fixed, it's an uneventful ride as, despite it being cold, the tailwind pushes me along helping with small climbs.

First flat tyre since Latvia

The last town before Anzac Cove is Buyuk Anafarta which has some mentions of the battles with a memorial wall, as otherwise, I wouldn't have known it is nearby. Even as I cycle in from the north on flat terrain and meet the sea, I still wouldn't know I'm near a World War One battle site.

As I begin following the shoreline south, on small hills on my left gradually coming into view are some stone memorials.

I soon pass a few New Zealand cemeteries, with information panels on the battles, before the Sphinx at the apex of the hillside comes into view. This famous natural landmark was named by ANZAC soldiers after they had been training in Egypt before the landing.

The Sphinx

My first stop is North Beach where the Anzac Day dawn service is held each year; it's smaller than I expected. Today it is just me and a busload of tourists reading the information panels on this cream bricked wall.

I'm trying to get an understanding of the landscape by using a combination of listening to an audio guide and an excellent New Zealand First World War Trail app which, with GPS enabled on my iPhone, helps me identify my location, while listening to stories about each outlined stop.

At one cemetery beside the beach among the numerous headstones, I find the name of A. W. A. Barber from Laen, a locality near Donald in Victoria, not far from home. The Barber surname is still around.

Cemetery beside the sea, with a name close to home

Near Shrapnel Valley cemetery is a small overgrown path which takes me up steps to Plugge's Plateau. Now I'm up higher I can see more clearly the terrain soldiers had to climb to get up to this ridge-line before they would have had to descend for a bit before climbing again to the next ridge-line. It would have been a tough climb through shrubs on a sandy hillside and I can see even higher points above me.

Back at my bicycle, I continue following the beach stopping at the only toilet block on the beach level but there isn't any toilet paper. From here I begin climbing on the one-way road up to the highest point called Chunuk Bair.

The wind is strong and cold in exposed places, but this doesn't stop me cycling despite being a headwind. The road has some short sharp climbs followed by gentle gradients, with many points of interest to stop at along the way which helps me pace myself up.

At many sites, there are information panels in both English and Turkish so it's easy to locate myself. I'm also still using both my audio guide and New Zealand War Trail app to guide me further. Some sites I have heard of like Lone Pine and the Nek, while others, in particular Turkish sites, I haven't.

An Ottoman carrying an Anzac

The main difference from the beach areas is the sudden increase in traffic with many large buses going past. It turns out more Turkish people than Australians or New Zealanders visit this war site. However, they appear not to visit the landing sites, instead concentrating on where the Ottomans defended from.

One of the first large statues is of an Ottoman soldier carrying an Anzac soldier, which sums up this area, in that visitors from both sides of the conflict are respected. I never felt like there is any resentment for me visiting. I assume visitors are a part of the local economy here.

The first cemetery on my way up is Lone Pine with a single pine tree in the middle, a large white stone monument and numerous graves.

This reminds me of Western Front cemeteries in Belgium and France I visited in 2013. Since I'm now high up I can see down to the beach where the

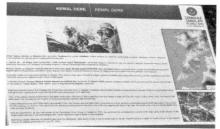

Information panels on the battles

Anzacs would have scrambled up from. It would be a challenging climb even without people trying to kill you.

Further along the road among pine trees, are some zigzagging trenches left over from the invasion. They are clearly not as deep as they were in 1915 but still deep enough for water to flow through like a channel. There are still logs here protecting underground entrances. It's not clear if the site is being left to naturally return to nature or being looked after.

Lone Pine Cemetery   *Remains of Anzac trenches*

Further on I'm passing more locations which ring a bell to me like Quinn's Post, along with more Anzac cemeteries but no Turkish ones.

Suddenly a large site with plenty of people around comes into view. With a few tour buses parked next to souvenir shops, a small café and toilets. Here they still play Islamic prayers on loudspeakers.

Across the road is the main Turkish memorial which is busy with Turkish visitors. This open aired memorial for the 57th regiment has a large cream brick archway entrance and at the back is a three-layered archway tower block. Inside this memorial are rows of numerous individual small cream headstones, each with a crescent symbol, their name, regiment, hometown and year of birth and death. I have been told the headstones are symbolic as there aren't any actual bodies buried here.

Something we often forget in Australia when talking about this conflict back home is that we were the invaders, and this directly affected Turkish people.

Main Ottoman Cemetery

View from the Nek

The biggest surprise is the Nek area which doesn't look like the end scene in the Gallipoli film. There may be more trees now, but it looks hillier and skinnier than I expected, with an Anzac cemetery nearby. From the Nek, I can see the back of the Sphinx and down to the beach.

Chunuk Bair, the high point, is the most impressive site with a large cream bricked monolith, surrounded by well-maintained log-lined trenches. New Zealanders in particular are remembered here as they captured this high point for two days before it was recaptured by Ottomans during the August Offensive. This is the only place where I can see the Dardanelles and was the only place where the Anzacs did too. I can also just see north of me is Suvla Bay, where the failed second landing in August 1915 happened.

Some places today made sense from reading about these battles years ago, while others require a lot of imagination to understand what happened. What surprised me is how small the whole battle area is, reinforcing just how pointless the campaign became once the initial attack was stopped.

With it being a one-way road up to Chunuk Bair via the front line, to get back down involves a road away from any war sites. It's quick back to sea level, where there is a large brand new looking museum which is closed today.

Chunuk Bair still has maintained trenches around the site

From here, it is only a short, flat ten-kilometre ride to Eceabat, the nearest town. I have to deal with some headwinds so it's not much fun on a cold overcast day. I wonder why the Anzacs didn't just race across this flat bit instead of climbing hills just north of here.

On the way into town, I spot the Boomerang Cafe Bar, so I go inside. I find an Australasian-themed bar with Australian and New Zealander flags, along with plenty of Australian native animal road signs, a poster of Australian films like Crocodile Dundee and many more references to back home.

Tomorrow I'm booked on a guided tour of the war sites, so I search for a place to sleep and to store my bicycle for two nights. I find the quiet Crowded House Hotel, another reference to back home.

Eceabat has a feeling of a port town as a ferry leaves from here to a visible Asia across the narrow Dardanelles Strait. There are a few small general stores rather than a supermarket in town and I find some tablets at a pharmacy to hopefully reduce my diarrhoea.

Near the foreshore is a large 3D map of the Gallipoli Peninsula campaign with flags marking where the front lines were. Next door is a display of life-size statues of soldiers from both sides fighting each other in close trench warfare.

I have tried finding an all-day guided tour of Gallipoli but all I can find are half-day afternoon tours which are timed for people coming from Istanbul for a day trip, who arrive in Eceabat for lunch.

However, one tour company, Crowded House, who owns the hotel I'm staying at, offers a morning tour of Cape Helles at the bottom end of the Gallipoli Peninsula, where the French and British landed in large numbers. I don't know much about what happened because it is only briefly mentioned when talking about Gallipoli in Australia.

Turns out I'm the only person on the tour so it becomes a private tour in a taxi with my guide Anil, a local man in his 60s with silver hair, dressed in his Fonzie leather jacket on this cold windy day.

We start with visiting Kilitbahir Fortress just south of Eceabat, which today has a complex of dirt bunker mounds where once were large artillery guns, which protected the narrowest part of the Dardanelles.

These guns, along with a similar set-up on the other side of the Dardanelles Strait, played a major part, along with sea mines, in stopping the British Navy ships from entering the strait. This then caused the alternative plan of the landings.

This site has its own Turkish story of a strong man lifting large shells from the arsenal to the large guns which is commemorated with a large statue of a man carrying a shell by himself.

Kilitbahir Fortress protected the Dardanelles

On the way south to Cape Helles, the landscape is flatter than where the Anzacs landed, as Alin explains how far inland the French and the British got, which wasn't far.

We visit one landing site called W Beach, where the British landed successfully at Cape Helles. Today, still visible in the water, is remains of a 103-year-old rusty pier with numerous rusting steel posts.

However, for the most part, it feels like I'm just being taken to cemeteries and monuments rather than focusing on battles. Still, it helps explain an area which is often forgotten in Australia because we focus on Anzac Cove.

The most surprising moment is seeing a French cemetery which is different in style to Commonwealth cemeteries. In this cemetery is one tall white monolith with many plaques on it, while the numerous graves are marked with individual steel Catholic crosses made from fence posts with a small diamond plaque marking where a person rests.

Some cross have been cut off

This assumed that everyone was Christian, when in fact many soldiers who came from African colonies were Muslims. This became an issue of disrespect when this was only recently pointed out to this predominantly Islamic nation. Therefore, many graves containing an African Muslim have had the Catholic horizontal cross-section cut off, leaving a single post.

The large Turkish memorial is busy with bus loads of Turkish people and there are numerous large Turkish flags. In this memorial, they don't have people actually buried here, just numerous individual metre high cement blocks packed in tightly next to each other. On each block are about twenty names, with an Islamic Crescent on a red background.

Busy Turkish memorial with plenty of headstones

Different styles of artwork around this memorial

There is also a large flower memorial in the centre, a decorative wall that shows people fighting and a large structure reminding me of the Arc de Triomphe in Paris in size. This structure has a large flat roof, held up by four large square columns, each with artwork referring to different armed forces who helped win the Gallipoli campaign.

While exploring the Turkish memorial unexpectedly my diarrhoea returns, causing me to slightly poo my pants. Thankfully, there is a modern toilet here with toilet paper, so I clean myself up and go commando as we return to Eceabat. While waiting for the afternoon tour with the same company to begin, there is thankfully enough time for a quick shower and change of undies.

Compared to my solo tour in the morning, the afternoon tour is with a large group with everyone else having travelled from Istanbul this morning. We start with lunch in a local restaurant, which is a pleasant change being able to talk freely in English with a wide range of people, the majority from Australia or New Zealand.

On this tour, I learn more about the campaign with a different guide who has maps and photos from 1915 to help explain it even more.

Photos of what it was like in 1915

However, we see less as we don't visit a couple of sites I was looking forward to learning more about, like the Nek, despite being advertised. There also isn't as much time to go on long walks or to stop at random places along the road as I could by bicycle. I did, however, enjoy being able to ask questions and compare photos taken in 1915 to what it looks like today, allowing more of a perspective.

From Eceabat it's a shorter, cheaper and a more frequent ferry crossing if I cycle five kilometres south to Kilitbahir. It's an easy cycle with the road beside the sea on this cold overcast day. The pier is just north of Kilitbahir with the fortress I went to yesterday visible as I cross by ferry from Europe to Asia into the larger city of Canakkale. Not that there is any noticeable difference so far between Europe and Asia, just I'm now in a busy city.

I'm still not feeling well, so I organise to leave my bicycle at an Airbnb and find a local bus out to the Archaeological Site of Troy.

Troy is quieter than I expected with only a handful of people around. What is left of the ancient city is in a small area, which only takes about half an hour to walk around on wooden boardwalks.

I admire different centuries of Troy's history in the layers of the stonework which have been uncovered. Beside certain remains are labels informing me which century they think it was built. Often different centuries are next to each other, with most dates being nearly 2,000 years ago.

Throughout the site are information panels with descriptions and pictures of what they imagine it looked like. The best example is of a stone ramp, still in

good condition, with an information panel next to it, of what the building that was attached to the ramp may have looked like. Often the low wall remains that are still here, allow me to imagine where buildings were. In some places, there are small round stone structures still in good condition which look like small chimneys.

Remains of a ramp

Imagination required to go back to ancient Troy

It's a pleasant small site but I wouldn't travel all this way just to see it.

Therefore, I'm back in Canakkale by lunchtime, which allows me to visit a few sites including the free "Sons of Gallipoli" display in a shipping container located near the ferry terminal. Inside there are videos showing both sides experience of the battles. I also hear from people who have relatives on both sides and people who research the battles

Sons of Gallipoli display

including my tour guide from yesterday afternoon.

Just south of the ferry terminal is Cimenlik Fortress, the eastern battery which protected the Dardanelles on this side and part of it is now a naval museum. After I go through military security, scattered around a courtyard is some naval equipment including remains of a submarine and various sea mines. Inside is information about various naval battles over the years including the 1915 campaign.

By midafternoon, I'm sick and tired from having diarrhoea, so I head to the local hospital. After being directed to the wrong people a few times, the front door receptionist who speaks some English takes pity on me and helps find me a doctor.

The doctor's English is poor but better than my Turkish, as we chat about his visit to Sydney. It cost me the equivalent of $11 Australian to visit the doctor and I'm given a script to obtain some stronger tablets. After a couple of days of using the stronger tablets, I started to feel better.

In the morning, since I'm still feeling fatigued from diarrhoea, the weather is still strong cold winds and my route is mostly freeway cycling, it's an easy decision to take a bus to Bandirma instead. This will allow me an extra 24 hours in Istanbul.

The bus operator has an office in town, but the actual large, busy bus station is way out of town near a freeway. It only cost me $7 Australian and all I have to do is remove the front wheel to put my bicycle under the bus. I wish Australian buses would be as accepting of bicycles.

On this modern clean bus, they have a waiter service handing out free food.

Putting my bicycle under the bus

When the staff realise I'm a foreigner, they take extra care to make sure I don't wander off when the bus stops for a short break.

I'm glad I'm on the bus, as cycling this busy freeway doesn't look that exciting as it follows the coastline with some steep climbs.

The bus drops me off at a bus station, well out of Bandirma, beside the freeway, which I assume is to save time by not driving into town.

The cycling component of my trip has basically finished so thanks for reading this and especially for anyone who supported me during this trip. I will be taking a ferry to Istanbul from Bandirma tomorrow before flying out of Istanbul back to Australia in a few days' time.

My Warmshower host in Bandirma has cancelled on me, due to dealing with issues with his pregnant wife which I understand. Instead I find a fancy hotel with butlers and a restaurant near the large ferry terminal with my bicycle left locked up in the underground garage.

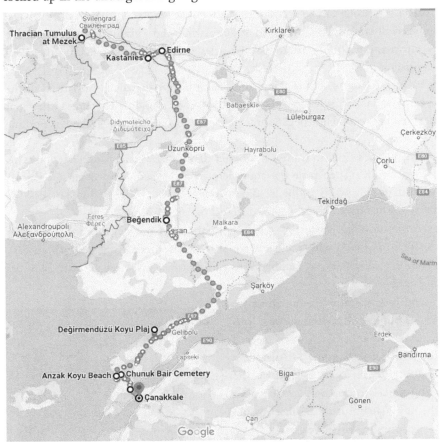

Edirne to Canakkale (Google Maps)

While waiting to board this passenger only ferry in the morning I see that people are bringing a wide range of stuff on board including a large pumpkin. I'm not the only cyclist, as a young man has a folding bicycle, so we chat for a short while in English about where I have cycled, which he finds hard to comprehend.

It's straightforward rolling my bicycle onto the ferry at Bandirma, where I'm directed to lock it up on an outside rail. Unfortunately, I'm not allowed outside in the fresh air, so I'm unable to see any decent views of the Sea of Marmara as we make a calm two-and-a-half-hour crossing. Having crossed back into Europe, the ferry arrives just south of Old Town Istanbul.

My Airbnb is close by, however, the number of people, cars and motorbikes on the narrow dogleg roads coming from every direction is noisy and overwhelming. I had heard Istanbul is the most populous city in Europe, but I wasn't expecting it to be this busy, so I'm glad once I find my accommodation.

My Airbnb is in an apartment with Elif, a lady in her mid-twenties. Having barely had any contact with Turkish women in rural areas, I wasn't sure how this would go. However, Elif speaks English, is like any other westerner and we get on fine.

To get to her floor requires me to carry my bicycle up a few flights of stairs and then it is stored it in empty spare room. I'm sleeping on a fold-out couch in the lounge room.

The apartment is located near a tram stop, making it an easy ride into the heart of Old Town Istanbul, right past Hagia Sophia and the main railway station called Sirkeci before the tram continues over the Golden Horn waterway into New Istanbul.

There is a small tourist office near Sirkeci Station, so I hop off a tram to learn more about Istanbul. Finding an extremely busy, noisy tourist area with numerous kebab shops, souvenir shops, restaurants and so many people, its claustrophobic.

After obtaining information on Istanbul, I find a bicycle shop nearby. I literally just walk into the shop and ask for a cardboard bicycle box and they give me one.

It's trickier getting my bicycle box back to my Airbnb, luckily it just fits on a tram.

After a couple of stops, the tram becomes packed, which was common in Istanbul.

Back in the apartment, I compare the bike box with my bicycle. It looks like it will be a tight fit so I will keep searching for a larger one.

Take a bike box on this packed tram

Once back on the tram I stay on it until the end as it travels over the Golden Horn into New Istanbul with the Besiktas Football Stadium nearby. From seeing scarves around I can tell a game is on tonight, so I head to the new round-looking stadium with plenty of security.

A few days earlier, I had looked online to see if any matches were going to be on, as there are a few clubs here. However, since I had been planning to arrive tomorrow, I hadn't considered tonight's match. There aren't any matches for the rest of my time in Istanbul, so I make my way to the stadium.

I soon learn that to get inside Turkish football stadiums I need to apply for a Fan ID. The ticket office can't help me, saying I'm supposed to have applied online earlier. People nearby hear me asking and so they offer to help but after they ask to see my passport and then mention inflated ticket prices, so it feels like I'm being ripped off with no guarantee I will get a ticket. I will continue exploring Istanbul instead.

After riding the underground funicular railway up a hill, I find myself in the busy Taksim Square, where I have just missed a free guided walking tour, so instead I go for my own exploration.

As I begin walking on Istiklal Avenue pedestrian mall, it looks like a tourist spot with souvenir shops, clothing stores, fancy restaurants and cafés. The sheer number of people becomes claustrophobic, so much so that as soon as I can I take a side road, Thankfully the number of people decreases considerably and I'm able to relax.

The sheer number of people in Istanbul and Turkish cities in general was the biggest challenge for me as I prefer more relaxing places. I always felt safe, I'm just not sure if I will ever go back.

During the walk, I can see a high round medieval tower with a pointy roof and just below that are windows going right around it, like it's a lighthouse, I soon learn it's called Galata Tower. I could climb up for a fee but with a busy line stretching out onto the street, I keep walking.

It towers over all other multistorey buildings in a built-up area.

After crossing Golden Horn on a pedestrian bridge, I begin randomly walking back towards my Airbnb with no real plan. Suddenly a large old stone structure with numerous double-level archways appears.

From one of the many tall white four-sided information posts around Istanbul, I learn this is the remains of a Roman Aqueduct called Valens which now only exists for a

Galata Tower   short section.

Valens Aqueduct

It is fascinating to see how well-built it was for something nearly 2,000 years old. They also had the foresight to design the individual archways for double-decker buses to go through on this multi-lane highway.

Nearby in an underpass are a few shops selling bicycles but none of their bicycle boxes are any bigger than what I have already found. Despite searching all over Istanbul, I never found one any bigger.

On the way back to my Airbnb apartment I call in at a random fast-food shop to try new food. My appetite is back as I am now feeling better and my diarrhoea has gone away. I end up enjoying Pide which is a pizza type dough with taco meat on top.

For my first full day in Istanbul, I start with seeing the underground Basilica Cistern in the centre of Old Town Istanbul. During the Roman era fresh drinking water was stored here but is now just for tourists. Inside I find a dark, damp place, with a few mouldy columns and scattered around the puddles are remains of statues, mostly heads. It's not that interesting and there is only a small area to explore.

Across the road is the large faded salmon-coloured Hagia Sophia which used to be the main church before being transformed into a mosque when Constantinople was conquered by the Ottomans in 1453. It was turned into a museum in 1935 and after my trip, is now a mosque again.

Having seen how long the lines were yesterday, I'm glad to get in early today, with a much shorter line but still plenty of people. Inside is interesting artwork but it's not as spectacular as the mosques in Edirne. Hanging from the walls are numerous large green discs with yellow Arabic writing, while there is plenty of artwork on every surface including the ceiling and the floor.

Hagia Sophia

Artwork inside Hagia Sophia is everywhere including on the walls, ceiling and the floor

Soon after leaving the Hagia Sophia, I find a free guided tour around Old Town Istanbul with a woman of similar age to me.

Where I learn about how the number of minaret towers isn't random because for a mosque to have more than one, you had to be royalty. Often new rulers would add new minarets. When the Blue Mosque nearby was built with six this caused controversy as the main mosque in Mecca in Saudi Arabia had six so the Sultan in Istanbul paid for an extra one to be built in Mecca.

The minarets original purpose was where they used to verbally announce prayers from; now it is done with loudspeakers as mosques compete with each other. Even the tour guide is annoyed when one loud prayer goes on far longer than needed.

Outside the Hagia Sophia is a large square which becomes busier throughout the day. There are a few statues in the middle including an Egyptian monolith cut in half and transported overland centuries ago and placed in the middle of a large Roman stadium called Hippodrome, which no longer exists except for some minor remains.

Our guide also points out around the outside of mosques are many Muslim headstones, which are a representation of the deceased person. She explains how they are decorated to show how important they were, so the more decorated presumably the more important or richer.

Islamic headstones

Behind the Hagia Sophia and towards the Golden Horn is the entrance to Topkapi Palace, the former main residence for Ottoman Sultans, with free entry to the first part. There are plenty of people lining up to enter through a tall, narrow, large archway entrance which clearly has an Arabic influence.

Once through, our guide takes us to a park, where I can see a popular palace further on but with long lines I stay away.

Entrance to Topkapi Palace

My afternoon continues with the same guide but this time I pay for a two-hour boat ride around the Bosporus, the waterway which separates Europe and Asia. As we start the tour, randomly there are elderly people swimming in the open water on this cold, overcast day.

From the boat, our guide points out numerous features including the remains of the city walls with many archways around waterside parts of Old Istanbul. Most of these walls don't look that well looked after, with the main railway line going behind it.

Our guide also points out numerous mosques with differing numbers of minarets, along with a few palaces, fancy hotels and various houses.

Remains of old city walls   *One of many mosques in Istanbul*

Our cruise ends on the Asian side, with no difference between Europe and Asia – both just as busy with people. Currently, there is no way to walk or cycle between Europe and Asia as bridges and a tunnel are for motorised traffic only. Apparently, a tunnel for cyclists and pedestrians is being built soon.

However, there are a few ferries and also a subway which travels under the water back to Europe.

Just like in Russia some subway stations are decorated, with the few having a sea theme. Yenikapi Metro Station has artwork showing how the subway was built under the Bosporus connecting Asia with Europe.

Artwork in Yenikapi Metro

The former southern gate

Having read Ghost Empire by Richard Fidler before leaving for this trip, I was inspired on my final full day in Istanbul to see the Roman era Theodosian Walls. This around six-kilometre-long wall went from the Marmara Sea in the south to the Golden Horn in the north, protecting the exposed western side of Constantinople for over a millennium. The rest of this compact city was protected by water.

The wall finally fell in 1453 when the Ottomans conquered Constantinople. This ended the Christian Byzantine Empire, which was the last remains of the once mighty Roman Empire and was when the city was renamed Istanbul.

Having my bicycle, allows me to cycle west away from the city centre to search for the remains of Theodosian Walls.

At the southern end of the former wall is an open red-bricked archway gate guarded by soldier statues holding a nondescript flag. Along the whole wall, there are a few gates each with different styles and sizes with most having a square tower above the gate.

They are often the best-preserved parts and I assume these gates were once busy places.

Now cars can freely cross through the numerous gates but there are also a few large gaps in the wall where roads now go through. Roads also follow certain sections of the inner side of the bricked wall allowing a close inspection.

The wall, especially in the southern section, passes through poor neighbourhoods where the wall and the road are both crumbling but in other places it looks well looked after as I go past modern buildings.

From what I understand, there was more than one line of walls to help defend the city along with a moat in front but since most of the time I'm on the inner side I'm mostly just seeing the tall inner wall.

In places the wall is derelict, other times it is in decent condition

Occasionally buildings are close to the wall, requiring me to divert around or cross to the outer side.

For most of the time, on the outer side of the wall is a freeway, which presumably was built where the moat was. Thankfully in places there is a path between the freeway and the wall, allowing me to safely admire it.

Veggie gardens inside the former walls

When I'm on the outer side I can see that in the spaces between two walls, locals have planted rows of vegetable gardens. Because there isn't any obvious sign of tourism along Theodosian Walls this makes it feel like a historic place left as it was when the Ottoman Empire broke through the wall in 1453.

The only tourism I know of is the Panorama 1453 Museum located halfway along the wall in a park on the outer side.

I enter from underneath to the middle of this one-tenth scale panorama which provides an uninterrupted view of a 360-degree painting, which shows in graphic detail the battle when the Ottomans finally conquered Constantinople.

In particular many parts of the wall are shown in the process of being destroyed by cannons, while people are fighting and dying.

On display directly in front of the painting are physical replica items from the battle, including large cannons, numerous boxes of equipment and weapons.

As I look right around in more detail, I can see there is depth to the painting, as it shows the sheer number of people involved in the battle. Along with the thousands of people fighting all along the wall, more soldiers are coming from the rear.

In the accompanying museum, they have a model of the panorama and information on the events leading up to, during and after the battle, all from the conqueror's perspective.

Part of the 1453 Panorama, while a model shows what it looks like

Narrow street near where my flat tyre was

After finishing seeing the wall at the northern end near the Golden Horn, I begin cycling back through Old Istanbul when suddenly I get a flat tyre caused by glass. A few locals offer to help but through miming I indicate I'm okay.

While patching the hole, I reflect on where I'm fixing a flat, thinking of my first flat tyre while on a tour in 2009 only a day's ride from home and now I'm getting flats in Istanbul. This flat occurs near some small local cafés located on narrow streets away from the busy tourist hot spots, so it feels like I'm eating local food for lunch rather than tourist food.

Once my bicycle is fixed, I cycle back to my Airbnb via a couple of mosques. Along the way, suddenly a group of school children come out on the street all covered in full black Islamic garments, not something I'm used to seeing and it is confronting. This reminds me of two things, firstly the Dementors in Harry Potter and a group of handmaids in The Handmaids Tale.

Just like in Russia, I struggled with religion influencing men and women how to dress and be treated differently. Most women I saw in Turkey, either dress like any other European women including Elif my Airbnb host, or just cover their hair which generally older women do. On yesterday's guided tour when we went into a mosque, the women in our group had to cover their hair, while men didn't. I and others, including women, asked our female guide around my age who was dressed like any other westerner if this is still fair in this nominally secular society. She tried to avoid the question and from her response I can see having grown up with this practice it is seen as normal.

After dropping my bicycle back at my Airbnb, in the afternoon I go for another explore of the city centre. Since each mosque I'm visiting requires me to take my shoes off, I just go barefoot and anyway, I feel like my feet need a break from shoes. I get weird looks from locals while walking through the main markets as I assume bare feet must be unusual.

Ceiling of a mosque

In a mosque I'm politely asked to leave because my feet are slightly dirty. Outside each mosque is usually a place to wash your feet but in this occasion, I forgot to do this first.

My focus is on admiring the artwork and architecture of each slightly different mosque. Some mosques having scenic views of the surrounding city, with many centuries old buildings to admire. Istanbul look like a much old city compared to Moscow.

In the evening, I disassemble my bicycle in my Airbnb apartment to see if it fits in the cardboard box. It just does but will see if I can find a larger box tomorrow morning. I also clean my bicycle, because when I arrive back in Australia, customs will ask if it's clean.

The view from a mosque of Istanbul

In the morning, before catching the train to the airport I use public transport to see the two former main railway stations, one on each side of the Bosporus. At one time, you could have gone by train from Iraq to France via a ferry across the Bosporus. Today all international trains have been moved out of the city and they don't travel as far.

On the Asian side the large Haydrapasa Station is under restoration, but it looks abandoned with railway tracks removed and ferries don't go directly to it anymore. I had to walk to find it.

Back in Old Istanbul there is a small free railway museum at Sirkeci Station and a small restaurant as this was the terminus for the famous Orient Express so there is memorabilia from when this was a famous station. However, the station complex looks abandoned with signs saying trains to Bulgaria now depart way out of the city. There is, however, a busy underground subway entrance here.

As for getting to the airport, there is a subway train to the airport and a station is only a short distance from my Airbnb. Therefore, my plan is to walk my bicycle and bike box together to the station. This is harder than I hoped as it's a struggle to walk my bicycle and box together as the box keeps falling off as I'm trying to balance it on top of my bicycle.

Thankfully once I finally get to the subway station, a station attendant helps me get down to the subway platform. Then it's a simple half-hour ride to the airport with no one caring that I have a bicycle on this relatively quiet train which drops me off close to the entrance.

There is one final challenge, in that to get inside the airport terminal all my gear has to go through metal detectors including my

On the train to the airport

bicycle. However, my bicycle is too big and security staff want me to take parts of my bicycle off for it to fit. However, the seat-post is jammed and won't budge so eventually I'm waved through. Disassembling my bicycle is relatively straight forward but it does take time to fit it all into the cardboard box.

I can see my plane so I will wrap this up and I hope the next 30 hours to get home will go quickly.

My route

Each dot on this Maps.me map represents a place I slept

I'm safely home now so will take the opportunity to thank anyone who offered support during the trip both in Europe and back home in Australia. A message can be encouraging, especially on challenging days.

People often ask how I cycle 8,753 kilometres in four months. I do it by taking each day at a time.

Since I got home, I have had many people ask me if I was scared in Russia, but other than a few hairy moments with cars overtaking towards me I felt safe. Sure, there was plenty of security, but I only found them friendly, helpful and really just doing a job that must be boring.

If you wish to follow me on social media including many other cycling trips, including hopefully future trips, search for

Itsnotaboutkms

My Second Book

IT'S NOT ABOUT HOW FAR I CYCLE

Joel Emonson

In 2019, with the FIFA Women's World Cup in France and both the Women's and Men's Ashes cricket series in England, it made sense for Joel to combine attending these sporting events with a five-month bicycle tour. He had some set dates where he needed to be, but for the rest, he made up the route as he went.

Joel spent time cycling as many rail trails and canal towpaths as he could in Spain, France, Luxembourg, Belgium and the UK. He also visited heritage sites, including numerous castles, battlefields, churches and a wide range of museums.

Travelling for months outdoors meant dealing with a range of weather, from the hottest day ever in France to rainy days in Spain to freezing summer days in Scotland.

He stayed with many helpful people but also camped in unusual places, from abandoned buildings to sporting fields to sneakily camping beside castles.

While on this journey he had a few issues with bags going missing, shoes falling apart and parts of his bicycle randomly breaking.

Lightning Source UK Ltd.
Milton Keynes UK
UKHW020654210322
400373UK00001B/2